A Concise History of Modern Europe

Liberty, Equality, Solidarity

Fourth Edition

David S. Mason

ROWMAN & LITTLEFIELD
Lanham • Boulder • New York • London

Executive Editor: Susan McEachern
Editorial Assistant: Katelyn Turner
Senior Marketing Manager: Kim Lyons

Credits and acknowledgments for material borrowed from other sources, and reproduced with permission, appear on the appropriate page within the text.

Published by Rowman & Littlefield
An imprint of The Rowman & Littlefield Publishing Group, Inc.
4501 Forbes Boulevard, Suite 200, Lanham, Maryland 20706
www.rowman.com

Unit A, Whitacre Mews, 26-34 Stannary Street, London SE11 4AB, United Kingdom

British Library Cataloguing in Publication Information Available

Library of Congress Cataloging-in-Publication Data Available

ISBN 978-1-5381-1326-4 (cloth : alk. paper)
ISBN 978-1-5381-1327-1 (pbk. : alk. paper)
ISBN 978-1-5381-1328-8 (ebook)

♾™ The paper used in this publication meets the minimum requirements of American National Standard for Information Sciences—Permanence of Paper for Printed Library Materials, ANSI/NISO Z39.48-1992.

Printed in the United States of America

*For students of history who use the lessons of the past
to build a better future*

Contents

Boxes, Illustrations, and Maps

BOXES

ILLUSTRATIONS

MAPS

Preface and Acknowledgments

I have tried to make this book interesting and accessible and to provide the basic contours of modern European history in a manner that does not overwhelm the reader with details. The book is written with a specific audience in mind: college undergraduates with little previous background in the subject. The project arose from a need at my own university for a short introduction to European history for a university-wide core course that focused on the tension between tradition and change at key points in world history, including Europe since the French Revolution.

Therefore, the focus of this book and the organizing principle are the periods of major change and revolution that shaped European societies. These included political revolutions, like those in 1789, 1917, and 1989, and also economic, intellectual, and scientific revolutions as well as wars. This narrative, therefore, touches on many of the interdisciplinary aspects of history: cultural, social, intellectual, political, and economic. These changes, in all of their manifestations, brought Europe, by and large, to liberty, equality, and solidarity (the subtitle of this book), as well as peace and prosperity. The European trajectory is fascinating and illuminating, and the accomplishment both amazing and marvelous.

The main challenge of writing this book was the effort to synthesize and abbreviate the history of a big region during an era of so much change. It is a testament to this challenge that few short histories of Europe are available to the general reader. One reviewer of the first edition praised the text for its "brevity, voice and value," so the publisher and I have tried to maintain those virtues in subsequent editions. This book is still, I believe, the shortest and least expensive text on modern Europe and one of the few written by a single author. Of course, this entails some compromises, so in a book like this one, half the length of most standard histories of modern Europe, there will inevitably be omissions and over-simplifications. In this, I hope I do not offend the amateur and professional historians among you.

Many people have contributed to the conceptualization, revisions, and editing of this book—many of them connected with Butler's core curriculum program. Professors Aron Aji, Bruce Bigelow, and Paul Valliere all encouraged me to undertake the first version of this book, and Susan McEachern, editorial director at Rowman & Littlefield, encouraged and supported the project in many ways through all four editions. Many friends and colleagues contributed feedback and suggestions on one or more of the chapters in this volume: they are acknowledged in the earlier editions of this book.

For this new edition, I received many valuable suggestions from four outside readers for the press: Christopher Brooks of East Stroudsburg University; Stephen Collins of Babson College; Thomas Porter of North Carolina Agricultural and Technical State University; and Marian Strobel of Furman University. At the conference in Poland organized by Andrzej Kamiński, "Recovering Forgotten History: The Image of East-Central Europe in English-Language Academic Textbooks," I received incisive and extremely useful feedback from five European scholars: Piotr Bajda, Spasimir Domaradzki, Krzysztof Lazarski, Andrzej Nowak, and Endre Sashalmi. My friends and colleagues Bruce Bigelow and Paul Hanson, and my wife Sharon, read and assessed some of the new material in this edition. Rebeccah Shumaker and Katelyn Turner, editorial assistants at the press, ably guided me through the revision process. To all of these wonderful people, I am deeply grateful.

A NOTE FOR STUDENTS

One advantage of a short text like this is that it allows time for students to sample important primary sources, such as documents, speeches, and literary works. I often refer to these in the text, and you can find many of them at the website of the Internet Modern History Sourcebook (based at Fordham University) and other places mentioned in "Suggestions for Additional Reading" at the end of this book. Boldface terms in the text (e.g., **absolute monarchy** on p. 13) are defined or identified in the glossary.

I have written this book for you, the student, and I hope that you enjoy it and learn from it. If you have comments, suggestions, or questions about the book, I would welcome hearing from you at dmason@butler.edu.

Introduction

Revolutionary Europe

The first edition of this book began with 1789 and ended with 1989, precisely two hundred years later. This fourth edition brings the story forward another quarter century, although those two years are still anchors for the book. Like all dates and periods in history, these are somewhat arbitrary, but these two years, 1789 and 1989, mark signal events in European history, arguably the two most important years in that continent's history. The first is the year of the French Revolution, which overturned the monarchy in France (albeit temporarily), institutionalized the ideas of the Enlightenment, and unleashed the forces of nationalism, revolution, and democracy all over Europe. The second is the year in which communism collapsed in Eastern Europe through largely peaceful popular revolutions that brought down one communist regime after another in the course of only about six months. These Eastern European revolutions stimulated the fragmentation and collapse of the Soviet Union two years later, with the consequent end of the Cold War conflict that had dominated international relations (and much of life in both the East and the West) since the end of World War II. The ending of the division of Europe between Eastern and Western, communist and capitalist, allowed for further movement toward unity and integration, marked by the expansion of the European Union (EU) from fifteen countries to twenty-eight by 2013. What Napoleon had tried to achieve by force of arms after the French Revolution—the unification of Europe under the revolutionary principles of "liberty, equality, and fraternity"—was achieved two centuries later through peaceful and mass protests and global economic integration.

In the years between 1789 and 1989, of course, Europe underwent many changes, some of them even more convulsive than the revolutions of 1789. Another seminal revolution in Russia, in 1917, brought to power a political party committed to another ideology, communism, which within fifty years was embraced by governments controlling half the population of the planet. Two world wars in the twentieth century, fought mainly on European soil, cost the lives of tens of millions of Europeans, both soldiers and citizens. Brutal totalitarian dictatorships emerged in Germany (Hitler) and Russia (Stalin), each causing misery and death on a scale unprecedented in human history.

At the same time, these two centuries were a period of enormous positive changes and creativity in Europe. The inventions of the mechanized spinning wheel, steam engine, and assembly line fueled the Industrial Revolution, which affected almost every aspect of daily life and transformed European society from agricultural to urban. Adam Smith's ideas about free enterprise spurred the growth of capitalism, while the rough edges and excesses of unfettered capitalism spurred Karl Marx to suggest an alternative way of organizing urban life with *The Communist Manifesto*. Charles Darwin revolutionized biology and science with his theory of evolution, in the process challenging traditional and religious notions about human creation. And in the midst of all this ferment, Europe produced some of the most marvelous writers, musicians, and artists of all time. To list them all would be both impossible and imprudent, but I will take the author's prerogative and mention only a few of the most universally known (and my own favorites): Tolstoy, Dickens, Goethe, and Flaubert; Beethoven, Mozart, Tchaikovsky, and the Beatles; Renoir, Van Gogh, Matisse, and Picasso.

These artists, like the philosophers of the Enlightenment and of revolutions, shaped the present-day culture of Europe and the world. In some respects, the spreading influence of European culture to the rest of the world was benign, for example, through emigration. Between 1840 and 1940, over sixty million people emigrated from Europe, the vast majority of them to the Americas, taking with them the values, cultures, and customs of their homelands. At the same time, European influence spread in less innocent, and often more harmful ways, with European imperialism, which reached its apogee in the latter half of the nineteenth century. Britain, Spain, France, Germany, Holland, Portugal, and other countries established colonies all over the world in the eighteenth and nineteenth centuries. The process was particularly rapid, frenzied, and competitive in the period from 1870 to 1912, in what is sometimes called the Scramble for Africa, when virtually the entire continent was carved up into European colonies. By 1912, only Liberia and Ethiopia remained independent African states.

Many of these colonies did not regain their independence until the 1960s or later, by which time European cultural influences, including languages, were deeply embedded in colonial areas. (French, for example, is still an official language in twenty-nine countries.) The movements for national independence in Africa, Asia, and elsewhere often involved a rejection of European values and even virulent hostility from colonial peoples toward the Europeans who had exploited them. Even so, the newly independent states almost always borrowed their models for political and economic development from Europe, and the major competing ideologies—liberal democracy and socialism—were both essentially European in origin.

An uninformed observer, looking at Europe today and Europe in 1789, might assume that there had been a steady development and incorporation of the ideals and ideas of revolutionary France and Enlightenment Europe. A draft of a new constitution for the EU, for example, made reference to the union's debt to "the philosophical currents of the Enlightenment." And indeed, the progress of the continent along this line has been quite remarkable: from a collection of states characterized by absolute monarchy, rigid social hierarchy, peasant agriculture, and endemic warfare to an incipient European community of twenty-eight states, all of them committed to democracy, human rights, welfare capitalism, free movement of goods and people, and peaceful interaction.

Progress toward the ideals of the Enlightenment, however, was not uniform or smooth. There were inherent tensions between values of liberty and equality, between freedom and order, between the needs of the individual and those of the community, and ultimately, between the forces for change and those for tradition. The French Revolution disrupted the old order, the *ancien régime*, but the chaos, instability, and violence that it unleashed frightened many people, especially other European monarchs and nobility. This led to the restoration of the monarchy in France and the establishment of the Holy Alliance among the European monarchs to ensure the maintenance of the traditions of monarchy, the church, and divine right. The Russian Revolution of 1917 led to the thorough remaking of Russian society and held out the Marxian promise of material abundance, social justice, equality, and workers' solidarity, both in Russia and worldwide. But the interim "dictatorship of the proletariat" turned out to be semipermanent, and the threat of communism scared the capitalist world and created a division in Europe—what Winston Churchill called an "iron curtain"—that impeded European growth and integration for generations. The economic insecurities and depression of the 1920s frightened enough people in Germany and Italy that they were willing to accept charismatic, but demagogic, leaders in Hitler and Mussolini, who promised to restore order and prosperity but in the process unleashed a world war that caused some fifty million fatalities in Europe alone.

By the end of the twentieth century, Europe had reached many of the goals set by philosophers and revolutionaries of the eighteenth century, but only after many detours and much suffering and trauma. This book is the story of that twisting path, from the Enlightenment to the EU, and the evolution of the ideas of democracy, progress, and human rights from the era of absolute monarchy and divine right to a Europe united and free. In tracing these developments, we will focus on major themes and ideas and how they affected the continent.

It should be pointed out that the definition of Europe itself has been a subject of debate and controversy among geographers, historians, and political leaders. Since Europe is a large peninsula that stretches from the Eurasian landmass out into the Atlantic, there is no completely clear border separating Europe from Asia. Since the early 1800s, however, most geographers define the eastern limit of Europe as being the Ural Mountains in Russia, which are about eight hundred miles east of Moscow. As Russia itself stretches thousands of miles eastward past the Urals, this raises the perennial question of whether Russia is part of Europe. The issue is political and cultural, as well as geographic. As the historian Norman Davies has put it, "throughout modern history, an orthodox, autocratic, economically backward but expanding Russia has been a bad fit" for inclusion in Europe.[1] But most Russian leaders, from the tsars through the communists to the present day, have viewed Russia as part of Europe, and the country has had enormous influence, both politically and culturally, on the development of Europe. In this textbook on European history, therefore, we will include Russia.

The term *Europe* has a prescriptive and even utopian dimension in addition to the purely descriptive one. As early as the eighteenth century, writers and philosophers pointed out the common foundations of European culture (especially the Christian ones) and the possibilities of a greater European community. Only recently, however, has this seemed possible. After World War II, Jean Monnet, the "father of Europe" and the inspiration behind the EU, admitted, "Europe has never existed. . . . One has genuinely to create Europe." The Cold War division of Europe into East and West seemed to postpone this goal. The Soviet leader Mikhail Gorbachev revived this hope when he began his program of reforming communism in the 1980s, thus raising the possibility of a "common European home":

> Europe "from the Atlantic to the Urals" is a cultural-historical entity united by the common heritage of the Renaissance and the Enlightenment, of the great philosophical and social teachings of the nineteenth and twentieth centuries. . . . A tremendous potential for a policy of peace and neighborliness is inherent in the European cultural heritage.[2]

Gorbachev's reforms unleashed the revolutions of 1989, which brought down communism in Eastern Europe and the Soviet Union, and paved the way for that vision of a united Europe. Ironically, though, Gorbachev's own country, Russia, is *not* part of the EU. Furthermore, the most serious crisis in Europe in recent years was in Ukraine, formerly a part of the Soviet Union, and centered on whether that country should be oriented toward Russia or toward Europe.

There is another definitional issue with the phrase "**Eastern Europe**." In this book, that terminology refers to the European Communist Party states during the Cold War—roughly from the end of World War II until the fall of communism in 1989. But that designation is controversial and slippery. Many in the region objected to this nomenclature (and still do), feeling that it consigned those countries to "the East" rather than to "the West" where they more properly fit historically and culturally. A more appropriate term, some argued, would be "Central Europe."[3] Furthermore, does it still make any sense to refer to these countries, like Poland and Hungary, as "East European" when they are now part of the EU?

In a short book like this, we cannot solve all these issues or cover the history of every single country in Europe. Rather, we will focus on particular countries during important turning points—for example, France in 1789, England during the Industrial Revolution, Russia in 1917, Germany during World War II, and Poland in 1989. We will begin our journey with France, in the eighteenth century, on the eve of the first great modern revolution.

Timeline of European History

1799	Napoleon Bonaparte seizes power in France
1804	Napoleon crowns himself Napoleon I, emperor of France
1812	Napoleon invades Russia
1814–30	Restoration; Bourbon monarchy in France
1815	Wellington defeats Napoleon at Waterloo
1815	Congress of Vienna
1825	First railroad runs in Britain
1825	Decembrist revolt in Russia
1830	Revolution in France deposes Charles X and establishes July Monarchy under Louis Philippe, who rules until 1848
1830	Revolutions in Belgium, Poland, and elsewhere
1830	Giuseppe Mazzini founds Young Italy movement
1832	First reform bill in Britain expands voting rights
1833	Slavery abolished in Britain
1837–1901	Reign of Queen Victoria in Britain
1838	People's Charter in England demands universal suffrage; Chartist movement
1848	People's Spring revolutions in France, Austria, Prussia, Hungary, and Italy; all repressed by 1849
1848	Marx and Engels publish *The Communist Manifesto*
1848–1916	Reign of Emperor Francis Joseph of Austria
1853–56	The Crimean War
1855–81	Reign of Alexander II (the Tsar Liberator) in Russia
1859	Charles Darwin's *Origin of Species*
1859	Cavour provokes war with Austria to win territory for Italy
1859–70	Unification of Italy under Victor Emmanuel II and Cavour
1861	Emancipation of serfs in Russia by Tsar Alexander II
1864–71	Bismarck's wars of German unification against Denmark, Austria, and France
1867	Dual monarchy established in Austria-Hungary
1869	Suez Canal constructed
1870s	Populist and nihilist movements in Russia
1870–71	Franco-Prussian War
1870–1940	Third Republic in France
1871–1918	The German Empire
1878	Serbia gains independence from the Ottoman Empire
1880s	Socialist parties founded in Europe
1883–93	French colonization of Indochina
1885	Berlin Conference on Africa
1885–1900	Scramble for Africa; intensive colonization by Europeans

1888–1918	Reign of Kaiser Wilhelm II in Germany
1894–1917	Reign of Tsar Nicholas II in Russia
1898	Spanish-American War; United States acquires Puerto Rico, Guam, and Philippines as colonies
1898	Russian Social Democratic Labor Party formed; soon splits into Bolshevik and Menshevik factions
1900	Sigmund Freud publishes *Interpretation of Dreams*
1904–5	Russo-Japanese War
1905	Bloody Sunday and revolution in Russia
1905	Albert Einstein publishes theory of relativity
1912–13	Balkan Wars
1914	Assassination of Austrian Archduke Francis Ferdinand in Sarajevo
1914–18	World War I
1917	United States enters war
1917	Russian revolution overthrows tsar and brings Bolsheviks (communists) to power
1918	Germany surrenders, ending World War I
1918	Fall of German, Austro-Hungarian, and Ottoman Empires and emergence of new independent states in Central and Eastern Europe
1918	Limited suffrage for women in Britain and full suffrage for women in Germany, Hungary, and Poland
1919	Treaty of Versailles
1919–21	Polish-Soviet war
1919–33	Weimar Republic in Germany
1922	Union of Soviet Socialist Republics (USSR) established
1922	Benito Mussolini seizes power in Italy
1922–43	Fascist rule in Italy under Mussolini
1924	Vladimir Lenin dies; soon succeeded as Soviet party leader by Joseph Stalin (rules until 1953)
1928	Stalin launches first five-year plan of planned industrialization in USSR
1928	Full suffrage for women in Britain
1929	US stock market crashes, leading to Great Depression of 1930s
1930s	Ukrainian famine
1933	Adolf Hitler appointed chancellor of Germany
1933–45	Nazi rule in Germany under Hitler
1936	John Maynard Keynes's *General Theory of Employment, Interest, and Money*

1936–38	Stalin's Great Purge in Soviet Union
1936–39	Spanish Civil War
1937	Rome-Berlin-Tokyo axis; Hitler signs treaties with Italy and Japan
1938	Munich Conference allows Hitler's takeover of Sudetenland
1938	Germany annexes Austria
1939	Nazi-Soviet nonaggression pact
1939	Germany invades Poland, leading to British declaration of war
1939–45	World War II
1940	Germans invade Norway, Denmark, Holland, Belgium, and France
1940	Winston Churchill becomes British prime minister; Battle of Britain
1940	Soviet Union annexes Lithuania, Latvia, and Estonia
1941	Germans invade Soviet Union
1941	Japanese attack Pearl Harbor; United States enters war
1942–43	Battle of Stalingrad; Russians turn tide against Germans
1943	Allies invade Italy; fall of Mussolini
1944	Allied invasion of France at Normandy
1945	Yalta and Potsdam Conferences of Allied leaders
1945	Hitler commits suicide; Germany surrenders
1945	United States drops atomic bombs on Hiroshima and Nagasaki; Japan surrenders
1945	United Nations established with fifty-one members
1945–48	Communist regimes established by Soviet Union in Eastern Europe
1947	Truman Doctrine and Marshall Plan commit United States to Europe
1948–49	Berlin blockade and airlift
1949	German Federal Republic (West Germany) and German Democratic Republic (East Germany) established
1949	North Atlantic Treaty Organization (NATO) founded
1949	Communists win power in China under Mao Zedong
1950–53	Korean War
1951	European Coal and Steel Community (ECSC) formed
1953	Death of Stalin in USSR
1954	France pulls out of Indochina; Vietnam partitioned into North and South Vietnam
1955	West Germany joins NATO; Warsaw Pact formed
1956	Uprisings in Poland and Hungary crushed by Soviet Union

1957	Soviet Union launches first orbiting satellite, *Sputnik*
1957	Gold Coast (Ghana) gains independence from Britain
1957	Treaty of Rome establishes European Economic Community (EEC)
1958	Fifth French republic established with Charles de Gaulle as president
1961	Berlin Wall erected
1961–75	US involvement in Vietnam War
1962	US-Soviet Cuban missile crisis
1964–82	Leonid Brezhnev in power in Soviet Union
1967	ECSC, EEC, and Euratom merge into European Community (EC)
1968	Prague Spring in Czechoslovakia crushed by Soviet Union
1970s	East-West détente; improvement of US-Soviet relations, arms-control agreements
1973	Britain, Denmark, and Ireland join EC, which then has nine members
1974	Revolution in Portugal ends dictatorship
1975	Death of Francisco Franco in Spain; constitutional monarchy established
1975	End of last European (Portuguese) empire in Africa
1975	Helsinki Conference on European Security and Cooperation
1978	Polish cardinal Karol Wojtyła named Pope John Paul II
1979	Soviet invasion of Afghanistan; end of détente
1980–81	Solidarity movement in Poland challenges communist rule
1982	Soviet leader Brezhnev dies
1985	Mikhail Gorbachev chosen leader of Soviet Communist Party; begins *perestroika*
1989	Hungary opens border to Austria; Solidarity wins elections in Poland; fall of Berlin Wall; fall of communist regimes in Eastern Europe
1990	Free elections in most of European postcommunist countries
1990	Germany reunified
1991	USSR dissolved; Warsaw Pact dissolved
1991–92	Croatia, Slovenia, and Bosnia declare independence from Yugoslavia
1992–95	Civil war in Bosnia finally ended with Dayton Accords of 1995
1993	Czechoslovakia divided into Czech Republic and Slovakia
1993	European Union (EU) born
2002	Euro introduced as currency of EU

2004–13	EU membership expanded with addition of thirteen new members, including eleven former communist countries
2006	Montenegro and Serbia declare independence, ending the state of Yugoslavia
2009–12	Debt crises in Greece and other countries prompt huge EU bailout plans
2014	Russia seizes and annexes Crimea during Ukraine crisis
2016	In Brexit referendum, Britain votes to leave the EU

1

The Old Regime
and the Enlightenment

The year of the French Revolution, 1789, marks the beginning of a new era of revolutionary change in Europe and the end of the **old regime** of absolutist **monarchy**, at least in France. But the overthrow of the old order in France had significance far beyond French borders for many reasons. In the eighteenth century, France was the most powerful country on the Continent, the most populous, and one of the most prosperous. French culture was admired and mimicked by the upper classes throughout Europe, and French was the language of the aristocracy and royal courts all over the Continent, including in Russia. The palace that France's King Louis XIV (r. 1643–1715) built at Versailles in the seventeenth century symbolized the grandeur, wealth, and power of **absolute monarchy**, and monarchs in other countries modeled their own palaces after it. Because of the French monarchy's influence across the Continent, its fall in 1789 sent shock waves across Europe. So it is important to understand the nature of the old regime in France and the factors that led to its downfall.

THE OLD REGIME IN FRANCE

Europe in the eighteenth century was composed almost entirely of absolute monarchies, countries run by a king or queen who inherited his or her position and would pass the crown to the eldest son or daughter. These monarchs knew few restraints on their power and claimed to rule on the basis of **divine right** as God's agents on earth. England was somewhat of an exception to this rule, as the Glorious Revolution of 1688 concluded a long struggle between Parliament and the Stuart kings and essentially replaced the absolute monarchy with a **constitutional monarchy**, in which laws limited the monarch's powers.[1] In most of the rest of Europe, throughout the majority of the seventeenth and eighteenth centuries, the powers of the European monarchs actually increased as powerful monarchs gradually broke the power of feudal lords, centralized power, and created unified, more modern **states**.

In France, Louis XIV spent much of his reign strengthening the power of the monarchy and centralizing political authority in Paris or, more accurately, at his magnificent palace built at Versailles, ten miles south of Paris. Versailles was meant both to reflect the grandeur of Louis—the Sun King—and to facilitate his centralizing policy. In the past, the kings of France and their royal courts had traveled widely in the kingdom, visiting the royal domains and the provincial chateaus of powerful nobles. Louis XIV ruled from Versailles, and those nobles who sought royal favor had to live at Versailles for much of the year. Versailles, then, became the symbol both of the power of the king and of France itself. The influence and significance of this was not lost on other European monarchs: Russian **tsar** Peter the Great and Prussian king Frederick the Great both built palaces modeled on Versailles.

Old regime France—the term *old regime,* or ***ancien régime,*** was introduced by the revolutionaries of 1789—was based on a rigid social hierarchy in which one's place in society was determined largely by birth, not by hard work or talent. The organization of society was explained by the Great Chain of Being, a concept prevalent since medieval times, which held that the entire world was organized hierarchically, from God and the angels at the top to inanimate objects, such as rocks, at the bottom, with human beings existing somewhere in between. At the top of the human chain stood the king, God's divine representative, expressed vividly in this 1766 proclamation of Louis XV (r. 1715–74): "Sovereign power resides in my person alone. . . . It is from me alone that my policies take their existence and their authority; . . . it is to me alone that legislative power belongs, without dependence or division; . . . all public order emanates from me."[2] Louis XV's great-grandfather, the Sun King, put it a little more simply when he allegedly proclaimed, *"L'état c'est moi"* (I am the state).

Beneath the king, the rest of French society was organized into three classes, or *estates,* each with a distinct social responsibility and each hierarchically organized. The First Estate, the clergy, enjoyed their high status by virtue of their spiritual function and proximity to God, although the clergy comprised less than 1 percent of the population.

The Second Estate, the nobility or aristocracy, provided military support for the king and constituted between 1 and 2 percent of the population. The nobility was actually quite a varied group. The wealthiest and most

Portrait of Louis XIV, the Sun King (1674), by Pierre Mignard, full of symbols of the power, majesty, and divine right of an absolute monarch. © BeBa/Iberfoto/The Image Works.

powerful nobles, numbering only a few hundred families and known as *Les Grands,* owned large landholdings and elegant chateaus and exercised considerable political influence as councillors of state and local judges. More numerous and less exalted were the provincial nobles, *seigneurs,* who owned estates, often with many peasants working their lands under various arrangements. There were also nobles who had few possessions and lived in genteel poverty, holding their titles and very little else.

The Third Estate, the remaining 97 percent of the population, comprised everyone else and was responsible for the production of goods and provision of services. France, like all of Europe at the time, was overwhelmingly a rural society; the peasantry made up about 85 percent of the population and therefore the huge bulk of the Third Estate. Compared to other European countries, the French peasantry was relatively prosperous. Even so, fewer than 40 percent owned their own land. Most French peasants rented their land from landlords, either as tenant farmers or sharecroppers.

The old regime economy was, therefore, overwhelmingly rural and agricultural and dominated by subsistence farming, with peasants producing barely enough to meet their own needs; any surplus production was absorbed by rent, tithes, seigneurial dues (paid to the lord of the estate), and taxes. In the late eighteenth century, there was neither a national currency nor a uniform system of weights and measures, nor even a truly national market. A good network of royal highways existed, but it still took at least five days to travel by coach from Paris to Marseilles (about eight hours by car today).

Alongside this traditional agricultural sector, in the seventeenth and eighteenth centuries, commercial trade was expanding, encouraged by royal policy. Since the seventeenth century, economic policy was guided by mercantilist theory, which held that the wealth of a nation could best be enhanced by the accumulation of precious metals like silver and gold. Countries that did not have native deposits of such metals, like France, had to rely on trade to acquire them. The monarchy encouraged the development of manufacturing industries to provide goods for the international market, and France developed an international reputation for producing luxury goods such as silk, satin, lace, perfumes, and tapestries. The development of manufacturing and trade led to the growth of a new social class, the **bourgeoisie**, or the middle class, and to the proliferation of many small merchants and shopkeepers, called the *petite bourgeoisie*. Near the end of the eighteenth century, the theory of **mercantilism**, with its emphasis on precious metals and government regulation, came under challenge both by alternative economic theories, such as Adam Smith's theory of a free market economy (see below), and by the bourgeoisie themselves.

Old regime France was overwhelmingly Roman Catholic, and Catholicism played an important role in the country, both as a religion and as an institution. Religion was pervasive in daily life, and religious services and celebrations were the most important events in most towns and villages. Those who attended school were taught by priests, and those without work depended on the church for charity. The church was also a powerful institution politically and was closely intertwined with the monarchy. French kings, as divine monarchs, were crowned in the cathedral at Reims, and the king appointed all bishops and other high officials of the church. The church owned extensive property, perhaps 10 percent of all the land in France, and the incomes from these properties were enormous, sometimes equal to half the annual income of the royal government.

This structure of state and society, described here for France, was similar to that of other European countries in the eighteenth century. Christian monarchs claiming divine right governed all of the major powers (the most important and powerful were France, Austria, Russia, Prussia, and England), which were characterized by a feudal or semifeudal and mercantilist economic system and a rigidly hierarchical social structure. The royal families of the European capitals, united by common bonds of religion, culture, and blood, were intent on preserving the old order and their positions in it. Since the middle of the seventeenth century, European monarchies had consciously pursued a policy of the balance of power, a system of shifting international alliances that prevented any one country from becoming too powerful. Wars were fought not so much for **ideology** or **nationalism** but to maintain the balance of power; consequently, these conflicts were relatively restrained. The victor did not want to crush the vanquished, as this would upset the balance; in any case, the defeated state might be a future ally.

This whole system, both domestic and international, was seriously challenged at the end of the eighteenth century and the beginning of the nineteenth, first by the ideas of the **Enlightenment**, then by the forces of the French Revolution of 1789, and later by the Industrial Revolution and the emergent power of the new middle class. Monarchy, Christianity, the church, hierarchy, and mercantilism would all be threatened with extinction at the turn of the nineteenth century. By 1815, order would be restored, but only temporarily.

THE ENLIGHTENMENT

The *ancien régime* in France and elsewhere in Europe was threatened not only by internal problems and tensions but also by new ways of thinking about society and the world. Emerging in the seventeenth and eighteenth centuries, the Enlightenment was both a movement and a set of ideas; it was also called the Age of Reason because of its emphasis on the power of the human mind to liberate the individual and improve society. Enlightenment philosophers argued that knowledge can be derived only from experience, experiment, and observation. They encouraged people to use their own critical reasoning to free their minds from prejudice, unexamined authority, and oppression by the church or the state. The German philosopher Immanuel Kant wrote in 1784 that enlightenment is "man's emergence from his self-incurred immaturity." "Immaturity," he wrote, "is the inability to use one's own understanding without the guidance of another." The motto of the Enlightenment, in Kant's words, was therefore, "*Sapere aude!* Have courage to use your own understanding."[3] The French Enlightenment philosopher Voltaire made a similar point when he wrote, "The most useful books are those to which the readers themselves contribute half; they develop the idea of which the author has presented the seed." The consequence of this appeal to reason, science, and self-reliance was, of course, a serious undermining of the authority of the established institutions of the old regime, particularly the church and the state.

The principles of the Enlightenment were in some ways a continuation of the discoveries and theories of the Scientific Revolution in the sixteenth and seventeenth centuries, when scientific observation and experiments challenged and threatened the worldview and authority of the church. In the sixteenth century, the Polish astronomer Nicolaus Copernicus proposed a theory of the universe that placed the Sun, rather than the Earth, at the center of the solar system. In the seventeenth century, the Italian Galileo Galilei constructed an astronomical telescope through which he confirmed Copernicus's heliocentric theory. Furthermore, his concept of the universe made God redundant, bringing him into conflict with the church's inquisition for his heresy. The English philosopher and mathematician Isaac Newton, in his treatise *Principia* (1687), derived the principles of gravity and motion; he described the universe as a machine and nature as governed by rational and consistent laws. Geologists in France discovered fossils that conflicted with the time scheme suggested in the Old Testament. All of these men used observation and experiments to draw conclusions that conflicted with the accepted wisdom of the time.

Enlightenment philosophers applied the methods of the Scientific Revolution to the study of society and of government rather than the material universe, believing that natural laws governed human behavior and institutions, just as they governed the universe. The principal forerunner of the Enlightenment was the Englishman John Locke (1632–1704), who first broached the notion that reason and knowledge are derived from experience. Human nature, Locke contended, is essentially good (unlike the biblical notion of original sin), and human character is a function of one's environment, upbringing, and education. It is possible, then, by shaping society and the environment and providing good education, to produce a better society. Locke also argued in his *Second Treatise of Civil Government* (1690) that man possesses natural and inalienable rights to life, liberty, and property. He wrote that political communities (i.e., governments) are formed by popular consent, implying a kind of contractual relationship between people and government that flew in the face of the widespread notion of divine right. Locke's ideas, and even his language, had an enormous influence on other Enlightenment-era political thinkers, including Thomas Jefferson across the Atlantic; these ideas are found later in both the US Declaration of Independence and the French Declaration of the Rights of Man.

Although the Enlightenment was a Europe-wide phenomenon, the movement was dominated by French writers, thinkers, and philosophers, who were referred to as *philosophes*. The Baron de Montesquieu (1689–1755), a critic of absolutist government, satirized the reign of Louis XIV, as well as elite society and the church (referring even to the pope as a magician). In his *Spirit of the Laws* (1748), he argued (in good Enlightenment fashion) that laws are derived from nature; he also developed the idea of the separation of powers—partitioning the executive, legislative, and judicial functions of government into separate institutions—another concept that was picked up by the Americans and incorporated by James Madison in his design of the US Constitution.

Another important French Enlightenment thinker, the philosopher Jean-Jacques Rousseau (1712–78), elaborated on some of Locke's ideas about natural rights and popular sovereignty. "Man is born free," wrote Rousseau, "and everywhere he is shackled." Society corrupts and distorts man's natural freedom and equality, Rousseau argued, but a reformed society and government can restore the balance through civil liberty and equality, negotiated between the people and the government through a **social contract**. Rousseau described this ideal society in his *Social Contract* (1762), which, like many Enlightenment publications, was banned in France.

The most important publication of the French Enlightenment was the *Encyclopedia*, an effort to compile a comprehensive and systematic collection of knowledge using the new gospel of scientific empiricism. Most of the important thinkers of the time contributed to the *Encyclopedia*, which was published between 1751 and 1765 in seventeen volumes, numbering 16,288 pages. It was principally through the *Encyclopedia* that many Enlightenment ideas were disseminated; those of Locke and Montesquieu, for example, appeared under entries such as "political authority" and "natural liberty" and encouraged democratic tendencies in France and elsewhere. The coeditor of the *Encyclopedia*, Denis Diderot, was credited

BOX 1.1
The Play That Sparked a Revolution: *The Marriage of Figaro*

The Marriage of Figaro (1786) is mostly known as a delightful comic opera by Wolfgang Amadeus Mozart. But the opera was based on a highly successful and controversial play written in 1778, by Pierre-Augustin Caron de Beaumarchais, a man who at various times was a musician, courtier, financier, diplomat, merchant, secret agent, publisher, and, one would have to say, an opportunist and something of a rogue. Even so, Beaumarchais was also a typical Enlightenment intellectual, a member of the nobility who satirized privilege and high society and a reformer, but not a revolutionary. At the time of the American Revolution, he urged the French king Louis XVI (r. 1774–93) to support (secretly) the revolutionaries against the British and managed almost single-handedly to raise money to purchase and ship enough military equipment to support twenty-five thousand men in the colonies.

In between his many projects and adventures, he managed to write a number of plays, including two whose reputations have lasted mostly through operas: *The Barber of Seville* (composed by Rossini) and *The Marriage of Figaro* (by Mozart). In *Figaro*, the story line is a comic attempt by the title character to frustrate the efforts of the count to exercise his *droit du seigneur*, the supposed right of the lord of a manor to bed any new bride in his employ. But the play also makes much fun of numerous institutions of the old regime, including social hierarchy, inherited privilege, incompetent officials, censorship, and the courts. When the play was first written, Louis XVI was so appalled by its impertinence that he asserted it could never be performed. However, after several modifications and revisions (including transferring the setting of the play from France to Spain) and numerous additional reviews by the censors, the play was finally approved and performed by the *Comédie Française* in 1784. Despite its four-and-a-half-hour length, it was enormously popular, ran for sixty-eight successive performances, and became the greatest success of eighteenth-century theater in France.

The revolutionary leader Danton credited *Figaro* with "killing off the nobility," and Napoleon characterized the play as "the revolution already in action."

with saying that salvation would arrive when "the last King was strangled with the entrails of the last priest." The French government twice attempted to suppress the *Encyclopedia*, but publication proceeded, and it became a best seller.

One more philosopher must be mentioned, not so much because of his impact on French revolutionary tendencies per se, but because of his broader impact on the development of Europe and the West: the Scottish philosopher Adam Smith (1723–90). Smith applied Enlightenment ideas about the natural state of things to the economy and the market, arguing that government interference in the economy violated the interplay of natural forces of competition and supply and demand. In his nine-hundred-page opus, *The Wealth of Nations,* Smith discussed how self-interest could work for the common good. By giving free rein to individual greed and the private accumulation of wealth, the "invisible hand" of the market would benefit society in the end, a formula sometimes characterized by the seemingly paradoxical aphorism "private vice yields public virtue." He argued for a system of *laissez-faire* (from the French, meaning "let do") in which the government abstained from interfering in the economy. These ideas shattered the prevalent doctrines of protectionism and mercantilism and became the basis for what would develop into capitalism. It is perhaps not entirely coincidental that *The Wealth of Nations* appeared in 1776, the same year as the US Declaration of Independence.

The Enlightenment is often treated as one of the causes of the French Revolution of 1789, but it is important to recognize that it was not *the* cause of the Revolution. Most of the *philosophes* should more properly be thought of as reformers than revolutionaries. They were mostly from the upper classes themselves, and although they satirized and criticized old regime society, they mostly favored the creation of an enlightened, or constitutional, monarchy rather than a popular, or representative, form of government. The *philosophes* themselves did not constitute any political parties or revolutionary organizations, nor did they propose any very specific reform programs or policies. None of them was involved very directly in the revolutionary events of 1789.

Even so, the ideas raised by Enlightenment thinkers were profoundly unsettling and challenging to old regime society and political order. The *philosophes* attacked the very assumptions on which the *ancien régime* was built, and they held the existing institutions up to ridicule. Their emphasis on reason and independent thinking undermined the habits of blind obedience to the authority of the church and the state. The assertions of Locke, Montesquieu, and Rousseau that the ultimate object of government was to promote the happiness and dignity of the individual created a whole new way of thinking about the political world, and not just in France. The very fact that these ideas were being aired and debated gave rise to a new phenomenon—public opinion—and the idea of government and politics as something "public."

Much cross-fertilization of ideas occurred between America and Europe at this time. Thomas Jefferson and Benjamin Franklin visited France, read the works of the *philosophes,* and were much influenced by the ideas of the Enlightenment. Similarly, the examples of the American revolutionaries, the Declaration of Independence, and the US Constitution (1787) inspired both reformers and revolutionaries in France.

THE IMPACT OF THE ENLIGHTENMENT

The impact of the Enlightenment went far beyond France and America, however, affecting virtually every country in Europe and all levels of society. Some European monarchs even embraced the Enlightenment (or at least some parts of it) and used its principles to introduce reforms; these "enlightened despots" included Frederick the Great in Prussia, Catherine the Great in Russia, and Maria Theresa in Austria. In Holland and Britain, liberals within the political establishment used Enlightenment ideas to effect change. In Spain and Italy, as in France, intellectuals used them to criticize and prod the old regime. Enlightenment ideas provided inspiration for political ideologies emerging in the eighteenth and nineteenth centuries, from **liberalism** to **socialism** and **communism**. The emphasis on reason, experimentation, observation, and empiricism laid the foundation for modern social science and the way we study and understand human society today. But most importantly, the whole tenor of the Enlightenment laid the foundation for human rights, popular sovereignty, tolerance, and respect for law, values that lie at the core of modern European society.

2

The French Revolution and Napoleon

The year 1789 marks a signal event in European and world history: the overthrow of a monarchy through a popular revolution. Like most historical markers, the use of this one particular year, 1789, is a shorthand that masks a much more complex reality extending over many more years. Although 1789 marked the storming of the Bastille and the Declaration of the Rights of Man, the king, Louis XVI (r. 1774–93), was not actually dethroned until 1792 and he was executed in 1793. And much of the impact of the French Revolution was felt elsewhere in Europe only after Napoleon Bonaparte seized power in 1799. The Revolution was not fully concluded until the defeat of Napoleon and the restoration of the monarchy in 1815 (nor was it truly defeated even then).

That these events occurred in France had special significance for the rest of Europe. As noted in the previous chapter, France was in many ways the most important country on the Continent at the time of the Revolution. Louis XIV (r. 1643–1715), the Sun King, had established a standard for a rigorous, powerful, and elegant monarchy, and his luxurious palace at Versailles was admired all over Europe. With some twenty-eight million inhabitants, France was the most populous country on the Continent. It was the leading center of arts and sciences and the focal point of the intellectual ferment of the Enlightenment. French was the most widely used international language, the language both of diplomacy and of most of the royal courts of Europe.

As with all revolutions, the causes of the French Revolution of 1789 included both long-term and structural factors, as well as more immediate events. The former included the socioeconomic changes of the eighteenth

23

century, the ideas of the Enlightenment, and weaknesses in the monarchy. The short-term factors were primarily economic: government debt, a financial crisis, and a bad harvest year. The financial crisis led the king to convoke a meeting of the Estates General in 1789, and from there events cascaded out of control.

During most of the eighteenth century, France experienced both economic stability and growth. Agricultural productivity and industrial production increased steadily in the middle part of the century, and the literacy rate of the population grew from 21 percent at the beginning of the century to 37 percent at the end. However, as we saw in the previous chapter, it was also a time of economic and intellectual ferment. Industry and commerce were transforming the economic landscape and fostering the growth of cities and a new middle class (the bourgeoisie), who were agitating for more influence both in the economy and in the political realm. Enlightenment writers were broaching ideas of religious and cultural freedom, representative institutions, and legal equality. And they were more generally pressing for change and progress. The eighteenth century saw a rapid expansion in the publication of books, periodicals, and pamphlets, which allowed wide dissemination of these new ideas and, with that, the early stages of public opinion.

By the end of the century, however, France was suffering serious problems. An inefficient system of taxation made it difficult for the monarchy to raise the money it needed. Furthermore, both the church and the nobility, which together owned much of the land in the country, were virtually exempt from taxes. The financial problems of the regime were made worse by the financial and material aid provided by France to the American colonies during their war of independence against Britain. For France, this was a strategic decision, rather than a moral or ideological one, as it was intended to weaken the country's chief rival, England, and to avenge the loss of French colonies in America and India during the Seven Years' War (the French and Indian War in North America). The combination of mounting debts and ineffective tax collection meant that, by 1787, payments on the debt absorbed about half of all the taxes that were collected.

The economic slump impacted the rest of the French population as well. The economic growth of the eighteenth century and the import of silver from the New World had fueled inflation in France, a phenomenon that was both new and alarming for many people. Between 1726 and 1789, the cost of living increased by 62 percent, whereas wages rose by only 25 percent. In the 1780s, increased competition from British textile manufacturers led to massive unemployment in the textile towns of northern France. Then, 1788 saw the worst grain harvest in France since 1709, causing increases in grain and food prices, food shortages, and even famine. All this provoked rising discontent in both the cities and the countryside.

One more problem was the weakness of the monarchy. Louis XIV had been a strong and vigorous leader, but his successors were neither, and Louis XVI was both weak and ineffectual. He was not able to control his ministers, and ministerial infighting made it difficult to deal with the financial crisis of the 1780s. Furthermore, Louis had become a virtual prisoner of Versailles, rarely leaving the Paris region, and he was consequently increasingly isolated from his subjects and the diverse regions of his kingdom.

1789: THE REVOLUTION BEGINS

In the face of the financial crisis and the refusal of the privileged classes to approve new taxes, Louis XVI decided to convoke the Estates General to address government reforms and the tax system. An assembly representing the three estates—the clergy, nobility, and the Third Estate—the Estates General had not met since 1614. The twelve hundred delegates of the Estates General met at Versailles beginning in May 1789, bringing with them the *cahiers de doléances*, or list of grievances, that voters had drawn up in the electoral assemblies that selected the delegates. The *cahiers* generally called for rather moderate reforms of the judicial, tax, and seigneurial systems and were not on the whole revolutionary. Nevertheless, the very process of drawing up the lists had politicized the population and focused national attention on the assembly in Versailles.

Even before the delegates assembled, a debate arose on how voting was to be conducted at the Estates General. Traditionally, each of the three estates sent the same number of delegates to the Estates General, and the voting there was by order, not by head, meaning that the Third Estate, representing 97 percent of the population, had only one vote of the three. But in some of the provincial assemblies meeting the previous summer, the Third Estate had been given half of all the delegates, and voting was by head, so there was some precedent for change. In an influential pamphlet titled "What Is the Third Estate?" a theretofore obscure priest, Abbé Sieyès, answered the title question, "Everything," and suggested a similar formula for voting. Sieyès's pamphlet discussed more than voting procedures, though, and hinted at even more radical changes: "If the privileged order were abolished," he wrote, "the nation would be not something less but something more."

In June, the Third Estate essentially adopted the program set out in Sieyès's pamphlet and declared itself the National Assembly. When they next tried to assemble, they found the doors of their meeting place locked, so they moved next door to an indoor tennis court, where they swore the famous Tennis Court Oath: "Wherever we meet, there is the nation," they proclaimed, and vowed not to adjourn until France was given a new constitution. As the delegates and the city of Paris became more unruly, the king began to move troops into the city. With rumors that the regime was intent on dissolving the National Assembly, armed militias began to form throughout the city. On July 14, a crowd of eighty thousand stormed the Bastille, the old royal prison, in hopes of seizing ammunition stored there. Royal troops opened fire, killing a hundred people, but the crowd prevailed, seized the governor of the fortress, cut off his head, and carried it about town on the end of a pike. The fall of the Bastille, like the fall of the **Berlin Wall** two hundred years later, became an important symbol of the Revolution, and that day, Bastille Day, is still celebrated as a French national holiday, complete with fireworks and parades.

The Bastille may have had mostly symbolic importance, but in revolutions, symbols are crucial. The vulnerability of the monarchy was exposed, and its authority quickly evaporated. Word about the fall of the Bastille spread to the provinces, where peasants followed the Parisians by raiding the chateaus of their landlords. In August, the newly styled National Constituent Assembly officially abolished the remnants of **feudalism** and freed peasants from their payments under the seigneurial system.

The assembly then turned to the task of determining the principles on which a new political regime would be based. The result, passed by the assembly on August 26, was the Declaration of the Rights of Man and the Citizen, similar in impact to the American Declaration of Independence and later the symbolic foundation of the French Republic. The declaration clearly reflects Enlightenment ideals and the ideas and language of Rousseau, Montesquieu, and Locke. It makes no mention of the authority of the monarch and declares instead "the natural, inalienable, and sacred rights of man." "Men are born and remain free and equal in rights," and these rights include "liberty, property, security, and resistance to oppression."

King Louis XVI refused to sign the declaration, and most of the deputies at this point still assumed that his signature was necessary before the document could become official. Once again, the Parisian crowd took action, feeling that the king would be more responsive to the will of the people if he were in Paris rather than Versailles. A crowd of six thousand women, aggravated by the short supply of bread in city markets, marched the fifteen miles to Versailles and escorted the king back to Paris.

For the next two years, a kind of stalemate prevailed, with the Constituent Assembly working on a new constitution, debating the powers of the monarchy, and wrestling with the country's continuing financial crisis, while Louis looked on as a sort of de facto constitutional monarch. In an effort to deal with the country's continuing debts, the assembly confiscated all properties belonging to the church. They enacted the Civil

Constitution of the Clergy, which required public election of clergy and bishops and forced the clergy to sign an oath of loyalty to the nation. Finally, in June 1791, the new constitution was presented to the public, providing for an elected legislative assembly and granting the king only a suspensive veto; that is, the power to delay legislation but not to defeat it.

Dismayed by these developments, Louis XVI fled Paris disguised as a commoner and attempted to reach the French border to rally those opposed to the Revolution. Among them were virtually all of the European monarchs, who saw events in France as an ominous portent for their own rule. The empress of Russia, Catherine the Great, declared that "the affairs of France were the concern of all crowned heads." But Louis was captured and brought back to Paris. The new constitution was put into force, and a legislative assembly was elected. Prussia and Austria soon joined in a war against France, and when their troops began to move into France, charges that Louis was in collusion with foreign monarchs provoked a new insurrection in Paris. New elections were called, and in September 1792, the newly elected National Convention scrapped the recent constitution, abolished the monarchy, and declared the establishment of the first French republic.

BOX 2.1
Women on the Revolution

Women played an important part in the revolutionary events in France, including the march on Versailles to bring Louis XVI back to Paris, where he would be more accessible and accountable to the people. But the leaders of the Revolution were mostly men, and not all women were pleased with the accomplishments of the revolutionaries. The Declaration of the Rights of Man, for example, made no mention of women at all, leading French playwright Olympe de Gouges (1745–93) to publish in 1791 a "Declaration of the Rights of Women," paralleling the articles of the original declaration, but replacing "man" with "woman." She addressed her appeal to the queen (Marie Antoinette) as a "mother and a wife," hoping to win support for her cause from this influential woman.

In Britain, the teacher and writer Mary Wollstonecraft (1759–97) welcomed the Revolution in France and saw in it the possibility of a representative government that would respect the rights of both men and women. But she also was disappointed with the Declaration of the Rights of Man and even more angered when the French assembly limited the right to education to men only. She published *A Vindication of the Rights of Women* (1792), in which she described marriage as "legal prostitution" and attacked educational restrictions that kept women in a state of "ignorance and slavish dependence." It was the first book in Britain advocating women's right to vote and hold public office.

THE RADICAL REPUBLIC AND THE TERROR

The fall of the monarchy marked the triumph of popular democracy and a return to universal manhood **suffrage** (introduced in 1789 but abandoned in 1791). In Paris, charismatic leaders like Georges Danton and Maximilien Robespierre jockeyed for power and influence. Political clubs (like the radical Jacobins) and factions formed. Meetings of the assembly were attended by crowds of regular folk who jeered, cheered, shouted, and threw things at political leaders and speakers. Such crowd participation had a dramatic influence on both the policies adopted and changes in leadership, of which there were many. In Paris and the provinces, local clubs and "section assemblies" drew large numbers of *sans-culottes* (those "without fancy pants") into almost daily political activity.

In the National Assembly, the first order of business for the newly elected deputies was the fate of the former king. Some argued that he should be tried for treason; others argued that he should be executed immediately without trial, whereas conservatives held that he enjoyed royal immunity from either trial or prosecution. The deputies finally decided on a trial, conducted by the National Convention itself. Louis appeared twice in his own defense, but after a month, the deputies voted unanimously to convict him of collusion with foreign powers and then, by a narrow majority, to execute him. In January 1793, he was beheaded on the guillotine, as was his wife, Marie Antoinette, nine months later. The guillotine, a mechanical beheading device recently introduced as a painless (thus, more humane) and efficient means of execution, became another symbol of the Revolution.

Within a month of Louis's execution, Britain, Holland, and Spain joined Austria and Prussia in the war against France. The threat that the French revolutionaries posed to the monarchies of Europe was made more immediate and personal by the fact that Marie Antoinette was the sister of the ruler of Austria. In France, the combined threats of counterrevolution and foreign war strengthened the hand of more radical factions within the National Convention, which set up a Committee of Public Safety to defend the gains of the Revolution and eliminate its enemies. Led first by Danton and then by Robespierre, the committee officially proclaimed the Terror, responding both to internal enemies and the threat of foreign invasion. Those who opposed the Revolution were now classified as suspects subject to arrest and trial. As Robespierre put it, "To good citizens revolutionary government owes the full protection of the state; to the enemies of the people it owes only death."[1] The guillotine was the usual method of execution. Overall, about forty thousand people perished during the Terror. Within a year, the Terror had run its course, but not before consuming its own. Upon being led to the scaffold, Danton told the executioner,

> **BOX 2.2**
> **Charles Dickens on the Guillotine**
>
> The legacy and meaning of the French Revolution are among the most hotly contested matters in all of history. It was, after all, a time of magnificent achievements but also of much suffering. In England, where political change had come in mostly peaceful ways, many people were appalled by the violence of the French Revolution. Charles Dickens, for example, who was born a generation after the Revolution, writes in *A Tale of Two Cities* of his revulsion of the worship of the guillotine during the Terror:
>
> It was the National Razor which shaved close. . . . It was the sign of regeneration of the human race. It superseded the Cross. Models of it were worn on breasts from which the Cross was discarded, and it was bowed down to and believed in where the Cross was denied.

"Show them my head; it is a sight worth seeing." A few months later, Robespierre followed him to the guillotine.

After the death of Robespierre, the convention dismantled the revolutionary dictatorship, wrote yet another constitution, and established a five-man Directory to hold executive power. The Directory would last for four years, trying to find middle ground between radical revolution and royalist reaction. Still at war with the rest of Europe and facing continuing political ferment, the Directory increasingly came to rely for support on the military as its own political legitimacy waned. The directors themselves supported a *coup d'état* in late 1799, placing the levers of power in the hands of a dynamic young military officer named Napoleon Bonaparte.

NAPOLEON AND EUROPE

Napoleon had been made a general in 1793 at the age of twenty-four. Two years later, he made a name for himself by putting down a royalist uprising in Paris. The next year, he was given command of the French army of Italy, where he scored victory after victory against the supposedly superior forces of Austria. He returned to France a hero, and even after the coup of 1799, his popularity remained high. He was elected first consul for life in 1802, and two years later crowned himself Napoleon I, emperor of the French. He was to hold that title for ten years, and during most of that time, he and France dominated Europe.

Within France, Napoleon pursued the middle course of the Directory, trying to preserve the major gains of the Revolution while avoiding a return either to radicalism or to monarchy. He emasculated representative institutions, censored the press, put down rebellions, and imprisoned or executed those caught in either royalist or republican conspiracies. He also made peace with the Catholic Church, signing a concordat with the pope and eliminating most of the harassment of the church and clergy that had been unleashed by the Revolution. Perhaps his most enduring legacy was the introduction of a new legal code, the Napoleonic Code, which remains today the basis for the legal systems of France and most of the rest of Europe (see box 2.3).

Napoleon formed mass armies and led them into other countries to spread the ideas of the Revolution and to enhance his own power and that of France. In 1805, he inflicted a punishing defeat on combined Austrian and Russian forces at Austerlitz, in Austria. The next year, he crushed the Prussian army at Jena, in Germany, and occupied Berlin. At the height of the Napoleonic empire in 1810–12, France controlled Spain, Italy, Belgium, Holland, Switzerland, and much of Germany, Poland, Croatia, and Slovenia.

Bonaparte Crossing the Alps (1801) by Jacques-Louis David. David was a supporter of the Revolution whose paintings contributed to the heroic image of Napoleon.

BOX 2.3
The Napoleonic Code

Before the Revolution, royal law and church law both competed with local-level traditions in many French provinces. Napoleon commissioned a battery of lawyers to help establish a uniform code of law and personally played a hand in the project. The code, over two thousand articles in length, institutionalized many of the gains of the Revolution, including equality before the law, freedom of religion, and the rights of property owners. It also reflected Napoleon's traditional views of the family, which he considered a crucial intermediary between the state and the individual. Napoleon once complained, "Women are considered too highly. They should not be regarded as equal to men. In reality, they are nothing more than machines for producing children."* The new legal code reflected this patriarchal view, with women and children legally subordinate to and dependent on their husbands or fathers, and with men assigned control of family property. However, the code also required that inheritances be divided among all sons and daughters, thus ending the practice of primogeniture, which assigned all property to the eldest son. As an unexpected consequence, French couples began to limit themselves to two or three children, so their property would not be further divided.

The Napoleonic Code, applied or adopted throughout much of Europe, is still the basis for the legal systems of much of the Continent, including secular but Muslim Turkey, as well as of the state of Louisiana, which was a French colony at the time of the code's inception. Napoleon himself felt that his code was his most enduring legacy: "My glory is not to have won forty battles . . . what nothing will destroy, what will live eternally, is my Civil Code."†

*Cited in John Merriman, *A History of Modern Europe*, vol. 2 (New York: Norton, 1996), 567.
†Merriman, *A History of Modern Europe*, 567.

Napoleon was not a revolutionary, but he solidified many of the revolutionary changes of 1789–91, and he himself supported most of the ideas and proposals of Enlightenment *philosophes*. Through his military conquests, he spread many of the ideas of the Enlightenment and the Revolution across the Continent. In many of these areas, Napoleon established satellite republics complete with constitutions, declarations of rights, elected legislatures, and civil equality, and he implemented financial, judicial, and administrative reforms modeled on those of the French. In every part of the empire, he undermined feudalism, introduced a legal code, fostered notions of representative government, and awakened the spirit of nationalism. The peoples of these areas did not exactly welcome French rule per se, but they saw French innovations as tools to be used against their own repressive monarchies. The monarchs, of course, saw Napoleon as a threat, both to the old order and to the balance of power in Europe.

BOX 2.4
The War of 1812

The War of 1812 between the United States and Britain was an indirect consequence of the Napoleonic Wars in Europe. The United States had remained neutral in the conflict between Britain and France, but there was much sympathy in the States for French revolutionary ideals and lingering gratitude for France's support of the American revolution a generation earlier. Continuing US trade with France during the European wars prompted the British to blockade US ports, intercept American merchant ships, and "impress" US seamen suspected of being British deserters. The United States declared war on Britain in 1812, although this dispute remained a sideshow for Britain, which was focused on defeating Napoleon. When this finally happened, the blockade ended, as did the impetus for the conflict with the United States, which was concluded in 1815. Many Americans celebrated this as the country's "second war of independence," and the lyrics to the country's national anthem were composed by Francis Scott Key in 1814 after he witnessed the British naval bombardment of Baltimore's Fort McHenry.

Eventually, though, Napoleon's extensive military conquests spread his power too thin. In 1812, he assembled an army of four hundred thousand soldiers and launched an attack on Russia. Napoleon had changed the nature of warfare in Europe by conscripting huge armies and infusing them with a commitment to fight for France and for "liberty, equality, and fraternity," the slogan of the Revolution. Almost everywhere, the size and spirit of these armies overcame the better trained, but mercenary, armies of European monarchs, whose soldiers fought for a salary rather than a cause. But the army of the Russian campaign dwarfed any previous one, and its size posed intractable problems of supply, movement, and logistics. By the time Napoleon's army reached Moscow, the Russian winter had set in and the city was in flames, probably set by the Russians themselves to deprive the French of shelter from the cold. In retreat, almost the whole French army either deserted or perished from cold, hunger, and guerrilla attacks by the Russians. Only seventy thousand made it back to France.

By this time, Austria, Prussia, and Britain were allied with the Russians against Napoleon, whose military fortunes began to wane. The allied armies pressed on, entered Paris, and forced Napoleon to abdicate, sending him into exile on the island of Elba off the Italian coast. He escaped within a year, rallied support in France, and confronted the allied armies again, only to be finally defeated by a British and Prussian army at the famous battle of Waterloo, in Belgium, in 1815. This time, he was banished to a small island in the South Atlantic, St. Helena, where he died in 1821.

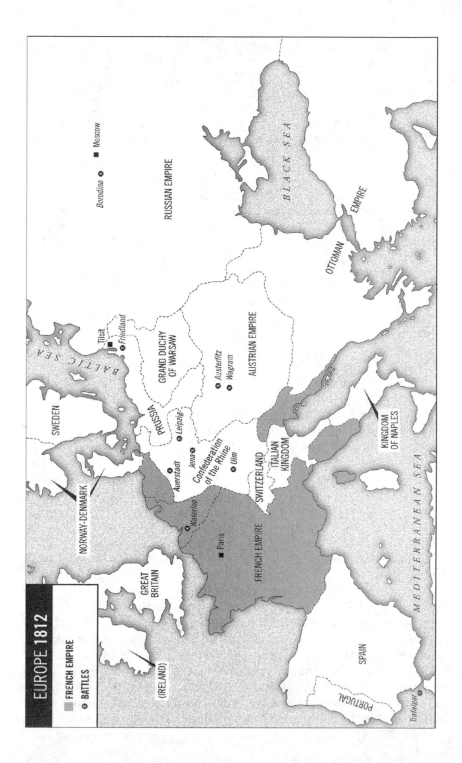

BOX 2.5
Beethoven and Napoleon

The German composer Ludwig van Beethoven (1770–1827) was also a revolutionary—in the world of music—and like many revolutionaries he had divided feelings about the French Revolution and Napoleon Bonaparte. Beethoven, himself a republican (favoring representative government), admired Napoleon as the embodiment of the values of the French Revolution and, in 1803, dedicated his Third Symphony to the general. But the next year, when Napoleon declared himself emperor of France, Beethoven became disillusioned and tore up the page dedicating the symphony to Napoleon, renaming it simply *Eroica*—the heroic symphony.

The way Beethoven wrote music, and the music itself, was revolutionary, and reflected the spirit of the times. His predecessors (including Franz Joseph Haydn and Mozart) had mostly written works commissioned by kings or princes, keeping the aristocratic audience in mind and performing in refined and elegant courts. Beethoven followed his own individual spirit, wrote with a passion and bombast that shocked his audiences, and performed at public concerts that people paid to hear. He took music to the streets. The *Eroica* symphony, like all of his major works, was a massive and lengthy composition, full of tension, emotion, tragedy, and joy. It was revolutionary music, and Beethoven himself became a symbol of freedom and individualism.

With the defeat of Napoleon, European monarchs attempted a restoration of the old order in France. Louis XVIII, brother of Louis XVI, was placed on the throne, thus restoring the Bourbon monarchy. The boundaries of France were returned to those of 1790. However, the revolutionary genie could not be put back into the bottle entirely. Louis XVIII issued a constitutional charter that incorporated many of the changes that had entered into French life and society since 1789, including a degree of freedom of speech and parliamentary government.

At the Congress of Vienna (1814–15), the four triumphant Great Powers (Britain, Austria, Russia, and Prussia) confirmed the restoration of the old order, with some modifications, and put back in place the balance of power with the intent of preserving monarchical power and maintaining a lasting peace. And indeed, no continent-wide wars occurred in Europe for the next hundred years. But the French Revolution and the Napoleonic wars had unleashed forces that would shake the foundations of European society. The first modern revolution occurred in 1789, and the 1792 French republic was the first modern experiment with democracy in Europe; these events have inspired democrats, liberals, socialists, and revolutionaries ever since. Napoleon spread ideas of democracy, liberty, and equality and planted the seeds of representative

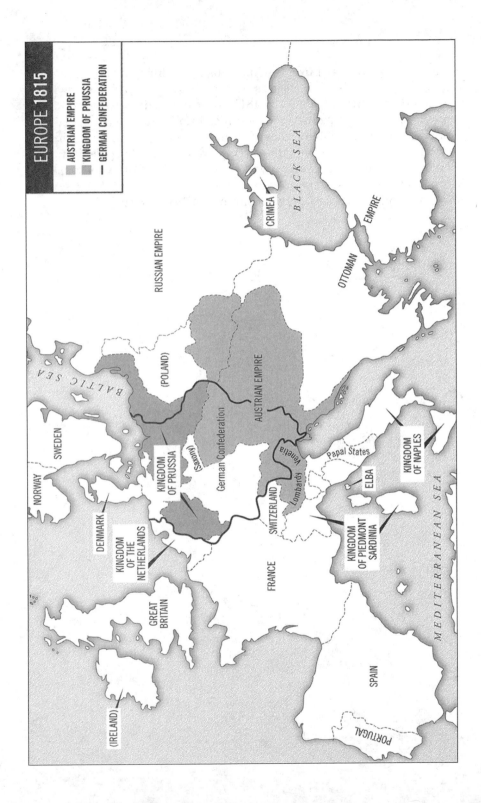

EUROPE 1815

AUSTRIAN EMPIRE
KINGDOM OF PRUSSIA
GERMAN CONFEDERATION

BLACK SEA

CRIMEA

RUSSIAN EMPIRE

OTTOMAN   EMPIRE

BALTIC SEA

(POLAND)

AUSTRIAN EMPIRE

NORWAY

SWEDEN

(Saxony)

German Confederation

KINGDOM OF PRUSSIA

Venetia

Lombardy

Papal States

ELBA

KINGDOM OF NAPLES

DENMARK

KINGDOM OF THE NETHERLANDS

SWITZERLAND

KINGDOM OF PIEDMONT SARDINIA

GREAT BRITAIN

FRANCE

MEDITERRANEAN SEA

(IRELAND)

SPAIN

PORTUGAL

government all across Europe while causing military destruction and the loss of hundreds of thousands of human lives. Even Russia, which withstood the French attack in 1812, was affected: Russian soldiers who pursued the retreating French armies into France were exposed to French civilization, Enlightenment thinking, and revolutionary ideology. Back in Russia, some of them attempted to establish a constitutional monarchy, in the Decembrist revolt of 1825. This effort was crushed, but the Decembrists were an inspiration for the revolutionaries who sparked the next great modern revolution, in 1917, in Russia.

3

The Industrial Revolution and the Birth of Capitalism

The Industrial Revolution refers to the era in which economic production shifted from the use of hand tools to the use of power machinery, fueled primarily by coal and steam. Most of this process took place between 1750 and 1850 in Europe, although the most intense changes occurred in Great Britain in the half century after 1780.[1] The Industrial Revolution occurred at about the same time as the French Revolution, although the two were quite separate. The former affected mostly England and mostly the economy; the latter affected France and the European continent, mostly in the political sphere. England was relatively immune from the French Revolution and the Napoleonic wars, and Europe did not fully engage the Industrial Revolution until after 1820.

The impact of the Industrial Revolution was at least as great as that of the French Revolution. It soon spread from England to western Europe, then to eastern Europe, and then to the rest of the world, initiating a broader process of modernization that was to extend through the nineteenth century and into the twentieth. The mechanization of production allowed a huge increase in productivity and economic output, thus laying the groundwork for modern industrial society. It also had far-reaching social and political consequences, with the advent of assembly-line factories, urbanization, the transformation of the family, and the rise of a new social class, the urban working class, or **proletariat**.

Chapter 3

CAUSES OF THE INDUSTRIAL REVOLUTION

When compared to the rest of late-eighteenth-century Europe, England seems a natural location for the birth of the Industrial Revolution. What's more, the attributes that fostered the Industrial Revolution there are the very same that helped secure England as the world leader in industrialization well into the nineteenth century. The island nation had an educated and mobile population; a ready supply of coal and iron; an extensive trade network of rivers, canals, and coastal sea-lanes; small internal distances; a growing population; and political stability. It also managed to avoid the disruptions of warfare and political upheaval created by the French Revolution and the Napoleonic wars.

The Industrial Revolution was preceded, and in part caused by, an agricultural revolution that had two components: the development of scientific agriculture and the **enclosure movement**. We saw earlier that the Scientific Revolution laid the groundwork for the Enlightenment; it also led to many practical inventions and innovations, including some in agriculture. In about 1700, Jethro Tull developed a seed drill that planted seeds in neat rows, replacing the much less efficient method of scattering seeds by hand. In the mid-eighteenth century, British farmers began planting turnips, which not only enriched the soil but provided food for livestock during the winter months, which previously had been slaughtered at the onset of winter. Scientific breeding of cattle and sheep was also introduced about this time. These new agricultural techniques dramatically improved productivity and made it possible for England (and the rest of Europe) to feed its rapidly growing population. The revolution in agriculture staved off, at least temporarily, the gloomy predictions of Thomas Malthus, the English economist who argued, in "An Essay on the Principle of Population" (1798), that poverty and famine were unavoidable because population increases geometrically whereas food production increases only arithmetically.

The other aspect of the revolution in agriculture was the enclosure movement. This involved the efforts of landowning aristocrats and country gentry to enclose common lands with fences, walls, and hedges, so that they could be used for private pastures and the production of grain. This gradually eroded the medieval practice, hitherto protected by common law, of providing free access to grazing lands and woodlands. In the late seventeenth century, however, when large landowners controlled the British Parliament, they pushed through hundreds of enclosure acts that legitimized this practice. Ownership of land thus became concentrated in the hands of a relatively few wealthy landlords. Overall farm sizes increased, allowing economies of scale, increased productivity, and greater food production. These changes in agriculture had two major consequences: with fewer people working the land, many left the countryside to find work in the cities, and the more efficient farms produced more food for the urban markets. Both of these processes fueled urbanization and industrialization.

Industrialization itself began in Britain with cotton. Before the mechanization of the textile industry, Britain produced mostly linen and wool at home and imported cotton textiles, primarily from India. In 1707, the British government banned the import of Indian textiles in order to protect and support the domestic cotton industry. This had the desired effect, but several important eighteenth-century inventions, namely the flying shuttle, spinning jenny, and spinning mule, increasingly mechanized the cotton spinning and weaving processes, making them vastly more efficient and thereby providing even greater stimulus to cotton output. Cotton clothing, less expensive and easier to clean than wool and other fabrics, allowed poor people to become adequately clothed, and quickly grew popular in all social classes.

The increased production of cotton in England eventually exceeded domestic demand, so for the industry to continue growing, it needed markets outside the country. It found these markets in the New World, especially after the American War of Independence. The growth of slavery in the United States generated a need for cheap cotton textiles, which British merchants supplied, in which to clothe the slaves. The cotton trade became a two-way enterprise after Eli Whitney's 1793 invention of the cotton gin, a machine for separating cotton seeds from fiber, a process previously done by hand. Before then, Britain had imported most of its raw cotton from the **Ottoman Empire** and the Caribbean, but the cotton gin made American cotton much less expensive. So after this point, British cotton manufacturers imported most of their raw cotton from the United States and exported their finished cotton textiles back to that country, thus creating a boom in British cotton-textile production and stimulating trade and economic growth in both countries.

Although the English spinning machines and the American cotton gin were important inventions for jump-starting the Industrial Revolution, the steam engine was the single most crucial invention of this era. Thomas Newcomen had created an early, but clumsy, version of the steam engine in England in 1711, as a practical solution to help pump floodwaters from coal mines. A Scot, James Watt, improved the machine immensely between 1763 and 1775. At first, the steam engine was used, as before, to facilitate the extraction of coal. But it soon became clear that the engine could be used for other purposes as well. In the 1790s, the cotton spinning mule was adapted to steam power, instantly increasing output to a hundred times that of a worker on a manual spinning wheel. This was indeed a revolutionary change in the single most important and widespread industry in Britain.

These new machines led to another innovation, the factory. Steam and water power required the concentration of labor close to the power source, and the heavy equipment (spinning machines, power looms, and steam engines) necessitated large buildings in which to house them. Manchester, a textile-manufacturing center in the English Midlands, became the first modern industrial city. With the proliferation of factories and the increased productivity afforded by mechanization and the assembly line, Manchester's output of textiles surged, and the city was soon outcompeting India. Although earlier in the eighteenth century an effort had been made to restrict trade through a ban on Indian imports, now that English cotton no longer needed protection, British manufacturers lobbied for free trade, a term that became a byword of early capitalism.

The steam engine became a motor of economic growth in other ways as well. In 1825, a steam engine was placed on a trolley that carried coal from a mine in Darlington to the port city of Liverpool along a seven-mile track. This was the beginning of the railroad, which was to revolutionize transportation just as it did industry. By 1850, more than six thousand miles of railroad track were laid in Britain. The railroad not only facilitated and accelerated transportation but also contributed to further industrial growth. Its rapid expansion fueled demand for coal, steam engines, iron, and steel. Each mile of newly laid railroad track, for example, used three hundred tons of iron. Between 1830 and 1850, the years of the so-called railway mania, iron output in Britain more than tripled. So the textile factories of towns like Manchester were soon followed by factories for the production of iron, steel, and steam engines, thus laying the groundwork for a modern industrial economy.

The innovations and inventions of the early industrial era were, by and large, the products of practical men searching for ways to increase efficiency and make profits. Hardly any of the inventions mentioned above were conceived by scientists. However, the intellectual and philosophical underpinning for industrialization and early capitalism had been provided by the philosopher and economist Adam Smith, in his 1776 publication *The Wealth of Nations*. We pointed out in chapter 1 how Smith's theory of the natural laws of economic exchange coincided with broader currents of Enlightenment thinking, but Smith was as much a creature of the Industrial Revolution as he was of the Enlightenment, and his book both reflected what was happening economically in England at the time and reinforced and legitimized these trends.

In *The Wealth of Nations*, Smith contends that there are natural laws of production and exchange and of supply and demand and that, if left to their own devices, these laws will naturally regulate the economy in the best possible way. Similarly, each individual should be allowed to follow

BOX 3.1
The Crystal Palace

The Great London Exhibition of 1851, the first world's fair, was a celebration of industrial progress and a symbol of both the Industrial Revolution and British power. The exhibition was held in the Crystal Palace, a huge iron and glass structure resembling a greenhouse and a triumph of prefabrication. It was 1,851 feet long—one foot for each year of the Common Era—with exhibits covering a wide range of industrial, commercial, and artistic products from all over the world. Six million people visited it during the six months of the exhibition. One of the most popular displays was the Hall of Moving Machinery, with newfangled steam engines and other mechanisms laid out like works of art or sculpture for the viewers. The exhibition also had many new mass-produced products for home use, such as elaborate furniture and silver-plated utensils, statues, and vases. In this sense, the Crystal Palace also celebrated and inaugurated the era of mass consumption. Similar exhibitions soon followed in Paris, Vienna, New York, and other cities.

Queen Victoria and Prince Albert opening the Great Exhibition of 1851 in the Crystal Palace. © Photo12/Archives Snark/The Image Works.

his own economic self-interest, unhampered by regulation. The natural laws of supply and demand will respond to the expressions of this self-interest, and the sum total of individual acquisitiveness will be an overall improvement in the general welfare (private vice yields public virtue). The government, in this view, should largely stay out of economic management or regulation, limiting itself to providing a stable environment for the economy: maintaining political stability, providing legal protection for private property and contracts, and enforcing the laws.

All of this, of course, was perfectly consistent with the interests of the new entrepreneurs in Britain, who chafed under the restraints of the old mercantilist system and favored free trade, legal protection for their new factories, and minimal government interference in their businesses.

SOCIOECONOMIC CONSEQUENCES OF INDUSTRIALIZATION

Industrialization transformed not only the economy of Britain but also the workplace, family, and daily life. Before the eighteenth century, most people lived on farms, in villages, or in small towns, and most work was done either in the field, in the home, or in small shops. With the emergence of the factory and urbanization, all of this began to change. Manchester, the quintessential early industrial city, grew tenfold in the last quarter of the eighteenth century, and the whole of Britain exploded with new, large cities during that period. In 1785, only four cities in England and Scotland had a population of fifty thousand or more; seventy years later, there were thirty-two cities of this size.

These cities were set up for industrial production but were not very pleasant places in which to live. Until 1835, no normal procedures existed in England to incorporate cities, so most of the new factory towns had no municipal government or provisions for taxation. Most of these new cities also had no representation whatsoever in the national parliament. So there were few financial and administrative resources to provide basic urban services like police protection, water and sewer, or garbage disposal. One source describes these new cities as follows:

> The new urban agglomerations were drab places, blackened with the heavy soot of the early coal age, settling alike on the mills and the workers' quarters, which were dark at best, for the climate of the Midlands is not sunny. Housing for workers was hastily built, closely packed, and always in short supply, as in all rapidly growing communities. Whole families lived in single rooms, and family life tended to disintegrate. A police officer in Glasgow observed that there were whole blocks of tenements in the city, each swarming with a thousand ragged children who had first names only, usually nicknames—like animals, as he put it.[2]

Work in the factories was unrelenting and grim. Factory hands often had to perform the same task over and over again, with few breaks or changes, during workdays up to fourteen hours long. The work was organized to be fast, coordinated, and intense, so there was little opportunity for socializing. The French feminist and socialist Flora Tristan, after visiting England, wrote that "in English factories, there isn't any singing, chatting or laughter. . . . The master does not want his workers distracted for a minute by any reminders of his life; he demands silence, and a deadly silence there is."[3]

The plants were usually fueled by coal, which meant that the factories, inside and out, were often covered in black dust. Wages were typically so low that a man could not support his wife and children. Therefore, children, some of them as young as six years old, often had to work in the factories as well. The brutal conditions of working-class life in England in the nineteenth century were immortalized in the works of Charles Dickens, as in his novels *Oliver Twist* and *Hard Times*. Dickens himself was a product of this environment. His father was almost constantly in debt, and when he was thrown into debtor's prison, Dickens was forced to leave school, at the age of twelve, and go to work in a bootblack factory to help support his family.

The concentration of workers in cities and factories had political consequences as well. The cramped and dirty working environments of the factories created both tension and the opportunity for laborers to gather and discuss these conditions and their common plight. As workers gained a sense of solidarity and potential power, they organized labor unions, even though these were formally illegal in England before 1825 (and the strike remained illegal for many years after that). Fearing the potential of revolution, Parliament passed an electoral reform act in 1832 that doubled the electorate, but even with that, only one in five adult, male citizens was able to vote. In 1838, a working-class group called the Chartists drew up a people's charter, which demanded universal suffrage for all adult males and the abolition of property requirements for elected members of Parliament. Even though over a million people signed a petition to the House of Commons in support of the charter, the Commons rejected it, and it was another thirty years before suffrage was significantly extended in Britain. This failure of the moderate parliamentary route to labor reform caused many workers to turn toward more radical solutions, including the ideas of socialism and the revolutionary overthrow of capitalism.

Friedrich Engels (1820–95), the German-born manager of a Manchester cotton business, provided a crucial link between industrialization and socialism. Even though he was on the top of the industrial hierarchy, Engels was shocked by the poverty in the city and wrote an account of his observations that was published as *The Condition of the Working Class in England* (1844). Shortly afterward, he met and befriended fellow German Karl Marx and brought him to England, where he began subsidizing Marx's research and writing. He introduced Marx to several leaders of the Chartist movement. In 1848, Marx and Engels collaborated in producing **The Communist Manifesto**, which ended with the phrase "Workers of all countries, unite!" This was one of the first steps in the formation of the communist movement, which would culminate in 1917 with the Russian Revolution.

Communism was just one of the "isms" that emerged in the first half of the nineteenth century. The period saw a proliferation of doctrines and movements of all kinds. More people were becoming involved in society and in social and political issues, and they began thinking more systematically about societal problems. Thus, the words "liberalism," "radicalism," "socialism," and "nationalism" all appeared for the first time in English usage between 1820 and 1850.

Romanticism was also born in this period, although, unlike the political "isms," it was a movement in literature and the arts. Romanticism was a reaction both to the Enlightenment and to the two revolutions of the eighteenth century, rejecting both the pure reason of the Enlightenment and seeking respite from the harsh political and social outcomes of the French and Industrial Revolutions. Romantics stressed the importance of feelings, intuition, and emotions as well as reason, and believed that the world could not be understood completely on the basis of reason and scientific evidence. "Feeling is all," proclaims the German writer Johann Goethe in *Faust*.

Romanticism affected artists and writers all over Europe, flowering in the first decades of the nineteenth century with poets and novelists such as Goethe (*Faust*), the Frenchman Victor Hugo (*Les Misérables*), Alexander Pushkin in Russia, and the English poets Samuel Taylor Coleridge, William Wordsworth, Lord Byron, and Alfred Lord Tennyson. Beethoven, with his stirring, stormy, crowd-pleasing symphonies, launched the Romantic era in music, followed by Chopin, Verdi, Tchaikovsky, and many others. Artists like Eugene Delacroix, J. M. W. Turner, and John Constable glorified nature or heroic figures—usually tragic ones—from history.

Many of these writers and artists struggled with the ambiguous results of the Industrial Revolution and the tensions between tradition and change. Industry had generated enormous wealth and progress, but it also produced misery and alienation. These were issues and tensions that would confront Europeans for generations to come.

THE IMPACT OF THE INDUSTRIAL REVOLUTION

The Industrial Revolution began in England but spread quickly to the rest of the world. Although the most important early inventions occurred in England, others followed elsewhere: in the United States, there was Robert Fulton's steamship and Cyrus McCormick's reaper, which revolutionized the harvesting of wheat, as well as the development of chemical fertilizers by Justus von Liebig and other German chemists. The railroad spread like a spider web all over Europe, linking the Continent together. It accelerated the western territorial expansion of the United States and the eastern expansion of Russia (which occurred at about the same time). In Germany, pig iron production quadrupled between 1825 and 1860; French coal and iron output both doubled in the same period.

In 1837, nineteen-year-old Victoria ascended to the English throne. She was to rule for the next sixty-four years, and that period has come to be associated with her name: the Victorian era. By the time of Victoria's coronation, the industrial era was well under way in Britain, and the newly emerging middle class was coming to dominate British society and shape its system of values. Although industrialism and urbanization may have been hard on the working class, it brought many benefits and many changes to the middle class. Many more consumer goods were now available to those who could afford them, and factories were busy producing "luxury" goods that had previously been accessible only to the aristocracy. Libraries, theaters, and symphonies were springing up in the cities to provide middle-class entertainment, and most major cities had their own newspapers.

BOX 3.2
Tennyson's "Locksley Hall"

A classic poem of the Romantic era, Alfred Lord Tennyson's "Locksley Hall" (1842) illustrates the raw emotions and passions of young love and makes conflicted observations about the human situation during the Industrial Revolution. In the poem, the speaker, a member of the English gentry, returns to his old home on the sea and reminisces about falling in love with Amy ("In the spring a young man's fancy lightly turns to thoughts of love"), then being rejected by her for a lover her parents found more suitable ("Oh my Amy, mine no more! / O the dreary, dreary moorland! O the barren, barren shore!"). Tennyson then draws the connection between the optimism of young love and the societal optimism of the early nineteenth century ("Men, my brothers, men the workers, ever reaping something new"), only to be filled with doubts and disappointment and the yearning for "Summer isles of Eden" where "methinks would be enjoyment more, than in this march of mind, / In the steamship, in the railway, in the thoughts that shake mankind." In the end, though, he opts for optimism and progress, with a nod to the railroad: "Not in vain the distant beacons. Forward, forward let us range, / Let the great world spin for ever down the ringing grooves of change."

As part of the socioeconomic transformation, gender roles were being redefined. Whereas in the preindustrial era a family often worked together in the field or in cottage industries, now the man was going to work in the city, and his wife was expected to take care of the home and children (although many working-class women remained in the workforce until late in the nineteenth century). Victorian values dictated the importance of hard work (even more than talent) and the stability and solidity of the nuclear family. Romantic marriages became the norm, and family sizes grew smaller.

Middle-class norms and Victorian values dominated British society for most of the nineteenth century and helped maintain relative stability and prosperity in that country. Underneath the veneer, however, were smoldering grievances and tensions, as depicted in the works of Dickens, Engels, and the Romantic poets. It was on the continent of Europe, however, rather than in England, where the French Revolution unleashed many of these tensions and the Industrial Revolution came to a head.

4

1848: The People's Spring

The year 1848 in Europe is sometimes called the People's Spring because, in the course of a few months, popular revolts and revolutions occurred all over Europe. These began in France but affected virtually every country except England and Russia. Monarchies were overthrown, constitutions proclaimed, or national independence declared in France, Austria, Hungary, Bohemia, Germany, Italy, and elsewhere. Never before in European history had there been such widespread and universal popular ferment, and since that time only the Eastern European revolutions of 1989 have shown a similar revolutionary contagion. All of the 1848 revolutions failed, however, and within a few years their accomplishments were mostly reversed. But the 1848 revolts further propagated the seeds of democracy and nationalism that were sown by the French Revolution of 1789.

As with all revolutions, there were both long- and short-term precipitants to the 1848 events. The Enlightenment had set the stage, with its ideas of individualism, human rights, and popular sovereignty. The Romantic movement in literature and the arts also stressed the individual and individualism and added the notions of heroism and heroic struggle to the mix. The Industrial Revolution set in motion enormous social and economic forces, including the increasing assertiveness of the new middle class and the proletariat, both of which had interests at odds with those of the social and economic structures of the old regime. While all of these currents of change intermingled, the social and political elites clung to tradition. As we have seen, the years after 1815 were a period of reaction as the monarchs of Europe tried to stuff the genie of revolution back into the bottle following the defeat of Napoleon. But the forces of change could not be contained. Already in the 1820s, national-independence movements were under way in Belgium (against Dutch rule) and Greece (against Turkey), and in 1830 Paris was once again convulsed by a revolution from the streets. All of these tensions were compounded by the great potato famine in the years after 1845, which contributed to a continent-wide economic recession. Yet another revolution in France in 1848 was the spark that lit the tinderbox.

EUROPE AFTER 1815: REACTION

With the defeat of Napoleon at Waterloo, the European powers gathered in Vienna, in 1815, to reassemble Europe following the old (pre-1789) map, although some changes were made. A new German confederation of thirty-nine independent states was created to take the place of an earlier confederation and the Holy Roman Empire.[1] Austria was given control of much of northern Italy. Russia's control of Finland, Lithuania, and eastern Poland was confirmed, and a separate kingdom of Poland was created ("Congress Poland"), with the Russian tsar as king. Almost none of the independent republics created by Napoleon were allowed to survive. As Russia's Tsar Alexander remarked at the time, "Republics are not in fashion."[2]

As one can see from the map of Europe in this period on page 35, the Continent was a hodgepodge of **nation-states**, empires, principalities, and mini-states. Portugal, Spain, France, and England were more or less unified nation-states by that time, but none of the rest of Europe had assumed the configuration of nation-states that it is today. "Germany" did not yet exist, and central Europe was divided among several dozen small and middle-size states, such as Bavaria and Prussia, with largely German populations. The Austrian Empire of the Habsburgs was a polyglot combination of German, Hungarian, and Slavic peoples. The Italians were distributed among various kingdoms, principalities, and Papal States. The Ottoman Empire controlled southeastern Europe, and Russia was a multinational empire with dozens of major nationalities, including Finns, Poles, and Ukrainians, and hundreds of smaller ones.

All the major European powers were controlled by monarchs with varying authority, from the constitutional monarchy of England to the thoroughly despotic **autocracy** of Russia. After the defeat of Napoleon, the victorious powers (England, Russia, Austria, and Prussia) formed a **Quadruple Alliance** to coordinate conservative efforts to squelch any new outbreaks of Bonapartism or revolution. After France was added to this alliance in 1818, it was referred to as the *concert system*. Prince Clemens von Metternich, chief minister of the Habsburg monarchy, was the conservative leader of Europe and the driving force behind the **Concert of Europe**. Metternich organized several congresses of the European leaders during the 1820s to discuss intervention against political unrest on the Continent, and the allies did actually intervene in both Italy and Spain in the early 1820s, to put down nationalist and liberal revolts.

LIBERALISM AND NATIONALISM IN THE EARLY NINETEENTH CENTURY

Arrayed against these forces of conservatism was the gathering strength of liberalism and nationalism, both of which had their origins in the Enlightenment and the French Revolution. Actually, two separate but related currents of liberalism existed: political liberalism and economic liberalism. Political liberalism grew out of the Enlightenment ideas of Locke, Rousseau, and others who favored government by consent and elaborated principles of popular sovereignty, constitutionalism (i.e., the powers of government limited by constitutions), and tolerance of divergent points of view. They promoted individual rights, respect for private property, the rule of law, and stronger parliaments, although most accepted the presence of a limited monarchy. The standard-bearer of nineteenth-century liberalism was the English philosopher John Stuart Mill, who argued in his essay "On Liberty" (1859) that one person's freedom could be restricted only if it impinged on the individual freedom of another: "The only purpose for which power can be rightfully exercised over any member of a civilized community, against his will, is to prevent harm to others."

Economic liberalism was related to Enlightenment ideas of private property, but derived more directly from Adam Smith (*The Wealth of Nations*) and David Ricardo (*Principles of Political Economy*), who emphasized *laissez-faire*, the "invisible hand" of the market, and free trade. Economic liberals, like political ones, wanted to limit the power of government, but especially in terms of its regulation of the economy. They favored a dismantling of the mercantilist system, in which governments controlled almost all foreign trade; the elimination of protectionist **tariffs**; and the reduction of government rules and regulations that inhibited or hampered commercial and industrial activity.

Political and economic liberals had much to agree about, although differences in emphasis did exist. John Stuart Mill, for example, defended *laissez-faire* economics, but only if the power of entrepreneurs was balanced with rights for employees and their trade unions. Both forms of liberalism grew stronger with the rapid emergence, in the nineteenth century, of the middle class, whose members advocated increased power and influence for themselves in both political and economic spheres.

Related to liberalism and another powerful driving force in nineteenth-century Europe was nationalism. The ultimate goal of nationalism is to create a unified nation-state, in which the citizens of that state identify with both the nation (the people) and with the state (the political community). The ideal of the nation-state was relatively new in Europe and in the world generally. Before the sixteenth century, most political communities were built on family dynasties (hereditary monarchies), with little regard for popular allegiance or national culture. In that century, powerful monarchs began to centralize political control within their countries and to distance themselves from outside control by emperors or popes. This movement coincided with the Protestant Reformation, which questioned and challenged the supremacy of the Roman Catholic Church. In England in 1534, for example, Henry VIII, in his efforts to divorce Catherine of Aragon and marry Anne Boleyn, signed the Act of Supremacy, which rejected papal authority and established the Church of England, with Henry in control. This was the beginning of the emergence of England as a nation-state and was followed by nation-state consolidation in Spain, France, and elsewhere.

The forging of centralized, unified, national states by monarchs, from the top down, is sometimes referred to as **civic nationalism**. **Popular nationalism**, the forging of states from the bottom up, is more recent still and is linked to the Enlightenment and uses the revolutionary ideas of the people as the source of power. This form of nationalism assumes that people who share a common language, culture, and identity—a nation—should be in charge of their own political destiny. It sees the people as a whole—rather than simply the elite—as the repository of culture. This kind of populist nationalism was apparent in France during the 1789 revolution, and was symbolized by people wearing their hair naturally, snubbing the use of wigs, and wearing common working trousers instead of silk breeches. In fact, ordinary working people, the emblem of the Revolution, were referred to as the *sans-culottes* (without fancy pants).

The political manifestation of nationalism is the demand for autonomous political communities based on the nation; it threatened primarily, of course, the multinational and autocratic states that still controlled most of Europe in the nineteenth century. Napoleon had helped spread these ideas, even creating new national states in Poland, Holland, and parts of Italy, but the Congress of Vienna abolished most of these states. The idea of nationalism remained widespread, however, and the precedent of the nation-state was established. In the years of reaction after 1815, Italian nationalist and revolutionary Giuseppe Mazzini (1805–72) popularized the principle of nationalism. In the 1830s, Mazzini founded a secret organization, Young Italy, committed to ridding Italy of foreign rulers and creating a unified Italian state. "Neither pope nor king," he declared, "only God and the people." Later, he created an international branch of his organization, Young Europe, which trained a network of conspirators across the Continent to agitate for democratic constitutions.

PRECURSORS TO 1848: THE 1830 REVOLUTION IN FRANCE

These liberal and national movements came together in revolts and revolutions in numerous places in the 1820s and 1830s, including Belgium (chafing under Dutch rule), Spain, and several Italian states. The best-known and most successful revolutionary movement before 1830, however, was the Greek revolt against Ottoman control. The Greeks won sympathy in Europe as a Christian nation struggling against Muslim domination and from the European sense that western civilization had begun in Greece. So, in contrast to other national insurgencies, the revolt in Greece actually won support from some of the monarchies in Europe, and the Greeks finally won their independence in 1830. (The British Romantic poet Lord Byron died while fighting for the Greek cause.)

But it was France, once again, that experienced the most important upheaval during this period—the July Revolution of 1830. The restored Bourbon monarch, Louis XVIII, had been succeeded by Charles X in 1824, who quickly moved toward a more absolutist regime, threatening to roll back most of the gains of the 1789 revolution. Legislative elections in 1830 brought in a legislature that opposed and resisted the reactionary tendencies of the king. In July, Charles declared the elections invalid, outlawed public assembly, and stepped up censorship. The response was immediate: barricades were thrown up and workers, students, and intellectuals massed in the streets, defying the army and the police. Most of the army refused to fire on the protesters, however, and Charles, not wanting to suffer the same fate as his brother (Louis XVI, who was beheaded in 1793), abdicated and fled to England.

In seeking a successor as king, the revolutionaries bypassed the Bourbon line and placed on the throne the Duke of Orleans. As a young man, the duke had served in the republican army of 1792, so he was assumed to be sympathetic to revolutionary ideals. He took the name Louis Philippe and called himself not the king of France, but the king of the French; he flew the tricolor flag of the Revolution, not that of the Bourbon lily. France still had a monarchy, but it was the end of the Bourbon monarchy, and this king owed his throne to the insurrection, not to his bloodline.

Word of the July uprising spread throughout Europe, sparking similar uprisings in Italy, Germany, Switzerland, Spain, Portugal, Belgium, and

Poland. The outcomes of these revolts were mixed. In Brussels, disturbances just a month after the Paris events led to demands for the independence of Belgium from Holland, which was finally granted the following year. A nationalist revolt in Poland against Russia, however, was brutally repressed. In the aftermath, Poland was dissolved and merged into the Russian Empire, once again disappearing from the map. (In the late eighteenth-century **Partitions of Poland**, the country had been dismembered and absorbed by its three neighboring empires—Russia, Prussia, and Austria.) Nevertheless, the 1830 events were a clarion call to revolution that was heard all over the Continent. The French novelist Victor Hugo wrote, in 1831, that he had heard "the dull sound of revolution, still deep down in the earth, pushing out under every kingdom in Europe its subterranean galleries from the central shaft of the mine which is Paris."[3]

THE REVOLUTIONS OF 1848

In France, with two revolutions in as many generations, the principle of popular sovereignty was increasingly affirmed and consolidated, at least in rough form. So when new hardships and renewed repression confronted the French in the 1840s, revolution was once again an option. A major economic recession and food shortages in 1846–47 fueled popular unrest. The economic problems affected every country in Europe, not just France, and were caused in part by a devastating failure of the potato crop. The potato blight hit especially hard in Ireland, causing widespread famine, a million deaths, and the emigration of another million from the country.

The economic depression was accompanied in France by a new round of political repression in the 1840s. The Chamber of Deputies did provide a certain check on the power of the monarch, Louis Philippe, but with only one man in thirty eligible to vote, the chamber was increasingly irrelevant and ineffectual. The king resolutely opposed a popular campaign for broader voting rights and other reforms. Peaceful protest demonstrations in Paris, in February 1848, prompted police action, which led once again to street barricades and revolution. Louis Philippe, like Charles X eighteen years earlier, abdicated and fled to England. For a second time, a Paris revolution unseated a monarch in three days.

This time, however, the ouster of the monarch was not enough. By the 1840s, France, and especially Paris, was in the throes of the Industrial Revolution, with the consequent emergence of a new and vocal urban working class. Many workers insisted on a social revolution as well as a political one, and the ideas of socialism were gaining currency in the cities of France and other countries. In January 1848, Marx and Engels published their call for socialist revolution in *The Communist Manifesto*.

BOX 4.1
Adam Mickiewicz: Romantic Poet and Revolutionary

The Polish national poet Adam Mickiewicz (1798–1855) symbolizes the close association between romanticism, nationalism, and revolution. He first gained attention with his *Ballady i romanse* (Ballads and Romances, 1822), which opened the Romantic era in Polish literature. His epic poetic masterpiece *Pan Tadeusz* is a nostalgic panorama of gentry society in its last days and the forces pulling it apart. In his fantasy drama *Dziady* (Forefathers Eve), Mickiewicz sees Poland as fulfilling a messianic role among European nations by embodying Christian themes of suffering and redemption. In this work and others, he glorifies resistance and rebellion. These romantic notions, and his image of Poland as "The Christ of Nations," became rallying calls for Polish nationalists all the way up through 1989.

Mickiewicz was a political activist as well as a brilliant writer. As a young man, he was enamored of Voltaire and other Enlightenment philosophers. He witnessed (and admired) the Napoleonic army when it entered his hometown on its expedition to Russia in 1812. His participation in patriotic literary clubs got him arrested and expelled from Poland, and he eventually ended up in Paris. He tried unsuccessfully to return to Poland in 1830, to support the doomed national insurrection against the Russians. During the People's Spring of 1848, he set off for Italy to organize a Polish legion there to fight for the liberation of Italians from Austria. He issued a set of principles for the legion that echoed those of the Enlightenment:

> Everybody in the nation is a citizen. All citizens are equal before the law. . . . To the Jew, our elder brother, esteem and help on his way to eternal good and welfare, and in all matters equal rights. . . . To every family, a plot of land under the care of the community. To every community, common land under the care of the nation.*

The 1848 revolutions failed, and Mickiewicz returned to Paris. He joined another heroic lost cause in 1855, traveling to Constantinople to join a Polish legion in the Crimean War to fight against Russia. He contracted cholera and died there. His body was returned to France, but in 1890 his remains were transported to Poland and buried with Polish kings in Wawel Cathedral in Kraków.

---

*Cited in Czesław Miłosz, *The History of Polish Literature*, 2nd ed. (Berkeley: University of California Press, 1983), 230.

In Paris, a provisional government had established national workshops to provide jobs for the unemployed, and these now became a source of demands from workers for improved working conditions. In April, elections produced a new National Assembly, based on universal male suffrage, but it was overwhelmingly conservative. In June, the assembly resolved to close the workshops, and workers took to the streets in protest. They stormed the assembly, declared it dissolved, established their own provisional government, and called for a social revolution to supplement the purely political one. The army and the police sided with the government, however, and restored the Constituent Assembly, which promptly declared martial law. Paris was convulsed with a raging class war in which armed workers confronted soldiers across barricades all over the city. In the bloody June Days of June 24 to 26, several thousand people were killed and eleven thousand insurgents were imprisoned or deported. The specter of socialist revolution had been suppressed, but the events of June sent a shudder through all the governments of Europe.

As with the revolutions of both 1789 and 1830, the gains of the 1848 revolution in France were short-lived and soon reversed. In the aftermath of the June Days, the Constituent Assembly began drafting a constitution for a new republic and called for the popular election of a president. One of the candidates was Louis Napoleon Bonaparte, the nephew of the great Napoleon. He claimed to be a friend of the common people and also promised to restore order, an attractive combination after the traumatic events of the summer. He was elected by a landslide in December 1848. But in the tradition of his uncle, he soon undermined the democracy that brought him to power. In 1851, he seized absolute control in a *coup d'état* and dissolved the assembly; the next year, he declared himself emperor and took the name Napoleon III. Once again, the French political pendulum had swung back to reaction.

REVOLT SPREADS THROUGH EUROPE

The influence of the events in Paris reached far beyond French borders. In 1848 and 1849, revolts spread to Austria, Prussia, Hungary, Bohemia, and parts of Italy. Some of these revolts contained either the liberal or socialist ingredients of the French experience, but some also reflected peasant grievances against landlords or nationalist aspirations.

The most serious and widespread revolts struck the Austrian Empire of the Habsburg monarchy, with its capital at Vienna. The Austrian Empire was the most populous state in Europe after Russia. It had three major geographic divisions, Austria, Bohemia, and Hungary, containing a dozen nationalities, including Germans, Czechs, Magyars (Hungarians), Poles, and Slovaks, so that the empire was vulnerable to both liberalism and nationalism. Soon after news of the February revolution in Paris reached Vienna, that city faced its own insurrection. Workers and soldiers invaded the imperial palace, forcing Prince Metternich, stalwart of the Concert of Europe, to flee the city in disguise and make for England. As the government in Vienna crumbled, national revolts erupted among Czechs,

Hungarians, and Italians under Habsburg control. Radical nationalists in Hungary declared a constitutional separation from the empire, and a few months later, moved their capital from Pressburg (now Bratislava), near the Austrian border, to Budapest, in the center of the country. The flustered emperor, Ferdinand, allowed a similar autonomous status to the Czechs in Bohemia. But by the fall, the revolutionary movement had spread so far and wide that he gave up, abdicated in favor of his eighteen-year-old nephew, Francis Joseph, and fled Vienna.

In Italy, nationalists drove out the Austrian garrisons and seized control in Milan, Tuscany, Sardinia, and elsewhere. Venice declared itself an independent republic. In Rome, Pope Pius IX fled the Vatican as a radical Roman republic was proclaimed, with Mazzini as one of its leaders. In Prussia, rioting in Berlin followed a few days after the insurrection in Vienna, compelling the Prussian king to promise a constitution. Finally, an assembly was called in Frankfurt, beginning in May, with the goal of uniting all the German states into a single, liberal, democratic state.

"GENTLEMEN! MAKE YOUR GAME WHILE THE BALL IS ROLLING."

"Gentlemen, make your game while the ball is rolling" (1848). As revolutions swept across Europe, the British satirical magazine Punch *depicted the European monarchs playing roulette with the ball as the world and the edges of the board marked with the threats to their rule, including "republicanism," "equality," and "constitutional government." © TopFoto/The Image Works.*

REPRESSION AND REACTION

During the 1848 People's Spring, virtually all of Europe was rocked by the tempest, with exceptions being the most liberal state, Britain, and the most reactionary one, Russia. The changes during those few months were phenomenal, with revolutionaries, nationalists, and patriots demanding constitutions, representative assemblies, responsible government, extended suffrage, jury trials, the right of assembly, and freedom of the press, and with stupefied governments allowing constitutional assemblies, independent nations, and the abolition of serfdom.

Within a year, however, the forces of reaction were back in control, and the revolution was over. As we have seen, in France, the revolution had run its course by the end of 1848, with the election of Louis Napoleon as president. In Austria, the Habsburg monarchy, after the initial shocks of March 1848, regained its footing and deployed the army against rebels in Bohemia, Italy, and Hungary. The Russian tsar contributed one hundred thousand Russian troops to the suppression of the revolt in Hungary. And in Italy, an intervention by the French army helped drive Mazzini and the republicans out of Rome and restore the pope to the Vatican.

The German assembly in Frankfurt was defeated by divisions from within and conservative reaction from without. Composed of elected representatives from all parts of German-speaking Europe, the assembly wrote a constitution for a united Germany. But the representatives were divided over whether Germany should include only German ethnic territory or should also include the Austrians, whose empire in eastern Europe was mostly non-German. In the end, the assembly decided to exclude the Austrians and to make the Prussian king the emperor of a newly united, all-German nation. By that time, however, the pendulum had swung back from revolution to reaction. Confident that he could contain the national movement by military force if necessary, the Prussian king declared that he would not "pick up a crown from the gutter"—a complete dismissal of the Frankfurt assembly and the popular-revolutionary-nationalist sentiment of 1848.

CONSEQUENCES AND LEGACY OF 1848

In the end, not one of the newly established republics survived. And in only a few small states were any real constitutional gains made from the events of 1848. In France, the monarchy was toppled, but Louis Napoleon soon undermined the very republican institutions that brought him to power, and within three years the country once again had an authoritarian emperor. National liberty had not been secured anywhere in Europe by the People's Spring.

Despite these defeats, important changes had occurred, and 1848 remains a watershed year in European history, both for individual countries and for the Continent as a whole. France moved one step closer to representative government, with the final abolition of the monarchy and the permanent establishment of universal manhood suffrage. Manorialism was permanently abolished in Germany and the Habsburg lands, eliminating the last traces of serfdom. Prussia got a limited parliament.

The 1848 revolutions frightened the crowned heads of Europe and caused several to abdicate. Those who remained were cognizant of the threats posed by liberalism, nationalism, and socialism, and some of them took steps in years afterward to allay the problems that contributed to revolutionary ferment. In Russia, a new tsar, Alexander II, began a series of liberalizing reforms including, most importantly, the emancipation of serfs in 1861. The Austrian emperor Francis Joseph also made some concessions and compromises to both liberals and nationalists, including the 1867 *Ausgleich*, in which the monarchy recognized the desire for Hungarian autonomy and established the dual Austro-Hungarian monarchy.

Most significantly, the ideas of revolution gained ground with the revolutions of 1848. That year showed that all the conservative monarchies of Europe were in jeopardy, not just the French king. Heretofore, revolution seemed to emerge only from that one country and had been mostly contained there. But by the spring of 1848, revolutionary passion had infected Belgians, Italians, Hungarians, Germans, Bohemians, Dutch, and Danes. The Concert of Europe was a system, and while it had the strengths of a system—in the common determination of the conservative monarchs to stifle revolution—it also had its weaknesses, including the tendency for change in one part of Europe to affect all other parts. This was particularly true of ideas, which had spread inexorably from England and France through the rest of the Continent. The basic liberal principle of government by consent was steadily gaining influence as the middle class grew in size and influence. The ideas of nationalism and national unification were frustrated in 1848, but gained currency in that year—and within a generation, they proved victorious in Germany and Italy. And socialism, which had raised the red flag in France, Hungary, and elsewhere, was now on the political agenda.

5

Marx, Marxism, and Socialism

The year 1848 saw not only the tide of revolutionary ferment during the People's Spring but also the appearance of *The Communist Manifesto*. Written by two German exiles, Karl Marx and Friedrich Engels, the *Manifesto* called for a worldwide workers' revolution that would overthrow capitalism and establish a society in which all property would be publicly owned. As discussed in the previous chapter, the revolutions of 1848 soon failed, and socialist or communist ideology was barely a factor in the events of that year. Nevertheless, the *Manifesto* marked the emergence of socialism as a powerful new force for political and economic change in Europe. By the time of Marx's death in 1883, Marxist-based socialist parties were challenging governments all over the Continent. In 1917, communist revolutionaries seized power in Russia, establishing the world's first government based on Marxist ideology, the **Union of Soviet Socialist Republics (USSR)**, or the **Soviet Union**.

The ideas of Marx and the communist ideology, however, were not creatures of 1848; they were tied to the Enlightenment, the French Revolution, and the Industrial Revolution. They reflected Enlightenment beliefs in science, historical progress, and the improvement of the human condition. They were inspired by the ideas, symbols, and events of the French Revolution, including the red flag and the slogan "liberty, equality, and fraternity." And the Industrial Revolution, in creating both great wealth and grinding poverty, established the preconditions for a revolution that aspired to create a new society based on material abundance and full equality.

KARL MARX

Karl Marx was born in 1818 to a middle-class family in Prussia (which is now part of Germany). Both parents were Jewish, although his father converted to Christianity just before Karl was born, and Karl himself was baptized when he was six. His father was a successful lawyer, a man of the Enlightenment, devoted to Kant and Voltaire, and an advocate for constitutionalism in Prussia. The young Marx was educated in Trier, Bonn, and Berlin and received a doctoral degree in philosophy at Jena in 1841. At the university, and especially in Berlin, he was exposed to the ideas of the philosopher G. W. F. Hegel and to radical political thought, both of which influenced him greatly.

In 1842, Marx became the editor of the *Rheinische Zeitung*, which soon became the leading journal in Prussia. But Prussian authorities soon closed down the publication for being too outspoken. The next year, Marx moved to Paris with his new wife, Jenny, to work for another liberal publication. At that time, Paris was the center of socialist thought and radicalism—and of the more extreme new sect that went by the name of communism. In Paris, Marx met Friedrich Engels, the German-born Manchester industrialist who was writing *The Condition of the Working Class in England* (see chapter 3), and began a collaboration with him that was to last forty years. The Prussian government prevailed on the French (both conservative monarchies, remember), however, and after only a year and a half in the country, Marx was expelled from France and moved to Brussels.

THE COMMUNIST MANIFESTO

In 1847, Marx and Engels joined a secret society called the Communist League, whose aim was "the abolition of the old bourgeois society based on class antagonisms, and the establishment of a new society without classes and without private property." They agreed to write the program for this fledgling organization, which was published in January 1848 as *The Communist Manifesto*, a twenty-three-page pamphlet meant for a mass audience. Although Marx and Engels later wrote thousands of pages in books and articles, *The Communist Manifesto* remains the best short presentation of the ideas of Marx and the communist vision.

The *Manifesto* opens and closes with dramatic, even frightening, proclamations. The opening lines were particularly prescient, given the events that followed in the months after the document's publication: "A specter is haunting Europe—the specter of communism. All the powers of old Europe have entered into a holy alliance to exorcise the specter: Pope and Tsar, Metternich and Guizot, French Radicals and German police-spies." Here, Marx and Engels invoke the bastions of conservatism and the old order in Europe—the **Holy Alliance**, the pope, the Russian tsar, and the conservative prime ministers of Austria and France—as well as their noncommunist rivals on the Left, the French radicals. However, in 1848, it was revolution, rather than communism, that haunted Europe, and French statesman François Guizot and the Habsburg dynasty's Metternich were among the first to be swept out of office in that year.

The first section of the *Manifesto* opens with the assertion that "the history of all hitherto existing human society is the history of class struggle." It goes on to develop in summary fashion the principal notions of

Karl Marx, London, 1875

historical materialism, class conflict, and proletarian revolution at the core of Marxist theory. Marx and Engels argued that history should not be understood as a story of great individuals or of conflict among states but of social classes and their struggles with each other. Each stage in a society's development, according to Marxist theory, was characterized by conflict between the dominant class and the subordinate class. In capitalism, these classes were the bourgeoisie, consisting of the owners of factories and capital, and the proletariat, who worked in the factories. Over time, conflict between these classes would erupt in a revolution in which the proletariat would overthrow the bourgeoisie and establish a classless, egalitarian society. The *Manifesto* concludes with a call to action for the working classes: "Let the ruling classes tremble at a communist revolution. The proletarians have nothing to lose but their chains. They have a world to win. Proletarians of all countries, unite!"

The Communist Manifesto was first published in London, in German, just a few weeks before the revolutions in Paris and Vienna forced the abdication of King Louis Philippe in France and Emperor Ferdinand in Austria. As the revolutionary movement gained momentum in Austria and Germany, Marx returned to Prussia and began writing again for a newly established liberal journal, advocating constitutional democracy. The June Days in Paris were seen by Marx and Engels as a confirmation of the imminence of revolution. But in Prussia, Marx took a more moderate line. He agreed with Engels to shelve the ideas of the *Manifesto* temporarily and to work instead on behalf of independent workers' candidates to the Frankfurt assembly, which was to draw up a constitution for a liberal, unified, and democratic Germany. When the conservative reaction set in during the summer of 1848, and the king of Prussia moved against some of the new democratic assemblies, Marx returned to a more radical line, calling for armed resistance against the government. As the revolutionary tide ebbed, Marx was banished once again. He returned to Paris, was duly expelled, and then returned to London.

His involvement in the People's Spring was the only real revolutionary activism of his life; for the next fifteen years, Marx spent most of his days in research and writing at the British Library in London, where a desk in the reading room is still inscribed with his name. Marx lived in poverty for most of these years, crowded into two small rooms with his wife and four small children. They often subsisted only on bread and potatoes and were once thrown onto the street for nonpayment of rent. Two of his children died. His main source of income was a subsidy from his friend Engels. But he made steady progress on his magnum opus, which was eventually published in German as **Das Kapital** (meaning "capital," in the sense of money).

In 1864, Marx became politically active again with the London-based International Working Men's Association, which is usually referred to as the First International (and an early antecedent of what would become the Communist Party of the Soviet Union in the next century). The International grew in prestige and membership, with about eight hundred thousand adherents by 1869. A number of factors, however, brought about its decline and dissolution. First, the International was split by yet another revolution in Paris, in 1870, that resulted in the establishment in that capital of a short-lived radical revolutionary government called the Paris Commune. Savage fighting between the Communards and troops of the Versailles government prompted the Communards to execute the archbishop of Paris, who was their hostage. With the defeat of the Commune, the government put to death some twenty-five thousand Parisians. Marx and Engels saw this as the first manifestation of a "dictatorship of the proletariat," the preliminary step toward full communism, and they supported the Paris Commune. But many in the International did not see it that way, and the appalling violence of the experience led others to turn away from the idea of violent revolution.

Another factor that weakened the appeal of the International was increasing possibility of evolutionary reform. The English Reform bill of 1867, for example, enfranchised part of the (male) urban working class and opened up broad new political opportunities for trade unions. At about the same time, in Germany, a new German Social Democratic Party was established, committed to socialist goals through cooperation with the state, not its overthrow. These evolutionary and reformist trends drew workers away from the more radical orientation of the International.

In the last decade of his life, Marx was beset by what he called "chronic mental depression." He saw little hope for proletarian revolution in western Europe. He increasingly looked to a European war to overthrow the Russian autocracy, the mainstay of conservatism and reaction, hoping that this would revive the political energies of the working class. (Something like this did occur long after his death, with World War I leading to the collapse of the Russian autocracy and the accession to power of the Russian communists.) Marx died in 1883 and was buried in Highgate Cemetery in London. At the graveside funeral, Friedrich Engels spoke of Marx's theoretical contributions, but added that Marx was "before all else a revolutionist." He was, Engels said, "the best-hated and most calumniated man of his time," but also "beloved, revered, and mourned by millions of revolutionary fellow-workers."[1] The inscription on his tomb reads, "Philosophers have so far explained the world in various ways: the point, however, is to change it."

MARXIST THEORY

It is difficult to summarize and synthesize the writings and theories of Karl Marx because these are so voluminous and because his ideas are rich, complex, and sometimes dense and even contradictory. But it is important to understand the basic principles of **Marxism** because they were so influential in the development of European socialism and remain important (albeit controversial) today.

The *Collected Works of Karl Marx and Friedrich Engels* number almost fifty fat volumes and occupy about six feet of library shelf space. The most important of these works for understanding Marxist theory are *The Communist Manifesto*, published in 1848, and *Das Kapital*, the first volume of which was published in 1867, and the second and third volumes of which Engels completed, edited, and published after Marx's death in 1883. In the early writings, many of them not published until many years later, Marx primarily set forth humanistic critiques of the excesses of capitalism in much the same way that Charles Dickens criticized urban capitalism in his novels. Marx's later work, however, was more historical and systematic, and attempted to create a "science" of history and economics. Marx wanted to create a sort of universal theory for human society, much like Charles Darwin had done for natural history (with his *Origin of Species*, published in 1859). Indeed, Marx considered dedicating the first volume of *Das Kapital* to Darwin.

Marx's "scientific" approach to the study of human society reflected mid-nineteenth-century trends in literature, the arts, and philosophy in which there was a breaking away from romanticism toward realism and materialism. After the failure of the 1848 revolutions, Marx offered a vision that was realistic and hardheaded, not idealistic and utopian. He branded other versions of socialism as utopian (and excoriated many of those in the *Manifesto*); his socialism, on the other hand, was "scientific."

A key component of this aspect of Marxist theory is historical materialism. Marx pointed to the material basis of all things, including historical development. He argued that one can understand history, and one's particular stage in history, by recognizing the *means of production* in that society: what it is that produces material things of value. So in a feudal society, which is based mostly on agriculture, land is the means of production, the factor that produces agricultural goods. In a capitalist society, it is capital, which mostly takes the form of factories, that produces material goods. In every society, the owners of the means of production dominate virtually every aspect of society and form the basis of the class structure of that society. In a feudal society, the owners of the means of production are the landowners (usually the nobility); in capitalist society, the bourgeoisie are the owners of the means of production, and the proletariat is the subordinate class of individuals who work in their factories.

These material and economic relationships constitute the foundation, or *substructure*, of society on which all else is built. The forms of economic production determine the dominant class, and the dominant class controls the economy, political system, social relationships, and culture of that society, all of which are part of the *superstructure* of society. As Marx wrote in his *Contribution to the Critique of Political Economy* (1859),

> The mode of production in material life determines the general character of the social, political, and intellectual processes of life. It is not the consciousness of men which determines their existence; it is on the contrary their social existence which determines their consciousness.

So even consciousness and human nature are parts of that superstructure and are, therefore, changeable; when the substructure changes, so too will all aspects of the superstructure, including human consciousness and our notions of human nature. Religion is also part of this superstructure, of course, and is simply a tool of the dominant class to keep the lower classes in their place in this world, with the expectation of a better existence in the hereafter. Religion, in the words of Engels, is the "opiate of the masses."

Marx saw all history of every society as proceeding on a predetermined path, moving from one stage to another after a clash between dominant and subordinate classes. "The history of all hitherto existing human society is the history of class struggles," he contended. All societies begin in the primitive-communal stage, move through a system of slavery (the dominant class being the slave owners), then feudalism, then capitalism, and eventually communism, at which point classes would no longer exist. A good deal of Marx's writing, then, was focused on the capitalist stage and the way capitalism would be overthrown by a proletarian revolution and replaced with communism. Marx believed that this process would occur naturally and inevitably in every society.

Marx believed that the decline of capitalism was already under way in advanced capitalist states like England, France, and Germany. He explained that capitalism, like every previous stage of history, both paved the way for the next stage and sowed the seeds of its own destruction in a process that Marx referred to as the **dialectic**.[2] The capitalist system, through factories and mass production, generates enormous amounts of material goods, enough to provide the basics for everyone, actually, if it weren't for the inequitable distribution of those goods. The underpaid workers often cannot even afford to purchase the very products that they assemble. The workers receive in wages only a fraction of the value of the products they produce. The factory owners (the bourgeoisie) keep the rest as "surplus value." This leads to the accumulation of goods that people cannot afford to buy and to periodic crises of overproduction in capitalist societies that force entrepreneurs to scale back production and lay off workers. This has two consequences: periodic and increasingly severe economic crises and the increasing "immiseration" of the working class as wages decline and more and more workers are unemployed. Economic crises and increasing immiseration foster growing **class consciousness** by the proletariat and the realization that they have nothing to gain from the system. Finally, during one of these economic depressions, workers will simply seize control of factories in a revolution that will displace the bourgeoisie and initiate a new stage in history.

BOX 5.1
Robert Owen, Karl Marx, and Indiana

In part 3 of *The Communist Manifesto*, Marx and Engels criticize alternative theories of socialism, including "reactionary socialism," "bourgeois socialism," and "critical-utopian socialism." In this last category, they mention Robert Owen (1771–1858), one of the first socialists and also one of the first cotton barons of Manchester and Scotland. Owen was appalled by the condition of workers in the mills, and especially of children. When he purchased four textile factories in New Lanark, Scotland, he tried to create a model community for his employees by prohibiting the employment of very young children, reducing working hours, establishing schools, and providing subsidized housing and factory stores. Owen argued (much as Marx did later) that a person's environment shapes his or her character, so the way to produce better people, and thus a better society, is to create the right environment.

Owen's increasingly radical ideas, including his negative views on religion, alienated him from many in Britain, so in 1825 he purchased land in southern Indiana and established a community there, which he called New Harmony. He believed that his utopia could more easily be achieved in the New World than in the Old and that New Harmony would be the seed for other such communities. The community was to be based on cooperative labor, communal upbringing of children, and free education and medical care. The experiment was soon overcome, however, by internal divisions, financial difficulties, and a plethora of opportunists and hangers-on. Within five years, Owen gave up on New Harmony and returned to Britain to work on social reforms and the development of trade unions.

Marx and Engels criticized the work of Owen and other socialists as utopian and as failing to recognize historical dynamics and class struggle sufficiently. They not-so-subtly criticized Owen's experiments in New Lanark and New Harmony as "pocket editions of the New Jerusalem."

THE IDEA OF COMMUNISM

According to Marxist theory, when the workers own the means of production, the entire economic substructure will collapse and re-form, as will the superstructure of society. Social classes will disappear. In the words of the *Manifesto*, "in the place of the old bourgeois society with its classes and class antagonisms, there will be an association in which the free development of each is the condition for the free development of all." Without the bourgeoisie to skim off surplus value, workers and peasants will benefit from the full fruits of their labor. Capitalism, with its mass production, had provided enough material goods to satisfy the needs of everyone, and with a more equitable distribution of goods under communism, everyone's basic needs will be satisfied. The governing principle of the new society will be "from each according to his abilities, to each according to his needs": each person will contribute to society what he or she does best and will get whatever he or she needs.

One might object that some greedy people will claim that they need more than they really do (i.e., what if someone needs a fifty-foot luxury yacht?), but the Marxist response to this is that human nature (part of the superstructure) will also have changed. Although capitalism requires human nature to be competitive, aggressive, and greedy (remember Adam Smith's notion that private vice creates public virtue), communism will foster human values of cooperation and solidarity. Without exploitation of labor and with adequate reward for one's work, workers will not feel the need to compete in the workplace. According to Marx and Engels, a "new man" will build a new society.

When social classes disappear, so too will poverty, exploitation, resentment, greed, and crime, so that there will be no need for a police force. Indeed, because government simply perpetuates the supremacy of the dominant class, without social classes there will be no need for government at all. The state, according to Engels, will simply "wither away." As states disappear, so will national boundaries, national conflicts, and wars, and the planet will evolve into a global community of workers joined in solidarity.

Marxist theory, then, was both relentlessly logical and, in the end, broadly appealing. Its rigor and science appealed to many students and intellectuals, and fit with the nineteenth-century ethos of progress, realism, materialism, and science. For workers of all kinds, it offered both an explanation for their plight and an attractive resolution to it. Nevertheless, communism remained a small and isolated piece of political thought throughout the remainder of the century and might have remained a footnote in history were it not for the Russian revolutionaries who revived and adapted it at the beginning of the twentieth century.

THE LEGACY OF MARXISM

Marxism, as we have seen, was a reaction to and product of the Enlightenment, capitalism, and industrialization. It contributed to our understanding of history and human society, and to the way in which we study those topics. Marx was one of the first social scientists, in terms of his efforts to apply scientific and systematic methods to the study of society. And even though modern social scientists have rejected many of his ideas, his notion of **economic determinism** (that the economy determines much else in society) has broad applications in contemporary sociology, political science, economics, and other disciplines.

But Marx's biggest impact, of course, was in the political realm rather than the academic. The writings of Marx and Engels were instrumental in the development of socialism and socialist parties in Europe, especially in the 1870s and 1880s. Although socialism never became much of a force in North America, it was a powerful political movement in Europe and remains so today, in the form of the socialist, democratic socialist, and social democratic political parties that play a major role in virtually all of the European countries.

From the nineteenth century forward, most of these socialist parties were parliamentary parties in the sense that they worked for socialist outcomes and programs within the legal constraints of their political systems. They favored broad-based equality, social welfare, and public ownership of the means of production, while rejecting the proletarian revolution that was intrinsic to Marx's theory. Communism, as such, was not a major political factor, or even much used in political vocabularies, until Russian radicals and revolutionaries resurrected it near the end of the century.

It was in Russia, of course, that Marxism eventually gained a foothold and a platform for expansion. Before 1905, tsarist Russia essentially had no parliament or democratic politics, so there was no room for legal political parties of any kind. The politics that did exist took the form of underground, illegal, or exile political organizations. This was how the first Russian Marxist party was formed, by Russian exiles in Switzerland, in 1883. *Das Kapital* had been translated into Russian just a decade before and attracted the attention of Russian radicals intent on transforming the stultified Russian autocratic state. Marxism seemed to provide both an explanation for Russia's backwardness and a solution to its problems.

Vladimir Lenin participated in the Second Congress of the Russian Social Democratic Labor Party (the Russian Marxist party) in Brussels and London in 1903, and he soon became the leader of the **Bolshevik** (majority) faction of the group. Russia's involvement in World War I (1914–18) gradually weakened the Russian autocracy and the Russian state, and the Bolsheviks seized power in November 1917. They proceeded to establish a government based on Marx's ideas, as revised for Russian circumstances by Lenin. The official ideology of the new state was Marxism-**Leninism**. The Bolsheviks became the Communist Party, and the Russian Empire became the Soviet Union. The last words of *The Communist Manifesto*, "working men of all countries, unite!" were emblazoned on the masthead of every newspaper published in the country (and on Communist Party newspapers all over the world). Communists ruled the country until its collapse in 1991. (All of this will be treated more thoroughly in chapter 10.)

After World War II, communism spread into Eastern Europe, China, North Korea, Southeast Asia, and Cuba, and the communist ideology and model became hugely influential throughout the **Third World**. Only eleven people attended Karl Marx's funeral in 1883. By the 1960s, half the world's people lived under governments that ruled in his name.

6

🌿

Darwinism and
Social Darwinism

A decade after the appearance of *The Communist Manifesto*, the English-man Charles Darwin published another revolutionary writing, *Origin of Species*. Just as Marx had produced a general theory about the history and development of societies, Darwin presented a universal theory about the origin and development of all living species. His theory of evolution by **natural selection**, backed by extensive evidence he had collected him-self, revolutionized biology, and the sciences more generally, and stimu-lated the development of the social sciences as well. Evolutionary theory also directly challenged key elements of religious thought at the time, including literal interpretations of the biblical story of creation and also natural theology, with its harmonious image of nature designed by God. Darwinism raised questions about the very nature of humankind and those beliefs that were so fundamental to religion. Eventually, as Darwin-ism gained acceptance, it effected changes in religion and theology, too.

Darwinism, like Marxism, was a product of its time and place. Dar-win's commitment to empiricism and science reflected both the Scientific Revolution and the Enlightenment. He was influenced by the ideas of Adam Smith and Thomas Malthus and by recent evidence and theories from geology and paleontology that raised questions about the age of the earth. And he was a product of his own upper-middle-class Victorian environment, which stressed the virtues of discipline and hard work but also often blamed the poor for their own circumstances.

Darwin's study of the origin of species spun off another set of theo-ries called **social Darwinism**. Popularized by the English philosopher Herbert Spencer, who coined the phrase "survival of the fittest," social

Darwinism applied Darwin's ideas of the evolution of species to a description of society and the "evolution" of particular groups, races, and nations. Unlike Darwinism, however, which was exclusively descriptive, social Darwinism included a prescriptive dimension and, in its rawest form, called for the elimination of any government programs that might assist the poor, weak, or "inferior," so that they might be allowed to die off in the natural struggle for survival. In the following decades, these ideas were marshaled in support of militarism, racism, **imperialism**, and the more virulent forms of nationalism.

CHARLES DARWIN

Charles Darwin was born in 1809, in England, the son of a prominent and successful physician. His mother died when he was eight years old, but otherwise he had a pleasant and privileged childhood. His father sent him to university to study medicine at first, but he was repelled by surgery performed without anesthetics and moved to Cambridge University to study divinity. He was not a particularly distinguished student but graduated in 1831.

That same year, Darwin was invited to sail as an unpaid companion of the captain on the HMS *Beagle*, which was to survey the east and west coasts of South America and continue from there to the Pacific Islands. The voyage was supposed to last two years but actually extended to five. During those years, Darwin kept meticulous notes and diaries and sent back to England geological and biological specimens. On board, he also read Charles Lyell's *Principles of Geology*, which argued that the features of the earth changed gradually over time through the cumulative effects of earthquakes, volcanic eruptions, erosion, and the like. This was a controversial theory at the time, a sort of geological evolutionism, but in his explorations, Darwin found evidence for Lyell's theory. He wrote three books about South American geology, based on his observations and collections, which brought him some fame even while he was still at sea.

After returning to England, he proposed to his first cousin Emma Wedgewood (after writing down a balance sheet of the pros and cons of marriage!), married her, and moved to the village of Downe, sixteen miles from London. They had ten children together, and Darwin, in comfortable circumstances from his father's fortune, was able to read and write there for the rest of his life.

While on the *Beagle*, Darwin had already begun formulating ideas about the evolution of species, and he began writing privately about these ideas in the years after the voyage. He kept his ideas secret, however, because they were not only radical in scientific terms but could potentially subject him to legal action under English laws governing blasphemy and sedition. England was in a very conservative period at the time, both in religious and political terms, partly in reaction to what were seen as revolutionary excesses in France and the rest of Europe. The natural world was seen as one in which the spirit of God was involved in the creation of new species of plants and animals.

Darwin's evidence conflicted with this interpretation. In 1838, he read Malthus's "An Essay on the Principle of Population" (see chapter 3), which argued that population increases geometrically, whereas food supply increases only arithmetically, and that periodic famines and disease hold population growth in check. Darwin recognized from this that, in the struggle for existence, "favourable variations would tend to be preserved and unfavourable ones to be destroyed"; from that idea he derived his idea of natural selection.

Finally, in 1859, Darwin's theory of organic evolution by natural selection was published in a book titled *On the Origin of Species by Means of Natural Selection, or the Preservation of Favoured Races in the Struggle for Life*. The first edition sold out immediately. His evidence and theories were greeted at first with skepticism, even by many scientists, and met with stiff opposition from the church. In *Origin of Species*, Darwin did not directly address the evolution of human beings, although most people applied his theory about animals and plants to human beings, which brought the theory into conflict with a literal interpretation of the Bible, and especially of the book of Genesis. Later, Darwin confirmed these hunches with the publication, in 1871, of *The Descent of Man*, which directly tackled the issue of human evolution. Furthermore, this book expanded the scope of **evolution theory** to include the acquisition of moral and spiritual traits, as well as physical ones, and pointed out humankind's psychological as well as physical similarities to the great apes.

THE THEORY OF EVOLUTION BY NATURAL SELECTION

From his observations of fossils and various species of plants and animals, as well as his understanding of the gradual and evolutionary change of the planet itself, Darwin first concluded that all species are mutable, that they can and do change over time. All species develop through small changes from those species that went before in a slow process of organic evolution. The changes occur through the process of natural selection, meaning that those organisms with the most useful characteristics tend to survive and pass those characteristics on to succeeding generations. Darwin saw a competition for survival within each species, such that within a local population, an individual with favorable characteristics for that environment—say a sharper beak or a brighter color—has a better chance of reproducing than others. As these traits are passed on from one generation to the next, they become predominant in that population. Those individuals possessing these advantageous characteristics survive and reproduce; those that do not possess them are more likely to perish and eventually to disappear from the population altogether.

Darwin's theories challenged both contemporary science and religion. Although other biologists had pointed to competition and struggle between different species, Darwin focused on the struggle for survival and competition within a single species. It was this, of course, that accounted for the changing nature of the species. And although the idea of organic evolution itself was not new, Darwin produced both evidence for such species changes and also the mechanism by which such changes occurred—the process of natural selection. In this way of thinking, the human being is not in a position of superiority within the animal world; humans have simply evolved in a different way than others. These were radically new ways of thinking about life (of all kinds) and constituted a genuine scientific revolution in the natural sciences, in much the same way that Copernicus's and Galileo's ideas revolutionized our thinking about the place of Earth in the solar system.

DARWINISM AND RELIGION

Darwinism posed a major challenge to religion and especially to the conservative and fundamentalist Christianity of Victorian England. But it was also a challenge to natural theology, a popular philosophical current in the eighteenth and nineteenth centuries, which understood God and his creations based on reason rather than Scripture. In this view, the beauty, complexity, and harmony of nature could be explained only by God's design. Darwinian theory, on the other hand, had no place for divine intervention in the creation or molding of species, including human beings. An utter incompatibility existed between Darwin's theory of evolution and a literal

A contemporary cartoon of Darwin contemplating human ancestry.

BOX 6.1
Darwin's Finches and Pigeons

During Darwin's voyage on the *Beagle*, he spent five weeks exploring the Galapagos Islands, a wild archipelago near the equator, 650 miles west of Ecuador. He was astonished at the number and variety of plants and animals on these small islands and assiduously cataloged them. Among those was "a most singular group of finches," consisting of thirteen different species, each with different characteristics. Darwin was particularly intrigued by the variety in shape and size of the beaks of these birds: "Seeing this gradation and diversity of structure in one small, intimately related group of birds, one might really fancy that from an original paucity of birds in this archipelago, one species had been taken and modified for different ends," he wrote in his diary.

Biology textbooks often display pictures of Darwin's finches in their discussion of evolution. But it was years after these observations on the Galapagos that Darwin began to conceptualize his theory of evolution by natural selection. Back in England, he became interested in the idea of plant and animal breeding and the ways in which breeders could cross different breeds to develop different, sometimes "better," varieties of orchids, roses, strawberries, dogs, or horses. At his home in Downe, two decades after the voyage of the *Beagle*, he began collecting and breeding pigeons; soon he had fifteen breeds under his care, including tumblers, trumpeters, laughers, fantails, pouters, polands, runts, dragons, and scandaroons, many of them so different from the others as to appear to be an entirely separate species. Yet all of them bore a resemblance to the rock pigeon.

Darwin hypothesized that all of his pigeon breeds descended from the rock pigeon and proceeded, through logic and the process of elimination, to rule out competing hypotheses. For example, if these fifteen breeds had not derived from one common ancestor over a period of time, then one would expect to find them descending from "at least seven or eight aboriginal stocks" because only that number could account for the variety of his existing pigeons. But there was no evidence, historically, in the wild or in captivity, of these seven or eight other kinds of birds. So in Darwin's view, they must have descended from one, either by natural selection or by artificial selection through breeding.

Natural selection and evolution are difficult to demonstrate by direct observation, as the changes in species occur over long periods of time, as in the case of the Galapagos finches. But people could understand the breeding of pigeons and even observe, to a certain extent, the results of selective breeding. For this reason, Darwin opened *Origin of Species* with a discussion of his pigeons.

interpretation of the Bible, particularly of the creation and Adam and Eve stories in Genesis. But the unpredictability of natural selection was also incompatible with the intelligent design argument of natural theology.

Well before Darwin, challenges were made to a literalist interpretation of the Bible: The theories of Copernicus and Galileo removed the Earth from the center of the solar system, and evidence from geology (especially by Lyell) and paleontology about the history of the Earth flew in the face of the shortened timetable presented in Genesis. But evolutionary theory was seen as more critical of religion because it focused on the nature of human beings, a central element to all religious doctrines. By the mid-nineteenth century in continental Europe, some critical evaluations of the Bible had been made, with a growing tendency to interpret some of the books and passages as allegorical rather than literal.

But in England, where a conservative reaction following the French Revolution had also affected religion, fundamentalism was still dominant among both the clergy and the population. A few years after the publication of *Origin of Species*, at Oxford University, a bastion of conservative theology, eleven thousand Anglican clergymen signed "The Oxford Declaration," declaring that if any part of the Bible were admitted to be false, the whole book might be brought into question. They stood, therefore, upon the absolute inerrancy of the Bible. This position, of course, left little room for accommodation or compromise with the new science of Darwinian evolution.

Over the years, people of faith gradually accommodated to the ideas of evolution, but the process was a slow and painful one. Not until the twentieth century did most churches and theologians come to terms with evolution by accepting that faith and science were separate spheres, but not necessarily incompatible ones. Increasingly, the English, like most Europeans, came to regard sections of the Bible, especially Genesis, as stories that contained truth, but were not necessarily literally true. Only late in the twentieth century (1996) did the Roman Catholic Church finally come to terms with evolution when Pope John Paul II formally acknowledged that the theory of evolution was "more than just a hypothesis." Faith, he said, could coexist with evolution, as long as it was maintained that only God can create the human soul. Because Darwin said nothing about the human soul, there seemed to be room for peaceful coexistence in those words. By the beginning of the new millennium, the conflict between evolution and creationism was no longer an active one in Europe; only in the United States was there still widespread skepticism about evolution.

SOCIAL DARWINISM

Charles Darwin's ideas about the struggle for existence and natural selection applied only to the biological evolution of animal and plant species, but these concepts had appeal for certain political thinkers and social scientists as well. Social Darwinism refers to the many and varied sets of ideas that try to apply Darwinian evolutionism to descriptions of the way society is, or should be, constituted. Some social Darwinists focused on the competition between social groups or nations, rather than just among individuals. And most preached not only that the fittest *had* survived but that only the fittest had the *right* to survive, so that the theory became a prescription for policy and not just a description of history and nature.

Many different people and ideologies adopted Darwinian theory for their purposes. The Irish playwright George Bernard Shaw wrote about Darwin that "he had the luck to please everybody who had an axe to grind."[1] But the most prominent advocate of social Darwinism was the English philosopher Herbert Spencer (1820–1903). Spencer had actually worked out his own theory of social evolution even before the publication of Darwin's *Origin of Species*; in fact, Darwin drew on Spencer's work in his own writing. In an 1852 essay, Spencer coined the phrase "survival of the fittest," which Darwin adopted and later added to one of his chapter titles in *Origin of Species*.

Spencer, like Darwin, was influenced by the writing of Thomas Malthus. Following Malthus, Spencer argued that population pressure on resources led to a struggle for existence among people, with the most intelligent people surviving this struggle. Spencer felt that this process would lead to increasingly intelligent human beings and increasingly strong societies, with modern capitalism as the pinnacle of human evolution. He therefore argued against any interference with this evolutionary process and the struggle for existence, especially by government. He opposed any government programs that might assist the poor or the weak, including state support for education or health care, antipoverty programs, or state regulation of housing. Without such programs, Spencer felt, the weakest would perish, the strong would survive, and society would improve. He allowed that there would be much suffering in this process but wrote that "the process *must* be undergone, and the sufferings *must* be endured." In his essay "Poor Laws," published eight years before Darwin's *Origin of Species*, he wrote unblinkingly about the necessity for the poor to endure the consequences of this struggle:

> It seems hard that widows and orphans should be left to struggle for life or death. Nevertheless, when regarded not separately, but in connection with the interests of universal humanity, these harsh fatalities are seen to be full of the highest beneficence—the same beneficence which brings to early graves the children of diseased parents, and singles out the low-spirited, the intemperate, and the debilitated as the victims of an epidemic.[2]

Spencer was an arch supporter of *laissez-faire* economics and the ideas of Adam Smith, who also opposed government involvement in the economy. His ideas, then, were often picked up and propagated by advocates of unfettered capitalism. This was especially true in the United States, a country born at about the same time as capitalism, where both individualism and the idea of limited government were strongly ingrained. The American industrialists Andrew Carnegie and John D. Rockefeller were both fans of Herbert Spencer. Rockefeller is quoted as saying in a Sunday school address,

> The growth of a large business is merely a survival of the fittest. . . . The American Beauty rose can be produced in the splendor and fragrance which bring cheer to its beholder only by sacrificing the early buds which grow up around it. This is not an evil tendency in business. It is merely the working-out of a law of nature and a law of God.[3]

SOCIAL DARWINISM AND EUROPEAN HISTORY

In the economic realm, social Darwinism probably had more influence in the United States than in Europe. But Spencer's ideas were also adopted in support of many other movements and philosophies in nineteenth- and twentieth-century Europe, many of them with sinister motives or catastrophic outcomes, including militarism, racism, imperialism, and **eugenics**.

Both Darwin's and Spencer's influential writings coincided with the rapid expansion of European **colonialism** in the second half of the nineteenth century. In that age of imperialism, European states created colonial empires all over the Southern Hemisphere, especially in Africa, during the closing decades of the century. England was the most active imperialist state during this period, and many people in that country justified their domination of other cultures, especially in Africa, with claims of racial superiority. The British mission in Africa was said to carry "the white man's burden" to bring European virtues, religion, law, and civilization to lesser, uncivilized races. Much of this claim to racial superiority was couched in the language of social Darwinism. European society was already at a more "evolved," or developed, stage than society in Africa, and spreading European influence in Africa would facilitate the evolution of those cultures.

It was not a far stretch from the arguments of social Darwinism to notions of racial supremacy to considerations of "cleansing," or the elimination of racial groups considered inferior. Many of these ideas had been around for a long time, of course, and had antecedents in other trends and philosophies, but they were given a certain scientific validation and respectability by Darwinism. A prominent nineteenth-century German historian, for example, wrote that "brave people alone have an existence, an evolution or a future; the weak and cowardly perish, and perish justly."[4]

Parallels exist between the thoughts of that historian and the ideas of Adolf Hitler (1889–1945). In his book *Mein Kampf* (My Struggle), published in 1926, Hitler drew on the ideas of the struggle for existence and the survival of the fittest to provide a quasi-scientific justification for the need for racial purity, which became a core doctrine of the Nazi movement. Hitler argued against the "crossing" of people who were "not at exactly the same level." Drawing indirectly on ideas from Darwin and Spencer, he wrote:

> No more than Nature desires the mating of weaker with stronger individuals, even less does she desire the blending of a higher with a lower race, since, if she did, her whole work of higher breeding over perhaps hundreds of thousands of years, might be ruined with one blow.[5]

Employing these ideas once he gained power in Germany, Hitler called for preserving the purity of the Aryan race by selective breeding and for the elimination of non-Aryans from Germany. This became the basis for his effort to exterminate all Jews—his "final solution" to the problem of racial mixing—and the consequent horrors of the Holocaust.

Perhaps it is unfair to attribute these repulsive philosophies and events to Darwinism, as usually they were based on a twisted interpretation of Darwin's theories, but Darwin did occasionally reveal some racist tendencies of his own, foreseeing, for example, that "at no very distant date . . . an endless number of the lower races will have been eliminated by the higher civilized races throughout the world."[6] Darwin was not alone in these beliefs, of course, which were pervasive in England and throughout much of Europe at that time. His theories about natural selection and survival of the fittest, though, reinforced and strengthened theories of white, European domination of the world.

THE INFLUENCE OF DARWINISM

Darwinism changed science, religion, society, and the way in which we think about ourselves as human beings. Its most dramatic impact was on the sciences; Darwin's theories of natural selection and evolution constituted a scientific revolution, with an impact equal to those sparked by Galileo, Copernicus, Newton, and later, Einstein. Indeed, one modern-day scientist, Neil deGrasse Tyson, calls Darwin's idea "the most revolutionary concept in the history of science."[7] Darwin's evidence for his theory of evolution was so persuasive that the theory was eventually accepted by virtually all scientists, and evolution remains the foundation of the biological sciences. Darwin's influence on science spread beyond biology, though.

His work stimulated the idea that scientific methods could be applied to the study of humans, as well as natural phenomena (as did Marx's work), leading to the emergence of the social sciences: ethnography, economics, sociology, anthropology, psychology, and political science.

Darwin's work and his theories separated science from faith and religion; science and religion were not necessarily incompatible, but they addressed different issues. Before Darwin, most people, including most scientists, viewed questions of human origins and human nature largely in religious terms. In this sense, Darwinism was another step in the gradual secularization of European society, and for that reason many churches and people of faith resisted it staunchly. Over time, though, most churches and most people, as well, came to accept evolution. Among developed countries, only in the United States did a substantial number of people continue to reject the theory of evolution. In the process, churches and theology also changed, moving away from literalist interpretations of the Old Testament and adapting to or incorporating evolution and other modern scientific findings. A revolution occurred in our understanding of ourselves as human beings, our development as a species, our relationship to our environment, and our place in the universe—issues central to all religions. Thus, paradoxically, Darwinism also changed religion.

As we have seen, Darwinism also had less benign consequences. The Darwinian spin-off of social Darwinism was employed to justify imperialism, racism, and ultimately, the Holocaust. Now social Darwinism is largely discredited, at least in Europe, but continues to live on in some conservative doctrines that flirt with the notion of the survival of the fittest, arguing against any government intervention on behalf of the poor, the weak, or the sick.

Darwinism can be compared to Marxism in that both attempted to develop scientific theories about human development that were comprehensive and universal in their application. Indeed, Friedrich Engels paired the two in his eulogy at Marx's graveside: "Just as Darwin discovered the law of development of organic nature, so Marx discovered the law of development of human history."[8] Both men had an enormous impact on the development of European society and on world history. Darwin's theories, however, have outlived those of Marx in terms of their contemporary influence. But even Darwin's authority had limits. At the time of his death in 1882, a British parliamentary petition won him a burial in Westminster Abbey, a mark of high honor. At his funeral, his cousin Sir Francis Galton, a professor and pioneer of the eugenics movement, suggested that Westminster Abbey's magnificent Creation Window be replaced by something more suited to evolution. It was not.

BOX 6.2
Sigmund Freud: Psychology and Civilization

Karl Marx and Charles Darwin both developed scientific theories about the development and evolution of societies or species, and both rejected religious thought as unscientific. The Viennese doctor Sigmund Freud (1856–1939) continued this tradition, using observation and experimentation to develop a new science of the human mind and a method for treating neuroses, which he dubbed psychoanalysis. Like Darwin, he was a multifaceted genius who drew on many disciplines to develop his ideas and theories. Freud emphasized the influence of the unconscious and the irrational in explaining human behavior, a theory that challenged contemporary emphasis on rational and cognitive processes. His work revolutionized our thinking about the motives and sources of human behavior and gave rise to a new form of treatment of mental illness and anxiety called "talk therapy." Many of his ideas and concepts have become mainstream in Western thought: the Oedipus complex, dream analysis, sexual repression, the pleasure-unpleasure principle, transference, and the mind's division into id, ego, and superego.

Freud used the language of both Marx and Darwin in thinking about the development and future of civilization, especially after the catastrophe of World War I. He dismissed religion's place in man's evolution "as a counterpart to the neurosis which individual civilized men have to go through in their passage from childhood to maturity."* He accepted Marx's emphasis on economic factors in shaping individuals and societies, but believed Marx left out the important psychological element. The future of civilization, he argued in *Civilization and Its Discontents*, would be played out in the struggle between Eros (love) and Thanatos (death). The purpose of Eros "is to combine single human individuals, and after that families, then races, peoples and nations, into one great unity, the unity of mankind." But this was counteracted by the death instinct. So the evolution of civilization would be a struggle between Eros and death, between the instinct of life and the instinct of destruction, as it works itself out in the human species. This struggle is what all life essentially consists of, and the evolution of civilization may therefore be simply described as the struggle for life of the human species.†

---

*Sigmund Freud, *New Introductory Lectures on Psycho-analysis and Other Works*, vol. 22 (London: Hogarth, 1964), 168.
†Sigmund Freud, *Civilization and Its Discontents* (New York: Norton, 1961), 77.

7

🌰

The Unifications of
Italy and Germany

With the unifications of Italy and Germany, the 1860s saw the emergence of two important new states in central Europe. At roughly the same time that a civil war was testing the unity of the United States of America, statesmen in Europe were using warfare and civic nationalism to forge powerful new nation-states out of a disparate collection of smaller political units. As we saw in chapter 4, the People's Spring of 1848 had unleashed forces of nationalism and liberalism, but these forces were contained and reversed by a conservative reaction and the reestablishment of autocratic rule. In 1848, nationalism was popular—from the streets—and this threatened and frightened the conservative establishments of Europe. But even within that establishment, there was support for the creation of unified, centralized states. A decade after the popular revolutions, strong figures in Germany and Italy acted to create national states from above, using the modern technology of warfare to do so. The creation of a united Germany and a united Italy changed the face of, and the balance of power in, Europe. After the completion of Bismarck's wars of German unification in 1870, Germany was the largest and strongest state in Europe.

NATIONALISM AND THE NATION-STATE

As we saw in chapter 4, the nation-state, a political unit bringing together most people of one nationality, had begun emerging in Europe in the sixteenth century, but the process was a slow one. Before 1860, there were only two major nation-states in Europe, England and France. Other nation-states like Portugal, Holland, and the Scandinavian countries existed, but these were mostly small and peripheral countries. In central Europe, most political units were mini-states, such as Hanover, Bavaria, Tuscany, and Sicily. From the sixteenth century, strong monarchs began forging strong national states by breaking the power of local lords and consolidating governmental power. After the French Revolution of 1789, popular nationalism became another force for national unity, independence, and the creation of nation-states.

The whole concept of a nation was relatively new and derived in part from Enlightenment ideas of popular sovereignty and the spread of literacy, which accompanied the Industrial Revolution and urbanization. A **nation** is a group of people with a common culture, a sense of identity, and political aspirations. Aspects of culture can include language, religion, ethnicity, traditions, customs, and history. Those common characteristics are not sufficient to constitute a nation, however, which also requires the psychological (or social psychological) element of identity and aspiration: a people must feel these common ties to be a nation.

This sense of national identity was fostered in the nineteenth century by artists, writers, musicians, and linguists in almost every national culture. In Poland, for example, which had earlier been "partitioned" by Russia, Austria, and Prussia, the Romantic and patriotic poet Adam Mickiewicz (see box 4.1) penned an epic poem called *Pan Tadeusz* (1834) that depicted a rural and idyllic society. At the end of this epic, young people don the uniform of the Polish Napoleonic army and proclaim the peasant a free citizen. The Finnish national epic, the *Kalevala*, was a compilation of folk stories and verses first published in the nineteenth century, at a time when Finland was dominated by Sweden and Russia. These literary works, like many others all over the Continent, helped define national groups and give them a sense of identity and pride. Musicians also contributed to this process, weaving folk tunes and themes into their compositions; witness, for instance, the mazurkas and polonaises of the Polish composer Frederic Chopin and the nationalist tone poem *Finlandia* by the Finn Jean Sibelius. At the same time, linguists began compiling dictionaries and grammars of many languages, many of them appearing in written form for the first time in the nineteenth century. As ethnic groups began acquiring a literary, artistic, and musical heritage, as well as a written language, they increasingly recognized their common identity, and this shaped their aspirations for their own political communities. This was nationalism.

When nationalism arises in multinational states or empires, such as the Ottoman, Russian, or Austro-Hungarian empires, national groups typically want to break away from the larger empire, which is dominated by other nationalities, such as the Turks, Russians, or Germans.

BOX 7.1
Verdi and Italian Independence

The great Italian composer Giuseppe Verdi wrote operas with nationalistic themes (including his popular masterpiece *Aida*), leading many to consider him the musical figurehead of the struggle for Italian independence and unification. In his third opera, *Nabucco* (1842), the chorus of Hebrews lamenting their captivity in Babylon was, for Italians under Austrian rule, a thinly veiled reference to their own longing for freedom. Verdi's name even became a kind of code word for those supporting Victor Emmanuel, then king of Sardinia, to assume leadership of all of Italy: *Vittorio Emanuele Re D'Italia* (Victor Emmanuel King of Italy). Victor Emmanuel did become king of Italy in 1861, and Verdi himself was elected a member of the newly created Chamber of Deputies.

This nationalist **separatism** constitutes a threat to the survival of the empire and so is naturally resisted by its rulers. Nationalism led to the breakup of the Ottoman Empire in the nineteenth century and the emergence of new nation-states like Greece, Serbia, Bulgaria, and Romania out of that empire. It also roiled the Russian Empire throughout the nineteenth century (especially in Poland) and almost brought down the Austro-Hungarian monarchy in 1848.

The popular revolts of 1848, sometimes tinged with socialism, had frightened European rulers and aristocrats and even the new middle class. However, currents of nationalism stirred within the middle and upper classes too. Often this nationalism took a very different form, called **irredentism**, which is the demand for territory belonging to another state, usually based on historical or ethnic claims. This top-down nationalism, used by national leaders making irredentist claims, fostered the creation of unified states in Germany and Italy.

PRELUDE TO UNIFICATION: THE CRIMEAN WAR

Before turning to the unifications of Italy and Germany, we should mention briefly another event that had some bearing on those events—the Crimean War (1853–56). This war was named after the Crimean peninsula, part of the Russian Empire that juts out into the Black Sea. Britain and France launched an attack there to assist Turkey in resisting Russian claims on Ottoman Turkish territory and the Russian tsar's efforts to extend protection over Christian subjects of the Ottoman Empire. The Kingdom of Sardinia also joined in the war against Russia, mainly to win support from England and France for the idea of a united Italy. Related to all of this was the issue of control over the Dardanelles, the critical straits that connect the Black Sea to the Mediterranean. The conflict was a nasty one of trench warfare, cholera, and huge casualties, a foreshadowing of what was to come a half century later in World War I. It was the first war covered by newspaper correspondents and the first in which women served as army nurses. Florence Nightingale became a legend when she commanded the British nursing services during the war.

Russia's defeat in the war led to the neutralization of the Black Sea, the extension of joint European protection over Ottoman Christians, and a European guarantee of the integrity of the Ottoman Empire. In addition, Romania and Serbia were recognized as self-governing principalities and soon thereafter became independent states. Even more important, however, was the impact of this war on the European balance of power. Russia's defeat in the war and Austria's abstention from it weakened the two states that were most determined to preserve the peace settlements of 1815 and to prevent change. Furthermore, the Sardinian gambit succeeded in advancing the Italian question.

MAZZINI, CAVOUR, AND THE UNIFICATION OF ITALY

Before 1860, the Italian peninsula was a patchwork of about a dozen large states and a number of smaller ones. Sardinia (also known as Piedmont), in the northwest, had the only native Italian dynasty in Italy. Lombardy and Venetia had, since 1814, belonged to the Austrian Empire, which also dominated Tuscany, Parma, and Modena. Across the middle part of Italy were a cluster of small Papal States controlled by the Roman Catholic Church at the Holy See in Rome. In the south, the Kingdom of the Two Sicilies (Naples and Sicily) was ruled by a branch of the Bourbon dynasty of France.

The Italian movement for national unification was known as *Il Risorgimento* (the resurgence) after a newspaper founded in 1847 by Count Camillo di Cavour (1810–61), the prime minister of Sardinia after 1852. It had earlier roots, though, in a number of secret independence societies and in the Young Italy movement of Giuseppe Mazzini (1805–72), whom we encountered in chapter 4, on the 1848 revolutions. Mazzini was a nationalist revolutionary and spent most of his life in exile in France, Switzerland, and England. "A nation," Mazzini proclaimed, "is the universality of citizens speaking the same tongue,"[1] so he favored uniting all Italians in one national state. Although Mazzini won support from some leaders in Sardinia and elsewhere, Cavour had little sympathy for Mazzini's revolutionary nationalism, preferring a more controlled movement toward unification under a liberal, constitutional monarchy.

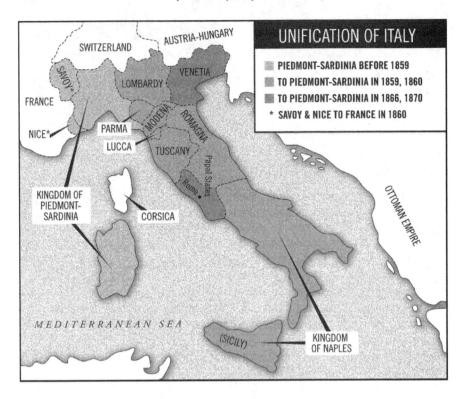

UNIFICATION OF ITALY

- PIEDMONT-SARDINIA BEFORE 1859
- TO PIEDMONT-SARDINIA IN 1859, 1860
- TO PIEDMONT-SARDINIA IN 1866, 1870
- * SAVOY & NICE TO FRANCE IN 1860

In 1848, as we saw in chapter 4, popular nationalism had erupted all over Italy, with independent republics proclaimed in Venice and Rome and rebellions in Sicily against the Bourbon monarch. All of these uprisings were crushed, however, as they had been elsewhere on the Continent. A decade later, though, the situation in Italy was different. Sardinia had won gratitude from France and Britain for participating in the Crimean War. Napoleon III of France was willing to support Sardinia's claims against Austria, which dominated much of northern Italy. With Napoleon's backing, Cavour provoked a war with Austria in 1859. Napoleon III himself led one hundred thousand troops from France into northern Italy to fight against Austria, which suffered major defeats. Tuscany, Modena, Parma, and Romagna drove out their Austrian rulers and were annexed to Sardinia. In the south, the Romantic revolutionary from Piedmont, Giuseppe Garibaldi (see box 7.2), led his thousand "Redshirts" in a seizure of power in Sicily and Naples. Plebiscites there confirmed popular desire to join with Sardinia.

In the peace settlement that ended the war, Austria held on to Venetia but little else; the pope still ruled in Rome but lost control over the Papal States, and France took Savoy and Nice. But Sardinia had won control

BOX 7.2
Giuseppe Garibaldi: Italian Nationalist and Romantic Revolutionary

The foremost military figure and most popular hero of the Italian unification movement was the flamboyant adventurer Giuseppe Garibaldi (1807–82).

Garibaldi was born in Nice, France (just across the border from Italy), and was largely self-educated. In his youth, he joined Young Italy, the movement organized by Mazzini to achieve freedom and independence for the Italian people. He was sentenced to death by a Genoese court for participating in an abortive insurrection in Piedmont, in 1834, but escaped to South America, where he lived for twelve years. There he led military actions in civil wars in both Brazil and Uruguay, helping to assure the independence of Uruguay from Argentina.

During the People's Spring of 1848, he returned to Italy to take part in the movement for Italian freedom and unification known now as *Il Risorgimento*. Organizing a corps of three thousand volunteers, he fought against the Austrians in Lombardy and supported the Roman Republic established by Mazzini. In defeat, having lost most of his forces, he fled Italy, moved to Staten Island, New York, and became a US citizen and a candle maker.

In the 1850s, Garibaldi returned to Italy to support Cavour and Victor Emmanuel in their wars of Italian unification. In 1860, he took a force of one thousand men, known by their uniforms as "Redshirts," to Sicily, which was then controlled by the Bourbon king of Naples. He conquered the island, set up a provisional government, and then crossed to the mainland and

After the pope's troops had been defeated by Cavour in 1860, the British satirical magazine Punch *depicted Garibaldi offering Pope Pius IX the cap of Liberty: "Take this cap, Papa Pius. You will find it more comfortable than your own."*

took Naples (which controlled most of the southern half of the Italian peninsula). This was a key piece of the Italian puzzle, enabling the establishment, in 1861, of the Kingdom of Italy with Victor Emmanuel as king. Garibaldi was dissatisfied with the exclusion of Rome from the kingdom, though, and fought several times over the next years to attach the Papal States to Italy. Eventually, Rome was annexed to Italy. Garibaldi was elected to Parliament in 1874 and died in 1882.

over the rest of Italy. In May 1861, an all-Italian parliament was convened in Turin and proclaimed the Sardinian ruler Victor Emmanuel II as king of Italy. Five years later, when Austria was at war with Prussia, Italy seized Venetia. In 1870, when France was distracted by the Franco-Prussian war, Italy seized the rest of the Papal States, including Rome, and limited the pope's dominion to the square mile of the Vatican. That completed the unification of Italy. The consolidation of territory, however, was only one part of the nation-building process. As one Italian nationalist remarked at the opening of the unification parliament in 1861, "now that we have created Italy, we must start creating Italians."[2] At the time, only a minority of people living in Italy spoke the Italian language, which had evolved from Tuscan. The challenge of creating a sense of common Italian identity, particularly between northern and southern Italy, has endured until this day.

BISMARCK AND THE UNIFICATION OF GERMANY

The unification of Germany proceeded in a similar fashion to that of Italy, with a strong leader, Otto von Bismarck (1815–98), of a powerful core state, Prussia, warring on neighboring states to consolidate other German territories under Prussia's dominion. As in Italy, the first stab at national unity had been stymied in the failed revolutions of 1848. A generation later, Germany was finally unified when the issue was pushed by the king of Prussia and his forceful chancellor, Bismarck.

Bismarck was a *Junker* (the landlord class) from Brandenburg, in Prussia, and was appointed chancellor (or premier) of Prussia, the most powerful of the German states, in 1862. Bismarck was neither a nationalist, nor a liberal, nor a democrat, but he wanted to strengthen the position of Prussia in Germany and of Germany in Europe. "The position of Prussia in Germany," he told the Prussian Parliament, "will be determined not by its liberalism but by its power. . . . not by speeches and majority votes are the great questions of the day decided—that was the great error of 1848 and 1849—but by iron and blood."[3] From this "blood and iron" speech and his forceful actions to achieve German unification, Bismarck became known as "the Iron Chancellor."

Bismarck essentially wanted a new German confederation, but one without Austria. He accomplished this through a series of short decisive wars against Denmark, Austria, and France, each time seizing pieces of territory and pushing those neighboring states out of German affairs. The first of these wars, in 1864, against Denmark was over the long-disputed territories of Schleswig and Holstein. These two duchies were ruled by the Danish king, although they were not formally part of Denmark. Because large numbers of Germans lived in them, the separation of Schleswig-

Holstein from Denmark became a passionate issue for German national-ists. Bismarck simply wanted to incorporate them into Prussia, but the issue of Schleswig-Holstein was arcane and complex. The British prime minister Lord Palmerston once said that only three men truly understood the problem: One was dead; one had gone mad; and the third, Palmer-ston himself, had forgotten it.[4] (And if Palmerston, a brilliant diplomat, could not figure out the details, I am not about to try to explain them here.) In any case, Bismarck's opportunity arose when Denmark decided to incorporate Schleswig. Bismarck organized an alliance with Austria, and together the two large states quickly defeated Denmark. Prussia took Schleswig, and Austria took Holstein.

For Bismarck, though, Austria was a bigger target than Denmark. He wanted to isolate Austria internationally and remove it from the German equation, so that Prussia would have a free hand in shaping (and domi-nating) a north German confederation. The opportunity to attack Austria came in 1866, when Austria and Prussia were quarreling over control of Schleswig-Holstein. Austria, as we have seen, was already relatively isolated after the Crimean War and its conflict with France during Ital-ian unification. In a startlingly swift victory, Prussia was able to defeat Austria in what became known as the Seven Weeks' War. Prussian suc-cess was due in large measure to the application of new technologies to logistics and warfare: the new breech-loading "needle gun" (which could be fired from the prone position) and the use of the railroad and the tele-graph to move and coordinate troops and supplies. In the aftermath of the war, Prussia annexed Schleswig-Holstein, Hanover, and a number of other territories, and Bismarck formed his North German Confederation of twenty-two states. The constitution for the confederation included a parliament with broad suffrage, a move that won widespread popular support for his emerging German empire.

The final piece of the puzzle for Bismarck was the addition to the empire of the southern German states (including Bavaria), but this was opposed by France, which understandably feared this expansion of Prussian power. In 1870, Bismarck provoked the French ruler, Napoleon III, into declaring war on Prussia over a minor issue involving the fate of the Spanish throne. The Franco-Prussian War lasted only six weeks, and the Prussian victory was so swift and unexpected that there was no French government left to surrender. Napoleon III was taken prisoner, abdicated, and took refuge in England. An insurrection in Paris (following those in 1789, 1830, and 1848) eventually led to the establishment of the French Third Republic (which survived until World War II). After six months of chaos, the French signed a humiliating peace accord, agreeing to pay huge reparations to Germany and ceding the territories of Alsace and Lorraine. Bismarck proclaimed the establishment of a new German empire, with Wilhelm I as emperor of

Germany. The site for this important proclamation was not in Germany, but in France, in the Hall of Mirrors at Versailles. (The French did not forget this humiliation and, after World War I, forced the Germans to sign their surrender at the same site.) As with Italy, Germany had been unified from above and with force. Unlike Cavour, though, Bismarck did not rely on popular plebiscites to ratify the consolidation of the state. Bismarck had created Germany through blood and iron.

THE DUAL MONARCHY OF AUSTRIA-HUNGARY

After the unification of Germany, one-sixth of all Germans remained outside Germany, mostly in the Austrian Empire. In the second half of the nineteenth century, Austria had steadily lost influence in Europe, first by its exclusion from the Crimean War, then by the loss of its Italian territories, and then in its humiliating defeat in the Seven Weeks' War. Furthermore, the empire was weakened internally by the multiplicity of nationalities and the growing forces of nationalism within it, particularly among the Magyars (Hungarians). There were at least twenty other nationalities in the Habsburg Empire, including Czechs, Slovaks, Poles, Slovenes, Croats, Romanians, and Italians. Germans constituted about one-third of the total population (mostly concentrated in Austria and Bohemia), and Magyars, mostly in the eastern part of the country, made up about a quarter of the total. The Magyars had long complained about the dominance of Germans in the empire and about German bureaucracy and centralization. The Prussian defeat of Austria in 1866 weakened Austria and quickened Magyar demands. The result was the *Ausgleich*, or compromise, of 1867 that created the **dual monarchy** of Austria-Hungary. Austria and Hungary each got its own constitution and parliament, but they were joined together under the common crown of the Habsburgs. This gave the restless Hungarians a considerable degree of autonomy without actually creating two separate nation-states. The nationality problem of the empire was not solved, however. Although the arrangement worked to the benefit of both Hungarians and Austrians, it did nothing to help other nationalities in the empire, especially the **Slavic** peoples, such as the Czechs, Slovaks, and Poles. The nationality problem would fester for the next fifty years, eventually contributing to the outbreak of World War I.

IMPLICATIONS OF NATIONALISM AND UNIFICATION

In Germany and Italy, civic nationalism, directed from the top, created unified nation-states after popular nationalism had failed in 1848. In both cases in the 1860s, the unification projects had the support of powerful states and leaders in Piedmont and Prussia and, in the Italian case at least, outside support (from France) as well. Elsewhere in Europe, nationalists were not so fortunate. The Poles, for example, who had uprisings against occupying powers in 1830, 1848, and 1863, had no outside support and no success. As the historian Norman Davies has put it, "The Polish national movement had the longest pedigree, the best credentials, the greatest determination, the worst press, and the least success."[5] The Poles had to wait until the conclusion of World War I to regain their statehood.

Nationalism had mixed success elsewhere on the Continent during the nineteenth century. The Greeks, Belgians, Romanians, and Norwegians got their own nation-states, but the Irish and the Czechs did not. The various nationalities of the Russian Empire had to wait another century before gaining independence. The hodgepodge of nationalities in the Balkans would provide the tinderbox that ignited World War I (and would remain problematic to the present day).

The unification of Italy and Germany fundamentally reshaped the map of Europe and the balance of power in Europe. The German Empire, in particular, was now the largest and most populous state on the Continent, next to Russia, and the most powerful one. The Industrial Revolution was advancing quickly in Germany, and with industry came military power. In Bismarck's wars of unification, the Germans had quickly and easily defeated the two other major military powers on the Continent, Austria and France. Bismarck's policies had created a Germany that was united, dynamic, and strong, and it was not the last time that Germany's leaders would use nationalism to advance Germany's interests.

8

✿

The Age of Imperialism
and the Scramble for Africa

In the last quarter of the nineteenth century, the European powers engaged in a competitive struggle to extend their influence around the
world. During this age of imperialism, more than a quarter of the land
surface of the Earth was claimed by six European states. The competition
was particularly intense in Africa, which until then had been largely free
of European influence and, except for coastal areas, mostly unknown
and unexplored by Europeans. In 1880, about 90 percent of Africa was
ruled by Africans. Twenty years later, after a period of competitive land
grabbing called the **Scramble for Africa**, virtually the whole continent
had been parceled out to the European states. Only Ethiopia and Liberia
remained independent.

The reasons for European imperialism are numerous and complex; they
include national pride; strategic competition; the search for new markets,
raw materials, and cheap labor; and a European sense of mission partly
based on social Darwinism. For Africans, the colonial experience brought
European technology, ideas, and religions, as well as a deep-seated resentment and bitterness bred of European exploitation and condescension.
The age of imperialism was relatively short-lived, and almost as soon as
the continent was carved up, African nationalists began campaigning for
independence. Within the first thirty years after World War II, virtually all
of the African colonies had become independent states.

EUROPEAN EXPANSIONISM BEFORE
THE NINETEENTH CENTURY

Imperialism can be defined as "the process by which one state, with superior military strength and more advanced technology, imposes its control over the land, resources, and population of a less developed region."[1] This phenomenon was not new to the nineteenth century, of course. With the Age of Exploration in the fifteenth century, Spain and Portugal became the first major colonizers, and over the next century, Spain established a huge empire in the Americas, including most of South America. The French explored and then colonized much of North America, but were eventually replaced almost everywhere by the British. The Dutch explored and colonized in the Pacific and Indian Oceans, especially in Indonesia. Beginning in the fifteenth century, the Portuguese began exploring the west coast of Africa and setting up settlements there for trade, especially in slaves, and missionary work. England, France, Spain, and other Europeans soon followed suit.

The first subjects of European colonization, however, were also the first to become independent. Britain's colonies in North America, what became the United States, revolted and gained independence at the end of the eighteenth century. In South America, revolts against Spanish rule began in the early nineteenth century due to events in Europe. Napoleon had invaded Spain in 1808 and placed his own brother on the throne, thus weakening Spanish authority and legitimacy in their American colonies. Within twenty years, revolts led by Simon Bolivar, José de San Martin, and others had secured independence from Spain and Portugal for almost every country in South America.

At the middle of the nineteenth century, only Britain had a large empire, stretching across the globe from Canada through India to Australia and New Zealand. The British proudly claimed that "the sun never sets on the British Empire." By the 1880s, only Africa, Indochina (in Southeast Asia), China, Japan, and some of the Pacific Islands remained unclaimed by Europeans.

THE MOTIVATIONS FOR IMPERIALISM

The primary motive for imperialist expansion was economic. The Industrial Revolution stimulated both production and demand in Europe and led to a search by entrepreneurs and governments alike for new sources of raw material for industry, new markets for the products of industry, and new supplies of labor, especially cheap labor. The drive for overseas markets was intensified by a long and deep economic depression across

Europe, beginning in 1873 and lasting until the mid-1890s. As their economies declined, one country after another imposed tariffs (taxes on imports) as a means of protecting their own industries from foreign competition. Such protectionism led to further declines in foreign trade and contributed to the deepening depression.

To get around this, European states sought "sheltered markets" free from such restrictions to trade and found them in the colonies they established in Africa and Asia. This nineteenth-century form of imperialism, however, was much more intensive and expensive than earlier forms and included substantial capital investments in the colonies in the form of mines, plantations, railroads, harbor facilities, banks, and the like. These investments necessitated a political and military presence to protect them, thus bringing soldiers, administrators, and settlers in increasing numbers.

A number of political and economic theorists pointed to imperialism as being a natural consequence of capitalism. In *Das Kapital*, for example, Karl Marx argued that, in capitalist society, the bourgeoisie required a constantly expanding market for its products. And the Russian Marxist and revolutionary Vladimir Lenin, in his booklet *Imperialism: The Highest Stage of Capitalism* (1916), asserted that imperialism was an inevitable stage in capitalist development. It would, however, bring the capitalist states into conflict with each other as they competed for colonial territory and would produce wars of national liberation in the colonies themselves against colonial powers. Lenin believed that imperialism was, therefore, a major cause of war among capitalist states (including World War I) and that it would eventually lead to the downfall of capitalism.

There were other motivations for imperialism besides purely economic ones. Both the *"Great Game"* of imperialist competition in the Middle East and the Scramble for Africa were driven in part by the strategic and diplomatic rivalries of the great powers in Europe. Britain and France had long been rivals on the European continent, and with the unifications of Germany and Italy in the 1860s and 1870s, those two countries were also drawn into the struggle for power and influence. Britain, in particular, wanted to protect its interests in India and Egypt from other Europeans. In the 1880s, Britain established a **protectorate** over Afghanistan as a buffer against Russian expansionism toward India; it established another protectorate over Egypt to protect its control of the recently built Suez Canal (which connected the Mediterranean and Red Seas). As the British statesman Lord Curzon put it, Turkestan, Afghanistan, and Persia were "pieces on a chessboard upon which is being played out a game for the domination of the world."[2] The same could be said of Africa, where each European country scrambled to acquire territory before any of its rivals could.

There was also a humanitarian element in European expansionism into less-developed countries, although this was often tainted by condescension and social Darwinism (see chapter 6). Many Europeans felt that their involvements in the colonies would help uplift and modernize the peoples of Africa and Asia. Christian missionaries wished to save souls and bring Christ to those they regarded as heathen and therefore lost. And many missionaries and reform-minded settlers sought to end real or imagined native practices that they considered barbaric, such as slavery, child marriage, polygamy, and cannibalism.

But much of this was motivated by the social Darwinist notions that the natural superiority of some races justified the conquering of "backward" peoples. The Englishman Herbert Spencer, the main advocate of social Darwinism, felt that Darwin's notion of the survival of the fittest applied to nations as well as to species. This condescension could take extreme forms: in 1904, a local zoo in Hamburg, Germany, for example, exhibited a group of Samoan women in one of its enclosures. The conjunction of social Darwinism and imperialism is illustrated by English writer Rudyard Kipling's famous poem "The White Man's Burden" (1899), in which he urges the United States to take up that burden in the Philippines after it had annexed them that same year:

> Take up the white Man's burden—
> Send out the best ye breed—
> Go bind your sons in exile,
> To serve your captives' need;
> To wait in heavy harness,
> On fluttered folk and wild—
> Your new-caught sullen peoples,
> Half devil and half child.

THE SCRAMBLE FOR AFRICA

The rapid and thoroughgoing colonization of Africa in the last fifteen years of the nineteenth century is referred to as the *Scramble for Africa*. The African continent constitutes about one-fifth of the globe's land area and was populated then by about one hundred million people; however, most maps of Africa at the time showed huge blank areas in the interior, thus leading to its name as the "Dark Continent." In fact, however, Africa contained about seven hundred autonomous societies, each with its own political structure. In many parts of Africa, there was "a high level of social, political and artistic sophistication in existence long before the coming of the Europeans."[3]

Before the nineteenth century, outsiders had barely penetrated the interior of Africa, and most contact between Africans and Europeans was along the coasts. Most of these early contacts were based on the slave trade: between 1450 and 1900, some twelve million people were transported as slaves from Africa to the Americas.[4] Slavery was outlawed in England in 1772, and trade in slaves was banned there in 1807. After that, most of that country's trade was in products such as sugar, coffee, cocoa, and gold.

European interest in Africa, especially North Africa, expanded after the construction in 1869 of the Suez Canal, which connected the Mediterranean and Red Seas (from which ships could travel to the Indian Ocean). The canal was a boon for shipping and world trade, especially between Europe and Asia. For England, especially, the Suez Canal cut shipping time to India in half and allowed ships to avoid the long journey around Africa and the treacherous waters at the southern tip of that continent. Britain soon purchased controlling shares in the canal and, in the 1880s, established a protectorate over Egypt (through which the canal was cut), even though that country was still part of the Ottoman Empire.

The scramble for the continent really began in 1879, when the Belgian king Leopold II (r. 1865–1909) sent the British-American journalist Henry Stanley to the Congo in central Africa. Stanley returned from his assignment in 1884, with treaties signed by some five hundred local chiefs giving Leopold control over the area.[5] In some alarm at this sudden acquisition of African territory by a European rival, the German chancellor Otto von Bismarck organized the Berlin Conference of 1884–85 to establish some rules on how Europeans would divvy up the African continent. The conference agreed to the establishment of the Congo Free State with Leopold II as its ruler. But it also set up guidelines for future colonization. A country could not just claim territory; it first had to establish "effective control" over an area. And the colonizing states had mandates to provide for the welfare of the native peoples. The Berlin Conference set off a mad scramble for territory in Africa, with each European state afraid of being beaten to the punch by others. Within fifteen years, by 1900, the entire continent had been divided up by European powers. Only Ethiopia and Liberia managed to escape colonization, and Ethiopia was the only native empire to do so. Liberia, founded in 1822 as a colony for emancipated American slaves, declared its independence in 1847 but in fact remained mostly under US control.

A key prize in the Scramble for Africa was South Africa, at the southern tip of the continent. The area was originally settled by the Dutch in the seventeenth century, and their descendants became known as the Boers. The British gradually assumed control in the middle of the nineteenth century, forcing the Boers to the north, where they formed the republics of

The Rhodes Colossus: Striding from Cape Town to Cairo. *An 1892 cartoon from the British satirical magazine* Punch *depicts the British entrepreneur and colonialist Cecil Rhodes astride Africa with telegraph wire from north to south.*

Transvaal, Natal, and the Orange Free State. The discovery of diamonds and gold in these areas in the 1860s brought many British prospectors and settlers into the Boer states. Friction between the Boers and the British mounted to a full-scale war (the Boer War), which lasted three years and to which the British committed some four hundred thousand troops. The eventual defeat of the Boers led to the creation of the British Union of South Africa in 1910. The government, including both Boers (also called Afrikaners) and British, soon established a policy of racial separation and inequality called **apartheid**, which suppressed and exploited the black population there until the end of the twentieth century.

THE COLONIZATION OF ASIA

Although European colonization in the nineteenth century was most frenetic in Africa, it extended all over the globe. Most of Asia was carved up by the European powers too, with only Japan remaining truly independent. The "jewel in the crown" of the British Empire was India, a huge and populous country and a rich source of cotton, tea, and opium. The British had defeated the French in India in the eighteenth century, and after that, the country was essentially ruled by the British East India Company, a trading company that answered to the British Parliament in London. After a number of native revolts against British influence, the British government took direct control over India, and Queen Victoria became empress of India.

France began colonizing Southeast Asia in the 1850s, gradually extending its control over the region. In 1887, it established the Union of Indochina, made up of what is now Vietnam and Kampuchea (Cambodia); subsequently, it added Laos. Vietnam later became a hotbed of national resistance to French rule, resulting in a war of national liberation that first drove out the French in the 1950s, then the Americans in the 1970s.

China had its own long-standing empire, so little formal European colonization occurred there. But the military and political weaknesses of nineteenth-century imperial China made it an easy target for its neighbors and for Europeans. Beginning in 1842, the European powers and the United States extracted concessions from China on over a dozen cities, including Shanghai, Canton (Guangzhou), and Hong Kong. These interlocking agreements, known as the *treaty system*, allowed Europeans to make their own settlements immune from Chinese law and imposed restrictions on Chinese citizens within the treaty ports. European and US gunboats patrolled the Yangtze River to protect their own citizens and commercial interests.

Later in the century, the carving up of China was intensified. Japan defeated China in the Sino-Japanese War of 1894, leading to an independent Korea and to Japan's taking control of Formosa (Taiwan), the large island just off the Chinese coast. Ten years later, Japan extended its control into Manchuria in northeast China. Russia extracted from China long-term leases over the ports at Port Arthur and Darien, thus gaining important strategic and economic outlets to the Pacific Ocean. The British compelled China to sign a one-hundred-year lease over Hong Kong, which became one of the most important commercial and trading centers in Asia. Even the new imperialist power of the United States got into the act. Not wanting to be left out of the lucrative Chinese market, in 1899, the United States declared an Open Door policy, calling for China to be open to trade with all foreign powers. All of these defeats and humiliations for the Chinese contributed to the overthrow of the Ching Dynasty in 1911 and a failed effort to establish a republic from the ashes of the oldest empire on earth.

PATTERNS OF COLONIAL RULE

The European states initially relied primarily on chartered trading companies to explore and develop colonial areas, expecting that the resulting colonies would essentially pay for themselves. Britain, France, and Holland all had East India companies that were chartered by their governments as early as the seventeenth century and that controlled the areas that they occupied. Eventually, though, administration of these areas was taken over by European governments. A similar pattern emerged during the Scramble for Africa in the late nineteenth century; in West Africa, for example, the Royal Niger Company was granted a charter from the British Parliament to develop Nigeria in the 1880s. But when the company went bankrupt in 1899, the British government took over administration of the area, and Nigeria became a British colony. In their colonies, the British practiced indirect rule, relying mostly on native princes and local troops to enforce their authority. The French used more direct rule, appointing Frenchmen as colonial governors and tying the colonies more directly to France. The important North African colonies of Tunisia and Algeria, for example, just across the Mediterranean Sea from southern France, actually became a part of metropolitan France and were heavily settled by French citizens.

Most colonies, however, were farther away from their European colonizers, so that colonization was made possible only by naval exploration and military force. England, with the largest navy in the world, also had the most extensive empire. The importance of naval power was made clear in an influential book published in 1890 by American admiral Alfred Thayer Mahan called *The Influence of Sea Power upon History, 1660–1783*, in which he argues that naval power is the key to a state's military, economic, and diplomatic influence. Mahan's book was particularly influential in the United States, whose navy, in 1898, seized a string of colonies from Spain, including Cuba in the Caribbean and the Philippines in the South Pacific, thus bringing the United States into the imperialist club. At the same time, Germany, recently united, began a program of shipbuilding to challenge Britain's dominance at sea, initiating a naval arms race that contributed to the outbreak of World War I.

THE LEGACY AND CONSEQUENCES
OF EUROPEAN IMPERIALISM

In 1500, European countries controlled 7 percent of the land surface of the planet; by 1800, they controlled 35 percent; by 1914, they controlled fully 84 percent. Britain had the largest empire, encompassing a quarter of the world's population in the early years of the twentieth century. France was not far behind, controlling about 3.5 million square miles, and Germany, Belgium, and Italy controlled about 1 million square miles each. At the turn of the twentieth century, Europeans truly dominated the world. Even the terminology of world geography reflected this domination: the terms *Near East* and *Far East* indicated the relative distances of these regions from Europe. And in 1884, an international conference located zero longitude, the prime meridian, at Greenwich, England, near London. Since then, all time zones across the world are expressed as Greenwich Mean Time (GMT) plus or minus x hours.

The European domination of Africa, Asia, and the Middle East had both positive and negative consequences for the subject peoples. For better or worse, European language, culture, and technology spread throughout the Southern Hemisphere in the nineteenth century. The English language became the *lingua franca* of the political and economic elites in countries like India, Nigeria, and South Africa, and an important source of unity and identity in countries riven by ethnic and religious differences. The same was true of French in much of North and West Africa. The Europeans built ports, roads, and railroads in their colonies, increasingly opening up these countries to European trade and technology. Cities and towns popped up in areas that had been primarily rural, and in the countryside, the production of cash crops (such as tobacco, coffee, and sugar) fostered the emergence of a cash economy. Among natives in the colonies, there was an increasing demand for European products like bicycles, radios, and clothing. A European system of education, both secular and religious, stimulated literacy and the development of an educated middle class. Missionaries spread Christianity.

All this, however, took a toll on the traditions, autonomy, independence, and pride of colonial peoples. The Europeans dominated, exploited, and subordinated the populations of Africa, Asia, and the Middle East and undermined the traditional systems of government in these areas. When the colonies eventually did achieve independence, they almost universally had difficulty establishing stable political institutions. Furthermore, a lingering resentment against the Europeans often poisoned relations between former colony and colonizer, hurting chances for trade and aid.

Ironically, the ideas of liberty and democracy that the Europeans brought with them to their colonies contributed to the end of their colonial rule. As these notions began to take hold, especially among the political and cultural elites in the colonies, they stimulated demands for freedom, democracy, and independence. National liberation and independence movements in the colonies accelerated after both world wars, when Europeans were absorbed with their own conflicts. After World War II, the cascade of independence became a flood (a topic that will be addressed further in chapter 12). Between 1947 and 1963, some 750 million British colonial subjects became citizens of newly independent states. In just one year in Africa, 1960, seventeen colonies won their independence from European states, and over the next two decades, virtually the whole continent became independent. The same was true of European colonies in South and Southeast Asia and the Middle East. All these newly independent states, many of them radically anti-Western, became members of the United Nations, thus shifting the balance of power in that organization and altering the dynamics of international politics. The *Third World*, those countries that adhered neither to the Western democratic capitalist states (the **First World**) nor to the communist bloc (**Second World**), became a pivotal arena in the **Cold War** struggles between East and West after World War II.

9

❧

World War I

The assassination of the Austrian archduke Francis Ferdinand, in Sarajevo in 1914, unleashed a catastrophic war that lasted four years, cost ten million lives, changed the face of the European continent, and set the stage for an even more global and destructive war a generation later. By the end of World War I, Europe no longer dominated the globe, and by the end of World War II, Europe itself was dominated by two powers outside the core of the Continent, the United States and the Soviet Union.

The Sarajevo assassination was a relatively minor incident in an obscure corner of Europe, and the resulting dispute was mostly between Austria-Hungary and Serbia, which was held responsible for the murder. But the incident quickly drew in most of the major European powers. The war was unexpected but not entirely unwelcome by many governments and citizens, and almost everyone expected it to last only a few months. It dragged on, however, in a stalemate and slaughter unprecedented in history, and did not finally draw to a close until after the intervention of the United States. With the end of the war, Europe had lost a generation of young men; the Russian, Austrian, Ottoman, and German empires were gone; a dozen new countries emerged; and Russia experienced a communist revolution.

EUROPE ON THE EVE OF WAR

At the beginning of the twentieth century, Europe's power and prestige were unrivaled. Europeans were world leaders in almost every arena—

science, culture, economics, and fashion. Their empires encompassed most of the planet. The last half of the nineteenth century had been a relatively peaceful one in Europe, managed by the balance-of-power system established after the Napoleonic wars and interrupted only by occasional wars with finite goals and of short duration (such as the wars of German unification). Most of the Continent was still controlled by monarchies, but as we have seen in earlier chapters, absolutism had been losing ground since the time of the French Revolution. In 1914, France was a republic and England a constitutional monarchy, but the other major powers—Austria-Hungary, Germany, Italy, Russia, and the Ottoman Empire—were all conservative monarchies of various degrees of rigor.

The balance of power was a system of shifting alliances meant to prevent any one country from becoming too powerful and threatening to the others, thus ensuring the overall stability of the Continent. In 1914, the main components of the balance of power in Europe were the **Triple Alliance** formed by Germany, Austria, and Italy, and the **Triple Entente** of Russia, France, and (minimally) England. Russia was also allied with Serbia in the **Balkans**, partly to counterpoise the influence of both the Ottomans and the Austrians in the region and partly as a way of extending protection over fellow Slavs. The Serbs, like the Russians, are Slavic peoples with a Cyrillic alphabet and a background of Eastern orthodox Christianity.

The balance-of-power system worked well through most of the nineteenth century but was strained both by Bismarck's wars of German unification and by the emergence of a strong and united Germany in the middle of Europe. In the 1860s and 1870s, the German chancellor employed short wars with limited objectives against Denmark, Austria, and France to secure territories that were to become part of the German Empire. Bismarck adopted the notion that "war is a mere continuation of policy by other means" enunciated earlier by the Prussian general and strategist Karl von Clausewitz. His quick and decisive wars seemed to prove this idea. Furthermore, Bismarck demonstrated how decisive the application of technology could be in warfare: Prussian generals relied on the railroad and telegraph to quickly move and coordinate their armies, as well as on new weapons like the breech-loading rifle. Thus, they were often able to outmaneuver and overwhelm their enemies, forcing quick surrenders with minimal loss of life.

Learning their lessons from Bismarck's successes, in the last decades of the nineteenth century, military planners all over Europe began developing military technologies and planning for short, decisive wars in which they would overwhelm the enemy. By 1914, most European states had the largest armies they had ever maintained in peacetime. The military buildup extended to the seas as well, with a major naval arms race between England and Germany that had lasted fifteen years. While all European states were busy enlarging and improving their militaries at the turn of the century, there was also a strong ethos of both state power and warfare. The Prussian field marshal Helmuth von Moltke, for example, wrote,

> Perpetual peace is a dream, and not even a beautiful dream. War is part of God's order. Without war, the world would stagnate and lose itself in materialism. In it, Man's most noble virtues are displayed—courage and self-denial, devotion to duty, willingness to sacrifice oneself, and to risk life itself.[1]

These sentiments were shared by many ordinary citizens all over Europe, and contributed to the widespread enthusiasm for the onset of war in August 1914.

War preparations and the arms race were shaking the stability of Europe at the end of the nineteenth century, but so were the forces of nationalism and their effects on the multinational empires that dominated central Europe. The Habsburg monarchy of Austria-Hungary had already been weakened by the revolts of 1848 and again by the loss of the Seven Weeks' War to Germany in 1866. The year after that, in what was known as the *Ausgleich* (compromise), the Magyars (ethnic Hungarians) and Germans separated into a dual monarchy constituting essentially two separate nation-states, with the Germans making up less than half the population of Austria, as the Magyars did in Hungary. All other ethnic groups in the dual monarchy, including Czechs, Slovaks, Slovenes, and Croats, felt left out and oppressed under the new arrangement.

THE TINDERBOX: NATIONALISM IN THE BALKANS

Ethnic nationalism can work to break up multinational states, as it was doing in Austria-Hungary, but it can also move to create new states made up of people of common ethnicity. The strongest nationalist movement at this time occurred among the Slavic peoples in the Balkan peninsula, who included Bulgarians, Macedonians, Serbs, Croats, Montenegrins, Bosnians, and Slovenes. For many of them, anxious to be out from under the control of Austrians, Hungarians, or Ottoman Turks, the goal was to create a single south-Slavic nation, what was eventually to materialize as Yugoslavia (which means "south Slav"). Serbia, which had gained independence from Ottoman Turkey in 1878, saw itself as the leader of south-Slav nationalism.

At its height, the Ottoman Empire controlled almost all of the Balkan peninsula, reaching even to the gates of Vienna. (They had been stopped there by an international coalition led by the Polish king.) But since the end of the seventeenth century, the empire had been in retreat, gradually shrinking toward its core, in what is now Turkey. As the Ottoman Empire weakened, other European states scrambled to fill the vacuum in southeastern Europe. At the same time, the various nationalities began asserting their own demands for autonomy or independence. Ottoman Turkish defeats at the hands of the Russians in the 1870s, for example, resulted in the creation of the new independent states of Serbia, Bulgaria, and Romania, all carved out of Ottoman lands. In 1908, Austria-Hungary annexed Bosnia, also a remnant of the Ottoman Empire, almost leading to a war with Russia and Serbia, which had its own claims on Bosnia. During 1912 and 1913, several regional wars erupted in the Balkans, all involved with the dismemberment of Turkey or the disposal of its European territory.

THE SPARK: THE ASSASSINATION

The European situation in 1914, then, was a tinderbox of growing rivalries among the major powers, huge armies prepared for rapid mobilization, insurgent nationalism, and a collapsing Ottoman Empire. The spark that lit this tinder was the assassination of the Austrian archduke Francis Ferdinand, heir apparent to the Habsburg throne, while he was reviewing troops in Sarajevo, the capital city of recently annexed Bosnia. The man who shot the archduke and his wife was a young Bosnian Serb nationalist named Gavrilo Princip. The Austrian government quickly blamed Serbia for the incident and demanded that the government of Serbia crack down on nationalist and terrorist groups within its borders. The Austrian emperor, Francis Joseph, was horrified at the murder of his nephew, but also concerned that the assassination was, in a way, an attack on all European monarchs and their empires. His military chief of staff was even more concerned about Austria itself:

> Austria-Hungary must draw the sword against Serbia. . . . It is not a question of a knightly duel with "poor little" Serbia, as she likes to call herself, nor of punishment for the assassination. It is much more the highly practical importance of the prestige of a Great Power. . . . The Monarchy has been seized by the throat, and has to choose between allowing itself to be strangled and making a last effort to prevent its destruction.[2]

Germany's Kaiser Wilhelm, a close friend of the murdered archduke and an ally of Austria, saw the situation in a similar light and gave a "blank check" to Austria to make military retribution against Serbia. Austria issued an ultimatum to Serbia that would have drastically compromised Serbian sovereignty, thus making it almost impossible for the Serbs to comply fully. Even so, Serbia yielded on almost all points of the ultimatum. Austria deemed the concessions insufficient, broke diplomatic relations, declared war on July 28, and the next day, began an artillery bombardment of Belgrade, the Serbian capital.

THE ESCALATION

This probably could have remained a localized war between Austria and Serbia were it not for the web of alliances and military mobilization schedules. Indeed, Austria foolishly expected that support from Germany would keep Russia (and others) out of the conflict. But the Austrian ultimatum against Serbia prompted Russia to mobilize its military, hoping this show of resolution would force Austria to back down. Germany demanded that the Russians halt their mobilization; when Russia did not, Germany began its own mobilization. To make matters worse, the German plan, envisaging a probable two-front war (because of Russia's alliance with France) called for German troops first to be deployed against France and, after a quick victory there, to be turned toward the Russians. Increasingly alarmed at the direction events were taking, the German kaiser initiated an exchange of telegrams with the Russian tsar, his cousin (they addressed each other as "Willy" and "Nicky"), attempting to head off the conflict. But military commanders in both countries asserted that the military mobilization schedules, once put in motion, could not be reversed. On August 1, Germany declared war on Russia; two days later, Germany declared war on France; and, within days of that, German troops advanced toward France through neutral Belgium, thus bringing England into the war. The incident in the Balkans had become a Europe-wide war, with the Central powers of Germany and Austria confronting the Allies of England, France, and Russia.

THE WAR

In August 1914, widespread enthusiasm for the war was evident in virtually every capital city. Young men flocked to military recruiting centers to enlist. Almost everyone expected the war to be a short one and that the soldiers would be home by Christmas. Events turned out otherwise, however, and in the end, the war was neither quick nor glorious. Because all sides now possessed new weapons and technology, nobody could quickly prevail, and military campaigns soon bogged down in trench warfare and attrition. The scale of the slaughter was unprecedented and horrific. Some single battles, for example those at Ypres and Verdun, saw tens of thousands of deaths *per hour* and hundreds of

A British World War I poster showing support for the war from the home front. © Canadian War Museum (CWM19720028-006).

thousands of casualties overall. The battle of the Somme, lasting for four months of 1916, cost the Germans five hundred thousand men, the British four hundred thousand, and the French two hundred thousand, and nothing of value was gained by either side.

New military technology rendered the conflict even more destructive and dramatically widened the scope of warfare, increasingly bringing civilians and noncombatants under fire. The newly perfected machine gun increased firepower on the ground a hundredfold. Poison gas proved so effective that, by the end of the war, half of all German artillery shells carried gas. During the war, over a million casualties were attributed to gas, with almost one hundred thousand fatalities. The German *Zeppelin* (blimp) raids on London in 1915 were the first deliberate attacks on civilian targets during warfare. And the submarine, first used by the Germans to attack supply ships on their way to Britain, ended up sinking passenger liners as well. The German sinking of the British liner

Lusitania in 1915, with the loss of 1,200 lives, including 118 American citizens, inflamed US sentiment against the Germans and helped draw the United States into the war.

The American historian and diplomat George Kennan sums up the brutal and demoralizing nature of the World War I battlefield:

> The deadlock was not long in establishing itself on the western front, and it is hard today to visualize the full hideousness and wastefulness of what ensued: those four long years of miserable carnage; that appalling phenomenon of great armies of men facing each other in the muddy trenches day after day, month after month, year after year, destroying each other hopelessly, systematically, with artillery barrages, with the as yet un-answered weapon of the machine gun, with trench mortars and barbed wire and even poison gas, until victory or defeat came to seem less a product of military leadership and skill and spirit than a matter of some grisly mathematics of cannon fodder and slaughter.[3]

In the end, some eight million soldiers were killed in the war, and probably only one in ten saw the man who killed him.

The end of the war came not so much from any particular military successes on the battlefield, but rather from general exhaustion and from two events occurring in 1917: the Russian Revolution, which was soon to take Russia out of the war, and the entry of the United States into the war. Russia had been battered from the start of the war, and Tsar Nicholas II was a bungling and incompetent ruler. At times, Russian soldiers, mostly peasants, were sent into battle without weapons and sometimes without even shoes. The enormous casualties, food shortages, and economic collapse increasingly turned the population against the war—and against the monarchy. In March 1917, in the capital, St. Petersburg, troops mutinied, workers went on strike, and the tsar was forced to abdicate. A provisional government took power but did not take Russia out of the war, thus eroding the new government's popularity. Meanwhile, the Marxist revolutionary leader Vladimir Lenin returned to Russia from exile, called for "peace, land, and bread," and in November led his Bolsheviks in an overthrow of the provisional government and a seizure of power in what became known as the October Revolution. The new government signed a treaty with the Germans in March 1918 and withdrew from the war. (The Russian Revolution is discussed more thoroughly in chapter 10.)

The closing of the eastern front allowed the Germans to turn all of their forces toward the west, but by this time, the United States had entered the war, and American troops were landing in France at the rate of 250,000 per month. The American president, Woodrow Wilson, had been reelected in November 1916, pledging to keep the United States out of the European war. The United States had become increasingly enmeshed in the conflict, however, supplying the Allies with both food and weapons. When, in

BOX 9.1
A Sweet and Honorable Death

At the outbreak of World War I, most people had a romantic image of warfare, and most literary works on warfare romanticized the glory, honor, and adventure of war. In Britain, for example, many schoolboys knew the line from the Latin poet Horace, *Dulce et decorum est pro patria mori* (It is sweet and honorable to die for your country). These notions were shattered by the grisly massacres and huge casualties of World War I, and this new realism was reflected in poems, novels, and stories that emerged from that war. Erich Maria Remarque, for example, after serving in the German army and being badly wounded, depicted the brutal, grim, and demoralizing experiences of ordinary soldiers in his *All Quiet on the Western Front*.

Wilfred Owen, poet, patriot, soldier, pacifist, in military uniform during World War I.

Another young writer, Wilfred Owen, enlisted in the British army in 1915, was wounded and sent home to England to recover, and then returned to the front in August 1918. One of his most moving poems, "Dulce et Decorum Est," depicts the horrors of poison gas, which seized one of his comrades:

> In all my dreams, before my helpless sight,
> He plunges at me, guttering, choking, drowning
> If in some smothering dreams you too could pace
> Behind the wagon that we flung him in,
> And watch the white eyes writhing in his face,
> His hanging face, like a devil's sick of sin;
> If you could hear, at every jolt, the blood
> Come gargling from the froth-corrupted lungs,
> Obscene as cancer, bitter as the cud
> Of vile, incurable sores on innocent tongues,—
> My friend, you would not tell with such high zest
> To children ardent for some desperate glory,
> The old Lie: *Dulce et decorum est*
> *Pro patria mori.*

Owen was killed in action exactly one week before the November armistice, at the age of twenty-five.

early 1917, the Germans resumed unrestricted submarine warfare, they sank several American ships, leading the United States to declare war on Germany in April "to make the world safe for democracy," in Wilson's words. The country mobilized quickly. In 1916, there were only 130,000 men in the US armed forces; by the end of 1917, 3.5 million men had enlisted, and by 1918, they were on their way to Europe. US intervention in the war tipped the balance and forced the Germans to sue for peace in November 1918, bringing the war to a close.

VERSAILLES, THE PEACE SETTLEMENTS, AND THE LEAGUE OF NATIONS

The Allied victors assembled in Paris in the winter of 1919 to draw up peace treaties dealing with each of the defeated states. The preeminent figure in these negotiations was President Wilson, who had arrived in Europe to a hero's welcome. Near the end of the war, Wilson had laid out his ideas for a postwar peace in his **Fourteen Points**, which trumpeted principles of democracy, liberalism, and nationalism and echoed the ideals of the Enlightenment, the French Revolution, and the People's Spring of 1848. Wilson called for **national self-determination** for the peoples of Europe and the redrawing of European borders along national lines. He also appealed for "a general association of nations," an international political organization to settle disputes among states and prevent war. Both of these ideas became central to the discussions at the peace negotiations.

Despite Wilson's lofty and idealistic goals, the peace treaty for Germany, the Versailles Treaty, was heavy-handed and punitive. Even though the origins of the war could hardly be laid at the feet of only one state, Germany was assigned blame for the war and was compelled to accept explicit responsibility for Allied losses in the war. German territory was much reduced in size, with Alsace-Lorraine returned to France and parts of the prewar state assigned to the newly established state of Poland. East Prussia was separated from the rest of Germany by a sliver of land, the *Polish corridor*, allowing Poland access to the Baltic Sea. The coal- and steel-producing areas of the Saar region (along the border with France) were placed under French control for fifteen years. Germany was stripped of her colonies in Africa and elsewhere, and they were assigned by the **League of Nations** to other states to administer as **mandates**. To prevent Germany from becoming a future military power, its army and military production were strictly limited. All of these were humiliating conditions for a country that had already suffered mightily through four years of war.

Although the Paris treaties reduced the German state, they also created a host of new central European states and drew a whole new geography

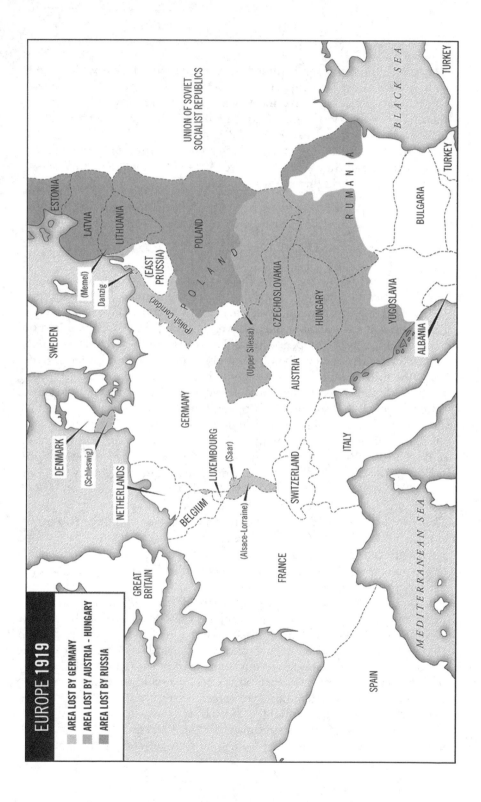

EUROPE 1919

Legend:
- AREA LOST BY GERMANY
- AREA LOST BY AUSTRIA - HUNGARY
- AREA LOST BY RUSSIA

UNION OF SOVIET SOCIALIST REPUBLICS

ESTONIA

LATVIA

LITHUANIA

(Memel)

Danzig

(EAST PRUSSIA)

POLAND

(Polish Corridor)

(Upper Silesia)

CZECHOSLOVAKIA

HUNGARY

RUMANIA

BULGARIA

YUGOSLAVIA

ALBANIA

TURKEY

TURKEY

BLACK SEA

SWEDEN

DENMARK

(Schleswig)

NETHERLANDS

GERMANY

LUXEMBOURG

(Saar)

BELGIUM

(Alsace-Lorraine)

AUSTRIA

SWITZERLAND

ITALY

FRANCE

GREAT BRITAIN

SPAIN

MEDITERRANEAN SEA

for the Continent. Out of the defunct empires were carved seven new independent states: Finland, Estonia, Latvia, Lithuania, Poland, Czechoslovakia, and Yugoslavia. Austria and Hungary were now small, separate states. Romania was enlarged by the addition of parts of Russia and Hungary. Greece acquired territory from Turkey. With the breakup of the Ottoman Empire, Turkey emerged as an independent republic, and Syria, Lebanon, Palestine, and Iraq were given as League of Nations mandates to France or Britain. Theoretically, these new states and border changes were all based on nationality, in accordance with Wilson's Fourteen Points. But central Europe was such a jigsaw puzzle of nations that some minorities inevitably remained in most states: Germans and Hungarians in Czechoslovakia; Ruthenians in Poland; Poles in Lithuania; Bulgars and Hungarians in Romania; and so forth. These areas became fertile ground for troublemakers and demagogues in the following years.

The other great brainchild of Woodrow Wilson was the "general association of nations," which emerged from the Paris meetings as the new League of Nations. The League was based on the principle of **collective security**, which held that all countries collectively would be responsible for protecting the sovereignty and independence of every other country. Member states pledged not to resort to war and to utilize the institutions of the League, headquartered in Geneva, Switzerland, to discuss and settle international disputes peacefully. As a universal organization with all nations represented, the League would replace the old system of alliances, balance of power, and war as an instrument of policy.

The League of Nations never lived up to this potential, however. The biggest problem was that the United States itself did not join the organization. When Wilson returned to the United States to promote the League, he was faced with a hostile Republican Senate and an isolationist public. The treaty failed in the Senate by one vote. Other crucial countries were also not involved in the League: the new communist regime in Russia refused to join an organization they considered to be dominated by bourgeois states; and Germany, as part of its punishment for the war, was prohibited from entering the League until 1926. Almost from the beginning, then, the League of Nations was fatally weakened, and when Hitler began challenging the European status quo in the 1930s, the League proved ineffectual.

CONSEQUENCES OF THE WAR

World War I, what the Americans called the "war to end all wars," altered Europe like no other war or revolution before or since. The human casualties alone were devastating: some eight million men were killed and another twenty million were wounded, many of them disabled or horribly mutilated. These losses were spread all around the Continent; each of the European Great Powers, except for Italy, lost at least a million men in the war. The US casualties, 115,000 killed and a similar number wounded, were light in comparison and were fewer than those the main combatants suffered in single battles like Verdun or the Somme. Europe lost, essentially, an entire generation of young men. As Winston Churchill wrote presciently about the war in 1929, "injuries were wrought to the structure of human society which a century will not efface and which may conceivably prove fatal to the present civilization."[4]

The duration and totality of the war transformed the home fronts in other ways as well. In every country, governments became more involved in economic planning and control as consumer economies were regeared for military production. With most men at the military fronts, women were brought into the workforce by the millions. (A 1916 British propaganda poster read, "Shells made by a wife may save a husband's life.")

This wartime upheaval in gender roles continued after the war and accelerated the movement toward women's suffrage in Britain and elsewhere. In Britain, women over thirty years of age gained the vote in 1918, and full female suffrage was extended in 1928. Women also won the right to vote in Germany, Scandinavia, the newly created states of Czechoslovakia, Hungary, and Poland, and in the new communist state of the USSR.

The war also marked the end of absolute monarchies in Europe, culminating a process that had begun with the French Revolution of 1789. With the defeat of the Central powers, the autocrats of Germany, Austria-Hungary, and the Ottomans were banished, and with the 1917 revolution in Russia, the tsar was ousted and then executed by the Bolsheviks. This time, unlike after previous revolutions and wars, the monarchies would not reappear. Out of the old empires emerged many incipient democratic states based on eighteenth-century ideals of popular sovereignty and nineteenth-century ideals of liberalism and nationalism.

This was a great advance for democracy, but many of these new states were weak, poor, and unaccustomed to democratic traditions of tolerance, compromise, and incremental change. The Bolshevik Revolution in Russia inspired unsuccessful left-wing revolutions in Germany, Austria, and Hungary in 1918–19, polarizing those populations between the Left and Right. Some states, Germany especially, chafed under the punishments and restrictions of postwar peace settlements. Perhaps in good economic circumstances the new political order in Europe could have gained a footing and flourished, but the worldwide economic depression of the late 1920s and 1930s dashed any such hope. In Germany, already weakened by punishing reparations payments after the war, the depression was devastating. With millions of Germans unemployed, impoverished, and resentful about Versailles, the stage was set for the rise of Adolf Hitler.

10

❧

The Russian Revolution and Communism

The Bolshevik Revolution in Russia in November 1917 took that country out of World War I and, in many respects, also took it out of Europe and launched it on a bold experiment: building a communist state based on the ideas of Karl Marx. The impact of the 1917 Russian Revolution was at least as great as that of the French Revolution of 1789 in terms of both its domestic consequences and its international implications. The year 1917, like 1789, was one of great political, social, and economic revolution. Also, like their French counterparts, the Russian revolutionaries claimed that their ideology was transcendent and universal, and they fully believed that the revolution in Russia would be the spark to ignite revolutions throughout the world.

The communist ideology of the new Russia was both anticapitalist and atheistic, so the Western governments, especially the United States, feared and distrusted it. The US government hoped and expected that the communist regime in Russia would fail and refused to extend diplomatic recognition to the new government until 1933. The fear and hostility between Russia and the West were intensified by the communists' stated desire to spread communism elsewhere in the world, including into western Europe and the United States. These tensions were muted somewhat during the interwar years because both the United States and the Union of Soviet Socialist Republics (USSR), the new name for the communist state, were focused on internal, rather than international, issues, and then during World War II because of their common alliance against Hitler's Germany. But with the end of World War II and the emergence of the United States and the Soviet Union as the world's two superpowers, those tensions re-emerged and dominated international politics during the Cold War.

TSARIST RUSSIA

To understand the Russian Revolution, however, it is necessary to understand the nature of the state in which it occurred. Russia at the beginning of the twentieth century was the last great **despotism** in Europe and the most conservative of the Great Powers. Although some liberalizing changes had occurred in Russia, as elsewhere in Europe, since 1789, Russia remained autocratic, economically backward, and mostly isolated from the rest of Europe. Yet it was a huge and diverse empire, covering a sixth of the land surface of the globe, dominated by the Russians but containing hundreds of other nationalities. These included other Slavic peoples, like Ukrainians and Poles, as well as non-Slavic Europeans such as Finns and Latvians, plus the largely Turkic Muslims of Central Asia. Many of these groups had been brought into the Russian Empire by imperial expansion or warfare, and the task of controlling and integrating them plagued the empire through much of its history.

A Slavic state, centered in Kiev (in present-day Ukraine), first emerged in the ninth century; soon thereafter, Prince Vladimir accepted Eastern Orthodox Christianity from Byzantium. From then on, the state and the Orthodox Church were closely entwined. During the three hundred years of Mongol occupation from the thirteenth to the sixteenth centuries, the church kept alive Russian culture, traditions, and identity. Russian rulers, who took the title "tsar" (the Russian version of the Latin *Caesar*), became the head of both the state and the Russian Orthodox Church. Moscow claimed the title of the "Third Rome" (after Constantinople), representing the center and the future of Christendom. The last dynasty of the tsars, the Romanovs, ruled from 1613 until the revolution of 1917.

Russia in 1900 was behind the other European powers, both politically and economically. The government remained a rigid and unrestrained autocracy, with the tsar at the head of both church and state. No local governments existed until the 1860s, and no national representative institutions until 1905, and even these were severely limited in their authority. The government prohibited political parties and kept dissent in check through a rigid system of censorship, a pervasive secret police, and an internal passport system that restricted people's movement around the country. Politically, Russia in 1900 was much like France in 1780.

Economic change was also slow to reach Russia. Until the emancipation of the serfs in 1861, Russia was still a feudal economy decades after feudalism had mostly disappeared from the rest of Europe. In 1900, peasants made up almost 90 percent of the population, and two-thirds of the population were illiterate. The Industrial Revolution and industrialization, which had begun in Britain at the end of the eighteenth century, did not take hold in Russia until the end of the nineteenth century. There was, therefore, not much of an urban working class, the group Karl Marx thought necessary for a revolution.

HINTS OF CHANGE AND REFORM

From the beginning of the nineteenth century, however, there were already hints of change and reform in Russia. The French Revolution and Napoleon's armies spread liberal, revolutionary, and Enlightenment ideas all across Europe, including Russia. In 1825, a group of former Russian military officers, some of whom had fought in the Napoleonic wars, been exposed to Western liberalism, and grown discontented with their own country's reactionary government, mounted an antitsarist revolt. The Decembrist revolt was crushed, but it sent a message and set a precedent for later protests and movements against the autocracy. The most important changes of the century, however, came from the top down rather than from insurrection or revolution. Tsar Alexander II (r. 1855–81), known as the "Tsar Liberator," launched a series of liberalizing reforms that included the creation of local self-government, modernization of the judiciary, and, most importantly, the emancipation of the serfs in 1861. Alexander II was assassinated in 1881, and his successors returned to more autocratic and draconian rule, but the freeing of the serfs, especially, stimulated enormous social and economic changes in Russia.

Many peasants were actually worse off economically after the emancipation, and many migrated to the cities in search of work. This fueled both urbanization and industrialization, which took off in Russia in the last decades of the nineteenth century. Between 1861 and 1900, pig iron production increased tenfold, and coal output increased forty-two-fold. Railroad mileage doubled between 1888 and 1913. The social fabric of the country began to change, too, with the growth of an urban working class (the proletariat), new industrial entrepreneurs (the bourgeoisie), and an emerging middle class. The overall population also grew dramatically, from some 73 million in 1861 to 170 million by 1914.

All of this political and socioeconomic ferment stimulated a number of bottom-up reform movements, too, including some revolutionary ones. "Westernizers" believed that Russia's future was tied with that of Western Europe and favored a constitutional political order and rapid economic development. **Slavophiles** (literally, "fond of Slavs"), in contrast, believed Russia to be culturally, morally, and politically superior to the West, so

A meeting of the village mir, *the traditional peasant council, made the basic unit of local government by the reforms of 1874.*

opposed Westernization and favored traditional institutions such as the orthodox Church and the peasant commune (*mir*). The **populists** (*narodniki*) also focused on the peasantry and wanted to base society on the *mir*, which they saw as an incipient form of socialism. In the 1870s, they launched a campaign of "going to the people" to educate the peasants in revolutionary ideas. An even more radical tendency was represented by the **nihilists**, who rejected institutions of all kinds, including government and the church, and favored freeing individuals from all religious, political, and family obligations. While all of these movements were gaining adherents in the mid-nineteenth century, Marxism, as such, had virtually no visibility in Russia and would not for many years to come.

Europeans during the nineteenth century were increasingly paying more attention to Russia, especially to its culture. Despite Russia's political and economic stagnation (or perhaps because of it), the country experienced a cultural renaissance in the nineteenth century. Russian novels became known throughout the world and included works of timeless and universal appeal, such as Fyodor Dostoyevsky's *Crime and Punishment*, Ivan Turgenev's *Fathers and Sons*, and Leo Tolstoy's *War and Peace* (which some consider the greatest novel ever written). Classical music by Russian composers became familiar to people worldwide (then and now) with works such as Pyotr Ilich Tchaikovsky's *Nutcracker* and *Swan Lake*, Modest Mussorgsky's *Pictures at an Exhibition* and *A Night on Bald Mountain*, and Nikolay Rimsky-Korsakov's *Scheherazade*.

1905: PRELUDE TO REVOLUTION

While Russian culture was flourishing in the nineteenth century and industrialization was transforming the economy, the autocracy remained rigid, backward, and increasingly ineffectual, both inside the country and in its foreign relations. Russia suffered a humiliating loss in the Russo-Japanese War of 1904–5, the first time in modern history that a European power was defeated by an Asian one.

In the middle of that war, an insurrection developed against the autocracy. It began with a large but peaceful demonstration in January 1905, led by an Orthodox priest named Father Gapon, in front of the tsar's Winter Palace in St. Petersburg. Guards fired on the protesters, killing hundreds in what became known as Bloody Sunday. The massacre precipitated nationwide strikes and demonstrations, which by the fall had paralyzed the country. The tsar, Nicholas II (r. 1894–1917), issued a conciliatory manifesto allowing the formation of an elected legislature (the Duma), and by the end of the year, the revolutionary movement petered out. The Duma was the first national representative institution in Russian history, and although it never had much power, it did allow the emergence of legal political groups and parties, including both liberals and socialists.

The reign of Nicholas II was a period of much change and development in Russian society. One historian has characterized this period as "a time of troubles" but also as a time of "self-scrutiny, experimentation with new institutions and dreams."[1] There were further economic reforms and advances, a growing middle class, and increasing numbers of independent farmers. After 1905, more freedom of expression was permitted in politics and the arts, and Russia became a center of the avant-garde in both music (e.g., Igor Stravinsky) and the visual arts (e.g., the abstract art of Wassily Kandinsky). But the more open environment also revealed the tensions that were so long repressed in the Russian Empire, including increasing pressures from political liberals and revolutionaries and increasingly assertive nationalism from Poles, Ukrainians, Latvians, Armenians, and the Turkic peoples of Central Asia. The twin forces that would finally topple the empire were Marxism-Leninism and World War I.

BOX 10.1
"The First Bolshevik" in Russian Literature

In nineteenth-century Russia, tsarist censorship and the secret police prevented most forms of political opposition, so literature and the arts became the main vehicle for social criticism and political dissent. Two of the most influential literary publications of the century were written by Ivan Sergeyevich Turgenev (1818–83), who was born and died in the same years as Karl Marx. Less known now than his contemporaries Dostoyevsky and Tolstoy, in the mid-nineteenth century Turgenev was the most famous writer in Russia and the first Russian writer to gain a reputation outside the country. His *Sportsman's Sketches* (1852), which depicted the miserable condition of peasants, was widely read in the country (including by Tsar Alexander II), provoked discussion and debate about the status of the peasantry, and probably contributed to the tsar's emancipation of the serfs in 1861. His masterpiece *Fathers and Sons* (1862) is at once a story of romantic love, generational conflict, and the tensions between change and tradition and between reform and revolution.

Turgenev himself was an example of many of these tensions. He grew up on a prosperous estate worked by serfs, part of an educated family that spoke French at home, and he spent many years in the West. After studying in Germany, he said, "I found myself a Westernizer," but he remained devoted to Russia and the Russian countryside. At the age of twenty-five, he fell in love with a young, but married, Spanish prima donna and spent the rest of his life following her around Europe in hopeless infatuation. He died in France, and his remains were transferred back to Russia for burial.

In *Fathers and Sons*, the main character is Bazarov, a young student and doctor who professes to be a nihilist, one who rejects everything that cannot be established by observation, experiment, and science. He repudiates all authority, in fact "everything," and believes that "the ground must be cleared" for the reconstruction of society. In the novel, he confronts and rejects romanticism, conservatism, and even liberalism. His host, Nikolai, a thoughtful and kindly owner of an estate, has freed his own serfs before the Emancipation required it, but Bazarov is both unsympathetic and rude to the older man. Bazarov's revolutionary rhetoric, uncompromising ideology, and commitment to science have led some critics of the novel to label him "the first Bolshevik," although Lenin's Bolshevik party was not formed until thirty years after the appearance of the novel.

MARXISM AND LENINISM

As we saw in chapter 5, the idea of communism was first developed by Karl Marx and others in the middle of the nineteenth century. The word *communism* basically disappeared from political discourse after the 1850s in most of Europe, although much of Marxism had been incorporated into the socialist movements and parties that thrived with the expansion of the urban working classes. In Russia, the absence of both a working class and parliamentary politics through most of the nineteenth century meant that Marxism had little influence in any form. It is somewhat ironic, then, that Marx's ideology of communism was revived not in an advanced capitalist state, but in Russia, the least developed of the major European powers.

The ideology of Marxism appealed for a number of reasons to people working for fundamental change in the Russian Empire. First of all, many Russian radicals had given up in frustration at trying to radicalize the Russian peasants (a goal of the populists in earlier decades) and liked the Marxist focus on urban workers, the proletariat, whom they thought would be more receptive. The scientific and antireligious elements of Marxism also had appeal to many Russian intellectuals, an instrumental group in the reform and revolutionary movements in the country. Marxism appealed to many because it had the potential to make Russia more modern and "enlightened." Marxist theory also helped explain Russia's backwardness as part of a process of historical development and not as some flaw in the Russian character. Finally, Marxism had some advantages tactically because the Russian regime and secret police thought it was harmless!

Russian radicals living outside Russia formed the Marxist Social Democratic Labor Party in 1898. Despite its small size, within a few years, the nascent party split into two factions, with the *Bolsheviks* (majority) pressing for a quick revolution in Russia and the *Mensheviks* (minority) arguing for a more gradual approach. It was the Bolsheviks, led by Vladimir Lenin, who in 1917 would seize power in the Russian Revolution.

Lenin was born in 1870 to a middle-class family. His older brother was hanged in 1887 for a plot to assassinate the tsar, and this contributed to Lenin's radicalization. He became involved in revolutionary activity, was arrested, and spent three years in exile in Siberia. From 1900 onward, he spent most of his time outside Russia, planning for an eventual revolution in his country.

For Lenin and other Russian Marxists, the Russian situation posed somewhat of a dilemma and a challenge. Marx had posited that a revolution would occur in an advanced capitalist state with abundant wealth and a large but exploited proletariat. Russia in 1900 was still a mostly rural country, just beginning to industrialize, with a working class that made up only 3 percent of the population. Lenin resolved this dilemma by proposing a number of modifications to Marx's original theories. In his 1902 essay "What Is to Be Done?" he argued that since the Russian working class was so small and weak, it was necessary to create a "vanguard of the proletariat," a small, disciplined elite that would help workers develop revolutionary consciousness and lead them to revolution. The Bolsheviks would play this role.

The other dilemma was the undeveloped state of Russian capitalism. Were Russian Marxists simply to wait for capitalism to evolve and develop its contradictions, as Marx seemed to suggest was necessary? For Lenin, the answer was for Russia simply to skip over the capitalist phase of development and proceed directly from feudalism to communism. For this to happen, though, the Russian communist state would need assistance from other wealthier states to provide the material abundance that was necessary for communism to work. He believed that this would happen because a revolution in Russia would break the weakest link in the chain of worldwide capitalism, which was sustained by Western imperialism. "Imperialism," Lenin wrote, was "the highest stage of capitalism" and the final one. Once the Russians established their revolutionary state, workers in other, more developed capitalist states would be inspired to conduct their own revolutions. These countries, then, could help to sustain the revolution in Russia, thus fulfilling Marx's vision.

These ideas of Lenin, who was in exile and marginalized, were at best airy theorizing and speculation. Few people in Russia paid much attention to the Bolsheviks, and when the 1905 revolution broke out, the Bolsheviks were hardly involved. But Lenin's ideas are important for understanding how the 1917 revolution came about and why the Soviet Union, as it eventually emerged, looked so much different from what Marx had in mind. When the leaders of the Soviet Union referred to their communist ideology in later years, they called it Marxism-Leninism.

WORLD WAR I AND THE TWO REVOLUTIONS

Lenin and the Bolsheviks might have disappeared into weighty history books were it not for the erosion and collapse of the Russian state during World War I. As we saw in the previous chapter, the war had a devastating effect on all European states, but on none more than the Russian Empire. The doddering political system was not up to the task, and the Russians suffered far more casualties than any of the other belligerents. Nicholas II, although a kind family man, was a weak and feckless leader. He spent most of the war at the front, attempting to direct military operations there. He left the operation of government to his wife, Alexandra,

---

BOX 10.2
The Bolsheviks and the Role of Women

When the Bolsheviks came to power in 1917, they expected that, under socialism, the family would "wither away," as would the state. They believed that capitalism was particularly oppressive for women, and they aimed to remedy that. Lenin envisioned the establishment of public dining rooms, kitchens, laundries, and kindergartens that would relieve the woman "from her old domestic slavery and all dependence on her husband."* Free unions of men and women would replace marriage, which would increasingly become superfluous. In the early years of communist rule, legislation (including legalized abortion) was crafted to liberate women and to encourage the disappearance of the family. In the 1930s (under Stalin), however, much of this social experimentation was reversed as the government emphasized more traditional family roles.†

The Emancipation of Women: From the Writings of V. I. Lenin (New York: International Publishers, 1966), 97–123.

†Wendy Z. Goldman, *Women, the State and Revolution: Soviet Family Policy and Social Life, 1917–1936* (New York: Cambridge University Press, 1993).

---

and an influential, but bizarre, monk named Grigory Rasputin, who had a hypnotic ability to stop the bleeding of Alexandra's hemophiliac son.

By the beginning of 1917, both the military and the country were near collapse. Soldiers were undersupplied and were sometimes sent into battle without weapons or even boots. Over fourteen million peasants were in military service, which contributed to widespread food shortages. In March of that year, bread riots (begun by women), strikes, and demonstrations convulsed the capital city of Petrograd (St. Petersburg was renamed during the war to avoid the German sound of it). Troops summoned to maintain order turned on their officers and mutinied. Nicholas was forced to abdicate. Three hundred years of Romanov rule had come to an end.

A provisional government established by the Duma promised to form a constitutional government and hold free elections. But it made a fatal error in not pulling Russia out of the war, which eroded its popularity and legitimacy. Meanwhile, throughout the country, workers and soldiers had established alternative governing bodies called *soviets* (councils). The Petrograd Soviet, where the Bolsheviks and other socialists had considerable sway, took over some functions of city administration and increasingly challenged the provisional government.

In April 1917, Lenin returned from exile to Petrograd, rallied the Bolsheviks, promised "peace, land and bread," and called for "all power to the Soviets," directly confronting the provisional government. Over the next months, the Bolsheviks gained strength in soviets around the country, and by the fall, had won a majority in the Petrograd Soviet and elsewhere. On November 7, Bolsheviks and their supporters in the Petrograd Soviet occupied the Winter Palace, disbanded the provisional government, and seized power. In his 1927 film, director Sergei Eisenstein depicted these events in the film *October*, showing hundreds of citizens shooting their way into the Winter Palace.[2] In fact, the real event was practically bloodless, and more damage was done to the Winter Palace in the filming of *October* than in the November 7 events themselves. Nevertheless, the Eisenstein version became the icon of the Russian Revolution, and November 7 was celebrated every year in the Soviet Union, with parades, speeches, and huge posters of Marx, Engels, and Lenin, as the day of the first communist revolution.

The Bolsheviks were not the largest or most popular of the political movements in Russia at the time of the revolution, but they were one of the best organized, and Lenin was a charismatic leader and influential theorist. In the chaos and virtual anarchy of the war and the collapse of the monarchy, these characteristics were enough to ensure a Bolshevik victory. Lenin moved quickly to consolidate power, to remove or neutralize rival parties, and to establish the soviets as the government. The Bolsheviks were renamed the Communist Party. To fulfill Lenin's promise, the new regime opened negotiations with Germany to end Russia's involvement in the war, signing the Treaty of Brest-Litovsk in March 1918. Russia had to concede most of Germany's territorial demands, losing a quarter of its prewar population and three-quarters of its iron- and steel-producing areas. Lenin believed, however, that these losses were incidental and temporary, as the Bolshevik seizure of power was only the first stage of worldwide revolution and Germany itself would not be far behind.

CIVIL WAR, NEP, AND CONSOLIDATION

The treaty with Germany ended one major problem for the new communist government, but almost immediately it was faced with a host of new ones threatening its very survival. Groups opposing the Bolsheviks, including supporters of the tsar, the provisional government, or other political parties, organized to resist the new government, causing a devastating civil war that lasted four years. Worried that Tsar Nicholas would serve as a rallying point during the civil war, the Bolsheviks executed him and his family in 1918.

The Bolsheviks also faced challenges from other quarters. The newly formed government of Poland, a creature of the Versailles settlements, moved into areas vacated by the Germans and clashed with the Russians. The Polish-Soviet War raged for twenty months, until Lenin finally sued for peace. Meanwhile, other nationalities that had been part of the Russian Empire were declaring independence and sometimes fighting against the Bolsheviks—in the Ukraine, Finland, the Caucasus, and the Baltics. To complicate and inflame matters even further, French, British, American, and Japanese troops became involved in some of these conflicts, usually fighting against the Bolsheviks.

"Comrade Lenin Cleans the World of Filth." (The word "filth" [нечисти] in Russian also connotes the devil.) This 1920 Soviet propaganda poster illustrates the party's commitment, later abandoned, to promoting world revolution.

By 1921, the communists had defeated most of the White Russian (anti-Bolshevik) armies and settled the conflict with Poland. Foreign troops had withdrawn from Russia. But the country was ruined by eight years of war, revolution, terror, civil war, and famine. Lenin called a truce on the domestic front as well, announcing a New Economic Policy (NEP) intended to revitalize the economy by allowing greater freedom in agriculture, industry, and trade. This was also a period of consolidation. In 1922, the communists established the Union of Soviet Socialist Republics (USSR, or Soviet Union), consisting initially of Russia, Byelorussia, Ukraine, and the Caucasus, but over the years expanding to include fifteen republics. In 1924, the Supreme Soviet of the USSR formally adopted a constitution, declaring the founding of the USSR to be "a decisive step by way of uniting the workers of all countries into one world Soviet Socialist Republic."

"Lenin Lived, Lenin Lives, Lenin Will Live!" A 1970s Soviet propaganda poster, reflecting the almost religious homage to the former leader. Photo by David Mason.

STALIN AND TOTALITARIANISM

The period of relative calm and recovery under the NEP was interrupted, however, by the death of Vladimir Lenin in 1924. His body was embalmed and placed in a glass sarcophagus in a mausoleum in Moscow's Red Square, where it remains to this day. There was no clear successor to Lenin, and after a sustained power struggle, Joseph Stalin (1879–1953) emerged as the leader of the Communist Party. Lenin may have laid the groundwork for an authoritarian state, with censorship, a secret police, and the elimination of rival political parties, but Stalin perfected it by attempting to extend party and state control over virtually every aspect of Soviet society. This began with the first **five-year plan**, launched in 1928, which focused on a rapid industrialization of the Soviet economy and the collectivization of agriculture. The five-year plans, which became a continuing feature of the Soviet economy, entailed lodging virtually all economic decision making—about wages, prices, and the output of every single product—in centralized government ministries. Supply and demand and other rules of the market had no role in the Soviet economy.

Collectivization, the amalgamation of individual peasant holdings into collective farms, was met by much resistance, especially from wealthier farmers, many of whom burned their crops and destroyed their livestock rather than contribute them to the collectives. By 1937, virtually all of the land had been collectivized, but at a tremendous cost: millions died of starvation or were sent to forced labor camps in Siberia.

Collectivization was primarily an instrument of Stalin's larger goal, the quick transformation of the Soviet Union from an agricultural country to an industrial power and the closing of the economic gap with the West. The quick development of heavy industry was facilitated by the collectivization campaign, which contributed to the migration of twenty million people from the countryside to the cities in the first decade of the five-year plans. In this goal, too, Stalin was largely successful. Between 1928 and 1939, iron and steel production increased fourfold, and by 1939, the USSR's gross industrial output was exceeded only by those of the United States and Germany.

By the mid-1930s, the dominance of the Communist Party and Stalin's leadership of it seemed unassailable. Stalin himself apparently did not feel that way, and from 1936 to 1938, he carried out the **Great Purge** to root out all potential sources of opposition to him and to the party. This began with a series of politicized show trials in 1936, in which all the old Bolshevik revolutionaries, men who had been Lenin's closest associates, were put on trial, accused of treason or subversion, found guilty, and executed. The purges then extended downward into the party and the army and through the rest of society; millions of people were executed or sent to Siberian labor camps. Soviet citizens grew afraid to speak openly even

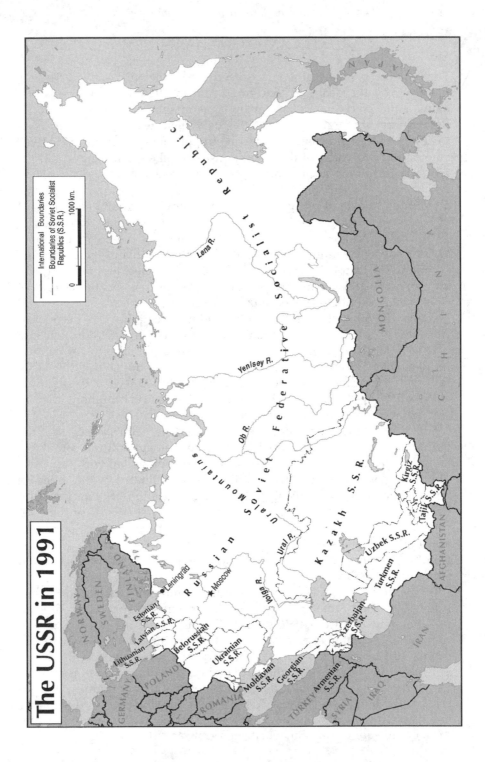

The USSR in 1991

International Boundaries
Boundaries of Soviet Socialist
Republics (S.S.R.)

0   1000 km.

GREENLAND

NORWAY

SWEDEN

FINLAND

GERMANY

POLAND

ROMANIA

Lithuanian S.S.R.

Latvian S.S.R.

Estonian S.S.R.

Belorussian S.S.R.

Ukrainian S.S.R.

Moldavian S.S.R.

Leningrad

Moscow

Russian Soviet Federative Socialist Republic

Lena R.

Yenisey R.

Ob R.

Ural Mountains

Ural R.

Volga R.

Georgian S.S.R.

Armenian S.S.R.

Azerbaijan S.S.R.

TURKEY

SYRIA

IRAQ

IRAN

AFGHANISTAN

Turkmen S.S.R.

Uzbek S.S.R.

Tajik S.S.R.

Kirgiz S.S.R.

Kazakh S.S.R.

MONGOLIA

CHINA

JAPAN

to close friends or family members for fear that they would be turned in to the NKVD, the Soviet security police. The Russian Orthodox Church was persecuted and subordinated to the state, and most churches and monasteries were closed or destroyed. By the end of the purges, the Stalin regime had virtually total control over the economy, media, church, culture, education, and even people's private lives, leading to the designation of Stalin's Soviet Union as a **totalitarian** state (i.e., "total" control). Stalin was to rule, unchallenged, until his death in 1953.

THE LEGACY AND MEANING OF THE RUSSIAN REVOLUTION

The French Revolution of 1789 was the first in Europe to overthrow a monarchy; the Russian Revolution of 1917 overthrew the last absolutist monarchy in Europe. This in itself marks the event as significant in European history, but the influence of the Russian Revolution was far more widespread, as was that of the French Revolution. Although the French revolutionaries attempted to put into practice some of the principles and ideals of liberalism and the Enlightenment, their Russian counterparts not only built on these principles but also based their state on the nineteenth-century ideals of Marxian socialism. In this, they had some successes, but at enormous costs.

On the positive side of the ledger, one can argue that the communists, particularly under Stalin, were able to transform Russia from a rural, economically undeveloped country into a major economic, political, and military power. By the 1960s, in fact, it was one of two global superpowers, along with the United States. If Stalin had not achieved his goal of industrial and military development, the Soviet Union probably would not have been able to repel the Nazi German onslaught of World War II, when it came in 1941.

Furthermore, the Soviet Union was able to achieve this economic development while simultaneously pursuing the Marxist goals of social welfare and egalitarianism. There was virtually no unemployment in the Soviet Union, and because of that, no hard-core poverty. Health care and education (through the university level) were free, and housing, food, and mass transit were heavily subsidized by the state and inexpensive for consumers. And although the government never tried to achieve complete equality (and many people complained of the privileged status of the communist elites), the differences between the rich and poor were far fewer than in capitalist countries. Marx would have been pleased with these achievements.

These gains, however, came with grievous costs in both human lives and human rights. The worst came during the Stalin years: several million lives were lost during the forced collectivization after 1929. Famine in Soviet Ukraine in 1932–33 claimed millions of lives, and Ukraine now refers to this catastrophe as "The Holodomor," a Ukrainian term meaning "murder by starvation." Millions more Soviet citizens died in the *Gulags*, the forced labor camps of Siberia and the frozen north.[3] The situation improved after the death of Stalin, but the Soviet political system remained throughout its history a single-party state, brooking no political competition, protest activity, or independent press. All books, periodicals, and mass media were censored. Most churches, synagogues, and mosques were closed or destroyed. People who dared challenge the regime or its policies were subject to arrest and possibly death in the Stalinist era and imprisonment or exile in the years after that. People had little choice about where they worked or lived, were restricted in their travel within the country, and could travel abroad only with difficulty.

Despite all this, the Soviet Union became increasingly powerful and influential on the world stage. Through the Communist International (the Comintern), Moscow helped establish communist parties and encourage revolutionary movements all over the world, including the Communist Party of China, which won power in that country in 1949. The Soviet Union bore the brunt of the losses from Germany during World War II, but it was the Soviet army that managed to liberate Eastern Europe from the Germans and to seize Berlin and force German surrender in 1945. This placed Moscow in a position of unparalleled strength in the center of Europe and brought it into conflict with the other new global power, the United States, in the emerging Cold War. Elsewhere in the world, the Soviet Union and its economic successes became a model for leftists, anti-imperialists, and revolutionaries all over the Third World. Indeed, by the 1970s, almost half the world's population was living under governments inspired or supported by the communists of Russia.

11

World War II and the Holocaust

The Paris Peace Settlements of 1919–20 brought to a close the bitter divisions and seemingly endless conflict of World War I. European participants in the war were devastated and exhausted and yearned for peace, stability, and normality, and many of the European governments (and the United States) retreated into **isolationism**, neutrality, or pacifism. The Paris agreements, including the crucial Versailles Treaty affecting Germany, had established national and democratic states in Germany, as well as the new states of Eastern Europe, and had created the League of Nations to protect the peace and ward off future wars. A sense of calm and relief spread through much of the Continent.

There were, however, storm clouds on the horizon even in those first postwar years, with economic distress and inflation, irredentist discontent with the Versailles Treaty (especially in Germany), and the unsettling presence of a new communist state in Russia. By the 1930s, things fell apart as a worldwide economic depression weakened governments everywhere, and many of the newly established European democracies were subverted from within or without. In Germany, Adolf Hitler (1889–1945) capitalized on economic distress and discontent, seized absolute power, and began constructing his **Third Reich**. His aggressive military moves to reclaim German territory and then to conquer all of Europe led to World War II, which was even more devastating than the previous war, and to the Holocaust. The United States finally intervened to help end the war, as it had in World War I, and the potent alliance of the United States and the Soviet Union finally crushed Nazi Germany. But with the end of the war, this wartime friendship deteriorated into rivalry, distrust, and a period of political and military tension known as the Cold War.

EUROPE BETWEEN THE WORLD WARS

Woodrow Wilson had brought the United States into World War I pledging to "make the world safe for democracy," and his Fourteen Points called for national self-determination and democratic politics in central Europe. In large measure, these goals were achieved with the Paris peace agreements, which carved from the old Habsburg Empire the new states of Austria, Hungary, Czechoslovakia, and Yugoslavia, and from the old Russian Empire the states of Poland, Finland, Latvia, Lithuania, and Estonia. All of them adopted written constitutions with legislatures elected through universal suffrage. In the city of Weimar, a German national assembly also adopted a constitution establishing a democratic republic, the **Weimar Republic**. In the ruins of the Ottoman Empire, a nationalist revolution led by Mustapha Kemal (later named Kemal Ataturk) abolished the sultanate and the caliphate and established a secular democratic republic of Turkey, the first Muslim country to separate religion from government. The 1920s saw democratic advances even in established democracies, for example, with the extension of voting rights to women in both Britain and the United States.

Germany was reconstituted as a democratic republic, but it was also forced to accept the terms of the Versailles Treaty, despite vigorous and sustained protests from every band of the political spectrum inside the country. The treaty not only assigned Germany responsibility for World War I and imposed reparation payments on the new government but also reduced the size of the country by restoring an independent Austria, returning Alsace-Lorraine to France, placing the Saar territory and the Rhineland under French or Allied occupation, ceding most of West Prussia to Poland, and establishing the port city of Danzig as a free city under the auspices of the League of Nations. In addition, the treaty placed German colonies (e.g., in Africa) under League of Nations control as mandates and limited the German army and armaments.

For Germans, the humiliation of all these provisions was compounded by the reparations payments, which eventually were set at the equivalent of $33 billion. The country simply could not make these payments (and in the long run paid only a fraction of them), so the government began printing more money, which contributed to unprecedented hyperinflation and rendered the German currency (the mark) almost worthless. By 1923, the exchange rate was four trillion marks to the dollar. German families had to cart wheelbarrows full of cash to the store just to purchase a loaf of bread.

The situation was stabilized somewhat the next year when the Dawes Plan, developed by an American board of experts, provided for a reduction in reparations payments, a stabilization of German finances, and the facilitation of German borrowing abroad. The ensuing years saw a period of economic growth and relative stability in both Germany and the rest of Europe. Germany was allowed to enter the League of Nations in 1926. In 1928, the Kellogg-Briand Pact, developed by the American and French foreign ministers and signed by sixty-five countries, renounced war as an instrument of policy. Once again, it seemed a period of peace and stability was at hand.

Then the US stock market crashed, leading quickly to a worldwide depression. By 1929, stock values in the United States had been driven to fantastic heights by excessive speculation. When the crash came in October, stock prices dropped by 40 percent in a month and by 75 percent within three months. Five thousand banks closed, and many companies went bankrupt. US investments abroad virtually ceased, and US trade declined precipitously, undercutting the foundations of the economic revival of Germany and much of Europe. Between 1929 and 1932, world economic production declined by 38 percent and world trade by two-thirds. Germany was particularly hard hit, suffering more from the Depression than any other country in Europe. But all over the Continent, as unemployment skyrocketed and food lines swelled, people began looking for answers and demanding economic security. The situation was ripe for strong leaders and demagogues. Newly formed democracies withered under the strain.

THE RISE OF MILITARISM AND FASCISM

Hitler emerged from this environment, but he was not the first or the only right-wing dictator to rise to power in interwar Europe. He was preceded, most importantly, by Benito Mussolini (1883–1945), who seized power in Italy in 1922 and established the first fascist dictatorship in Europe in a country that had maintained parliamentary government since unification in 1861. Mussolini, born the son of a blacksmith in 1883, had in his youth dabbled in both revolutionary activity and radical journalism. He served in World War I, and after the war, organized a fighting band, made up mostly of ex-soldiers whom he called "fascists." **Fascism** emerged as a political ideology that was anticommunist and antisocialist, militantly nationalist, and in favor of economic security and law and order, if necessary through dictatorial rule.

In the years after the war, Italy, like Germany, suffered from wartime debts, economic depression, and unemployment. In 1921 and 1922, when widespread strikes and demonstrations practically paralyzed the country, Mussolini and his fascists, dubbed "blackshirts," threatened a takeover of the government and promised to restore order and stability. Under the threat of Mussolini's ultimatum, the king appointed him prime minister. The parliament then granted him a year of emergency powers to restore order in the country. Within a few years, Mussolini had emasculated the parliament, put the press under censorship, and abolished all political parties except his fascists. He took the title "*Il Duce*" (the leader).

Adolf Hitler's early life paralleled that of Mussolini in some ways, and after Mussolini's seizure of power, Hitler consciously imitated Mussolini's tactics and success. Hitler was born in Austria, the son of a customs official, but lost both of his parents during his teenage years. He spent his early years in Vienna and Munich, a frustrated artist, mostly unemployed and poor. He welcomed the onset of World War I and served with distinction, becoming a corporal and receiving the Iron Cross for bravery. After the war, he founded the **National Socialist German Workers' Party**, which became known as the **Nazi Party**. In 1923, the year after Mussolini's March on Rome, Hitler and his Nazis made a similar attempt to seize control of the government in Bavaria, in southern Germany, in what became known as the Munich Beer Hall Putsch. The coup attempt was put down by the army, fourteen Nazis were killed, and Hitler was sentenced to jail.

During his year in jail, Hitler wrote his rambling memoirs, *Mein Kampf* (My Struggle), which was published in 1925 and became a best seller. The book was a strange conglomeration of autobiography, racism, nationalism, theories of history, and anti-Semitism. In this book, fifteen years before the gassing of Jews at Auschwitz, Hitler unveils his ideas of racial hierarchy and supremacy. Borrowing some of the language of social Darwinism and eugenics, he inveighs against the "crossing of breeds" in humans, which is "contrary to the will of Nature for a higher breeding of all life." In a chapter titled "Nation and Race," which is mostly an invective against Jews and communists, and which ends with a call for "a German state of the German nation," he writes, "The stronger must dominate and not blend with the weaker, thus sacrificing his own greatness. Only the born weakling can view this as cruel . . . for if this law did not prevail, any conceivable higher development of organic living beings would be unthinkable."

The trial of Hitler for the putsch and the publication of *Mein Kampf* made him a political figure of national prominence. But the years after his release from jail were ones of relative prosperity and stability in Germany (following the Dawes Plan), and Hitler and his Nazis lost appeal and supporters. When the economic depression hit Germany in 1930, however, Hitler had new fodder for his charges against Versailles, Jews, communists, foreigners, and the Weimar Republic. As the economy collapsed and unemployment rates rose to 30 percent, Germans began looking for radical solutions from both the Left and the Right, and support grew for both the communists and the Nazis. In legislative elections, votes for the Nazis jumped from 3 percent in 1928 to 18 percent in 1930 to 37 percent in 1932. By that time, the Nazis were by far the largest party in the legislature, the *Reichstag*, although they did not have a majority of the seats. No other political party wanted to collaborate with Hitler in forming a coalition government, and the traditional conservative parties, led by President Hindenburg, all thought they could control Hitler by allowing him into the government and hemming him in with their own people in the cabinet. So in January 1933, President Hindenburg appointed Hitler chancellor (prime minister) of the German Republic.

Hitler's appointment sparked a wave of brutal Nazi attacks on socialists, communists, Jews, and others who opposed Nazism. Hitler began to consolidate power in much the same way that Mussolini had in Italy a decade earlier. When a fire consumed the *Reichstag* building a week before elections, Hitler blamed it on the communists, frightening legislators and citizens alike with a Red scare and claiming a national emergency. The legislature voted to give him dictatorial powers. In July, Hitler declared that

Adolf Hitler and Benito Mussolini during the Italian dictator's visit to Munich, Germany, in September 1937. © Pictures From History/The Image Works.

the Nazis were the only legal party. He initiated a public works program (and rearmament), which soon absorbed almost all of the unemployed in Germany. When President Hindenburg died the next year, Hitler merged the offices of president and chancellor under his control. He proclaimed the establishment of the Third Reich. Like Mussolini, he took the title of *Führer* (leader). The groundwork was laid for a third totalitarian state, along with those of Stalin and Mussolini.

HITLER'S AGGRESSION

Hitler had gained both notoriety and popular support by condemning the Versailles Treaty and calling for a restoration of German honor, pride, and power and the recovery of lost German territories. Within a few months of becoming chancellor, he began to fulfill those promises in a steadily escalating series of aggressive moves. In October 1933, he pulled Germany out of the League of Nations and denounced the disarmament negotiations that were then under way. By 1935, he began rearming Germany, contrary to the provisions of Versailles, and had introduced compulsory military service. The League censured Germany but took no other action. In 1936, Hitler moved German troops into the Rhineland (on Germany's western border), an area that had been permanently demilitarized by the Versailles Treaty. The same year, Hitler signed mutual defense and assistance treaties with both Mussolini's Italy (the Rome-Berlin axis) and with the military government in Japan. And during the Spanish Civil War of 1936–39, when government forces were pitted against Francisco Franco's rebel fascists, Hitler and Mussolini cooperated in assisting Franco, providing a testing ground for their troops and weapons (see box 11.1).

By 1938, Hitler was prepared to press his demands to bring all Germans into the greater German Reich. In March of that year, he marched German troops into Austria, announced the *Anschluss* (merger) of Austria with Germany, and drove to Vienna in triumph. Even after this, neither the League nor the Western powers responded, in part due to a growing sentiment that there was some justification to Germany's nationalist claims. The annexation of Austria had added about six million Germans to the Reich, and now Hitler began making noises about the supposed intolerable conditions of the three million Germans living in the Sudetenland region of Czechoslovakia. As rumors spread that Germany was about to invade Czechoslovakia, the governments of France, England, and the Soviet Union issued warnings to Hitler. In September 1938, Hitler invited the prime ministers of England and France, Neville Chamberlain and Edouard Daladier, plus Mussolini, to a conference in Munich to discuss the situation. In the resulting agreement, the four powers renounced war on each other, ceded the Sudetenland to Hitler, and guaranteed the territorial integrity of the rest of

BOX 11.1
Picasso's *Guernica*: Art, War, and Politics

One of the most famous paintings of the twentieth century, Pablo Picasso's *Guernica* vividly depicts the horrors and suffering of war in the painter's homeland, Spain, during that country's civil war of 1936–39. The war pitted the democratically elected (and leftist) Republican government against the right-wing and military forces (the Nationalists) under the command of General Francisco Franco. Franco's forces were assisted by Mussolini's Italy and Hitler's Germany. In 1937, the German *Luftwaffe*, in support of Franco, bombed and strafed the little Basque village of Guernica, a Republican stronghold, killing more than sixteen hundred men, women, and children. This was the world's first aerial bombing of civilians, and a prelude to what was to come in World War II.

This massacre of innocent civilians shocked the world, including Picasso, who was living in Paris at the time. His large painting, more than eleven feet tall and twenty-five feet wide, employs the same black, gray, and white of the newspaper photos depicting the tragedy. It is a stark, hallucinatory nightmare. One woman grieves over a dead child in her arms; another screams as she is surrounded by flames. A shrieking horse, run through by a spear, represents the suffering Spanish Republic.

The painting was a sensation; its tour throughout the world brought attention to the Spanish Civil War. But it also became a global antiwar icon, symbolizing the tragedy of war and the suffering it inflicts on individuals, especially innocent civilians.

Picasso refused to have the painting delivered to Spain, until democracy was established in that country. That took a long time. Franco, who won the civil war and took power in 1939, survived almost forty years as ruler of Spain. As the rest of Europe recovered and grew after World War II, Spain remained relatively poor and undeveloped, separate and isolated, and outside the European Union. Only after the death of Franco in 1975 and the reestablishment of democracy there did *Guernica* return to Spain. But by then, Picasso too was dead.

Pablo Picasso's Guernica. © *2018 Estate of Pablo Picasso/Artists Rights Society (ARS), New York.*

Czechoslovakia. Prime Minister Chamberlain returned to London asserting he had achieved "peace with honor." Six months later, Hitler invaded and annexed the rest of Czechoslovakia.

Since that time, the names Chamberlain and Munich have been associated with the appeasement of aggression. But in 1938, none of the major powers was prepared to confront Hitler militarily. The old balance-of-power system of alliances had collapsed in World War I, and in any case, the traditional counterweight to Germany, a flanking alliance of England and/or France with Russia, was impossible because of Western distrust of the communists of the Soviet Union. The replacement for the balance of power, the League of Nations, had already proved ineffectual in countering the military aggression of Japan, Italy, and Germany. Alarmed at the unchecked militarism of Nazi Germany, the Soviet leader, Joseph Stalin, bought some time by signing a nonaggression and friendship pact of his own with Hitler in August 1939. This agreement was public, but in a secret protocol, the Germans and Soviets agreed to divide Poland between them in the event of war and sanctioned Soviet influence in the Baltic states. One week after the signing of the Nazi-Soviet pact, the Germans invaded Poland with a massive army of over one million troops. Britain and France immediately declared war on Germany. For the second time in a generation, Europe was at war.

THE WAR

By this time, Hitler's goals went beyond the recovery of "German" territory to the acquisition of *lebensraum* (living space) in Eastern Europe for his expanding "master race"—thus his interest in Poland. The German attack on Poland, in September 1939, employed the new military tactic of **blitzkrieg**, lightning warfare using massive amounts of manpower, airpower, and armor so as to achieve rapid annihilation of the enemy. Poland fell within a month, and Hitler set about the occupation of the western half of the country. Meanwhile, the Soviet Union, invoking the secret protocol, invaded and occupied eastern Poland, an area they had fought over in the Polish-Soviet war of 1919–20. In the spring of 1940, Nazi troops invaded Norway and Denmark, then launched another *blitzkrieg* across Holland, Belgium, and Luxembourg and into France, forcing a French surrender within six weeks. With stunning speed and ease, Hitler had taken over most of Europe.

In the summer of 1940, England was the only country that remained at war with Germany. Winston Churchill had replaced Neville Chamberlain as prime minister, promising nothing but "blood, toil, tears, and sweat" in an implacable war against "a monstrous tyranny, never surpassed in the dark, lamentable catalogue of human crime."[1] Hitler launched an air campaign against Britain, with bombing raids on London and other cities, as a prelude to a full-scale invasion. But the British Royal Air Force was able to prevent German supremacy in the air, and with Churchill's inspiration, civilian morale held up in spite of the death, destruction, and privation.

Unable to subdue Britain, Hitler shifted his attention to his more important objective, the Soviet Union, which from the beginning he had intended to invade and occupy, in spite of the 1939 nonaggression pact. The military assault on the Soviet Union, Operation Barbarossa, was launched on June 22, 1941, with three million men along a two-thousand-mile front. Within a few months, German troops had encircled Leningrad and got within twenty-five miles of Moscow. For the next three years, until the Allied invasion of the mainland of Italy (September 1943) and France (June 1944), the struggle between Germany and the Soviet Union was the only real fighting in the European theater. The overwhelming majority of all casualties from the war were Soviet, and the Soviet Union sustained some eight million military losses and at least eighteen million civilian deaths. At the battle of Stalingrad, in the winter of 1942–43, a turning point victory over the Germans, the Soviet army lost more troops than the United States lost in the whole of World War II in all theaters combined.

St. Paul's Cathedral in London stands among burning buildings during the German air raids of December 1940. National Archives (306-NT-3173V).

Soldiers from the Red Army hoist the Soviet flag over the German Reichstag (parliament building) after the capture of Berlin in May 1945. © Keystone/The Image Works.

After Stalingrad, the Soviets made steady gains, pushing the Germans out of the Soviet republics of Ukraine and Byelorussia, then advancing head-on through Poland toward Berlin. At the same time, Soviet forces moved southwest into Romania, Bulgaria, and Hungary, all of which were allied with Nazi Germany. Meanwhile, the June 1944 Normandy invasion ("D-Day") landed 130,000 British, US, and Canadian forces onto French beaches in one day and a million within the month. By March 1945, the Allied forces had crossed the Rhine River into German territory, and Soviet forces had taken Budapest and Vienna and would soon occupy Berlin. Hitler committed suicide, and the German government surrendered in May 1945. The European war was over, although fighting continued in the Pacific theater against Japan until the atomic bombings of Hiroshima and Nagasaki forced a Japanese surrender in August.

THE HOLOCAUST

At the end of the war, as Allied troops liberated Nazi-controlled areas, they stumbled upon the concentration camps of Dachau and Buchenwald and the gas chambers and crematoria of the death camps at Auschwitz, Treblinka, and elsewhere. It was only then that the full extent of the Nazi policy to exterminate the Jews became public and clear.

The anti-Semitism of Hitler and the Nazis, however, was perfectly clear from the beginning and is vividly displayed in *Mein Kampf*, in which he systematically baits and demeans Jews and refers to them as un-German and subhuman. At first, though, the policy of Hitler's Nazi government was to encourage or intimidate Germany's six hundred thousand Jews to leave the country, rather than to kill them. The 1935 Nuremberg Laws identified Jews as subjects but not citizens, banned them from the professions, and placed restrictions on intermarriage and sexual relations between Jews and non-Jews. Official anti-Semitism became violent in November 1938, with *Kristallnacht* (the night of broken glass), when Nazi storm troopers looted and smashed Jewish shops and synagogues, beat up thousands of Jews, and rounded up tens of thousands to be sent to concentration camps. After this, a campaign of threats and intimidation was carried out to force Jewish emigration.

The actual slaughter of the Jews, what was later to become known as the Holocaust, began with the mass killings of Jews in German-occupied Soviet territory in 1941. About the same time, Nazi leadership decided that the "Final Solution of the Jewish Question" was to take the form of annihilation. In early 1942, decisions were taken to accelerate experiments with Zyklon-B gas; to establish dedicated death camps at Treblinka, Auschwitz, and elsewhere; and to organize the systematic transport of

Jewish citizens during the German destruction of the Warsaw Ghetto in Poland 1943.
National Archives (238-NT-282).

Jews from all over Europe to these camps. Over the next three years, some six million Jews perished in these camps, including almost all of Poland's three million Jews and perhaps two-thirds of all the Jews in Europe.

THE CONSEQUENCES OF WORLD WAR II

If the ten million deaths of World War I had seemed horrifyingly unimaginable, the losses of World War II were far worse: in Europe alone, there were probably fifteen million military casualties and almost twice that many civilian deaths. More than twenty million died in the Soviet Union, more than 10 percent of the entire population. Nobody really knows the exact count, but some estimates place the overall casualties from the war, in both Europe and Asia, at sixty million men, women, and children. The numbers are so huge in part because this was the first war in which civilians were deliberately and systematically targeted—from the German aerial attacks on London and Coventry, to the Allied firebombing of Dresden and Tokyo, to the Nazis' systematic "liquidation" of Warsaw in 1944, to the nuclear incineration of Hiroshima and Nagasaki. The scope and scale of warfare had changed forever.

With the war years, much of Europe seemed to have reversed course from the steady evolution that had begun at the end of the eighteenth

BOX 11.2
Survival in Auschwitz

Auschwitz (in Polish, Oświęcim), located in southern Poland, was the worst of the German Nazi death camps and has become a symbol of the Holocaust. Although the numbers are still in dispute, probably 1.5 million men, women, and children were killed at Auschwitz and nearby Birkenau, including about 1 million Jews. The museum there includes a heart-rending children's barracks that has entire rooms filled with shoes, clothing, eyeglasses, and hair taken from the hundreds of thousands of children who were gassed and cremated on the premises.

Most survivors of Auschwitz were understandably loath to talk or write about their experiences, and many others did not want to hear about it. When an Italian Jew, Primo Levi, first published his Auschwitz memoir *If This Is a*

Man (later appearing in English as *Survival in Auschwitz*) in 1947, it was barely noticed. A decade later, it was published again, about the same time as another Holocaust memoir, Elie Wiesel's *Night*; for the first time, Europe began to confront the Holocaust.

Survival in Auschwitz renders in shattering detail the horror and brutality of the camps and the tenuous nature of humanity in such circumstances. Prisoners compete, and even kill, for a scrap of bread or a piece of clothing in their struggle to survive. Levi explains the thin

Child survivors of Auschwitz, wearing adult-size prisoner jackets, standing behind a barbed-wire fence during the Soviet liberation of the camps in January 1945. US Holocaust Memorial Museum, courtesy of Belarussian State Archive of Documentary Film and Photography.

veneer of civilization:

> Imagine now a man who is deprived of everyone he loves, and at the same time of his house, his habits, his clothes, in short of everything he possesses: he will be a hollow man, reduced to suffering and needs, forgetful of dignity and restraint, for he who loses all often easily loses himself.

In the end, though, a good-hearted civilian coworker named Lorenzo inspires Levi himself to persevere and survive by convincing him that "there still existed a just world outside our own, something and someone still pure and whole, not corrupt, not savage, extraneous to hatred and terror; something difficult to define, a remote possibility of good, but for which it was worth surviving." After the war, Primo Levi returned to his hometown, Turin, to become manager of a chemical plant; he retired in 1977 to devote himself to writing. But his life was troubled, and he suffered from depression. In 1987, he toppled over the railing of a stairwell in his home and died from his injuries in an apparent suicide.

century. The totalitarian regimes of Hitler, Stalin, and Mussolini rejected the notions of individualism, natural rights, and common humanity that had derived from the Enlightenment. Indeed, as depicted so movingly in Elie Wiesel's *Night* and Primo Levi's *Survival in Auschwitz*, the Nazi death camps called humanity itself into question. But with the deaths of Hitler and Mussolini in 1945, and of Stalin in 1953, totalitarianism was no longer a force in Europe. At the Allied trials of Nazi leaders held at Nuremberg after the war, the policy of genocide was defined as a "crime against humanity," thus reestablishing a sense of common values and morality.

The end of the war also signaled a major geopolitical shift in both Europe and the world, with the emergence of the United States and the Soviet Union as the dominant powers on the Continent. As a result of the end-of-war military operations, the Soviet Union ended up occupying eastern Germany (including East Berlin) and most of eastern Europe. US forces, having moved toward Germany from the south (North Africa, then Italy) and the west (Normandy) controlled western Germany and most of western Europe. It was as if these two geographically peripheral players had been sucked into the vacuum of central Europe created by the collapse of Germany and Italy. And where they met, in the middle of Germany, is where the Cold War began.

12

🌰

Europe Divided, the Cold War, and Decolonization

At the conclusion of World War II, Europe was ruined, exhausted, occupied, and divided. The death and devastation from the second war of the century was even greater than that from the first. The major European powers, having dominated the Continent for centuries, had all been occupied, bombed, ravaged, or defeated. The victorious armies of the United States and the Soviet Union, each with millions of men in uniform, stood astride the Continent. But the wartime alliance between them that had defeated Nazi Germany soon broke apart over differences on the treatment and future of Germany and other occupied lands. The tensions between the United States and the Soviet Union became known as the Cold War: a war, in that they viewed each other as mortal enemies, but cold in that they did not engage in actual military conflict.

As the Cold War emerged, Europe became divided in almost every way, including nomenclature: Western Europe and Eastern Europe. The United States assisted in the economic recovery of Western Europe and promoted the development there of liberal democracies. The Soviet Union imposed communist political systems in Eastern Europe and came to control and dominate that region. Germany, caught in the middle of the Cold War, was itself divided into East and West, as was the former capital of Berlin. The Berlin Wall, running through the center of the city, came to symbolize the division of Europe and the Cold War itself. The East-West tensions that were centered in Europe shaped much of world politics for the next half century. Not until the collapse of communism and the fall of the Berlin Wall in 1989 was the Cold War brought to a close.

The weakness of Europe after World War II, in combination with the rise of national liberation movements in Europe's overseas colonies, forced the European imperial states to cede independence to their colonies. This process of **decolonization** began at about the same time that the Cold War was developing and continued for the next two decades. Decolonization compelled West Europeans to become more dependent on the United States, and on each other, eventually facilitating the economic integration that evolved into the European Union.

THE DIVISION OF EUROPE

In February 1945, Franklin Roosevelt, Winston Churchill, and Joseph Stalin met at the Soviet resort town of Yalta to plan the final stages of World War II and to negotiate the postwar order in Europe. The Anglo-Americans were not in a very strong bargaining position because they had liberated only France, whereas the Soviet army had pushed the Germans out of most of Poland, Hungary, Yugoslavia, Czechoslovakia, and Romania and were only about one hundred miles from Berlin (which they would take three months later). Among the provisions of the **Yalta Agreements**, as these negotiations came to be known, were the movement of Poland's borders some one hundred miles westward (leaving parts of eastern Poland to the Soviet Union), the temporary division of Germany into occupation zones (with the Soviets occupying the eastern part), and the agreement that the nations of Eastern Europe were to be democratic and "friendly" to the Soviet Union. The three leaders also agreed to begin work on a new international organization to be called the United Nations (UN).

In later years, Yalta became a symbol of betrayal for many of the peoples of Eastern Europe who felt that the Allies had given Stalin a free hand in the region. Indeed, in the three years following the Yalta Conference, the Soviets systematically undermined democratic politics and established Soviet-style communist regimes throughout the area. Given the circumstances of 1945, however, it was almost inevitable that the Soviet Union would come to dominate Eastern Europe. As a result of postwar military operations, by the time of the Nazi surrender in May 1945, the area was almost completely under Soviet military occupation. So just as the American, British, and French forces swept the Germans out of the western part of Europe and initiated Western-style democratic governments in those countries, the Soviets occupied Eastern Europe and established "people's democracies" that were "friendly" to the Soviet Union. From the Soviet point of view, and especially from Stalin's, "friendly" meant "socialist"—a capitalist state would by nature be hostile to the communism of the Soviet Union.

Conference of the Big Three at Yalta makes final plans for the defeat of Germany. Prime Minister Winston S. Churchill, President Franklin D. Roosevelt, and Premier Joseph Stalin, February 1945. National Archives (111-SC-260486).

Furthermore, for the Soviet Union, the lands of Eastern Europe were far more important strategically and ideologically than they were for the West. Most of these countries bordered the Soviet Union, and this region historically had constituted the principal route of invasion into Russia and the Soviet Union by numerous armies, including those of Napoleon in 1812, the Poles in 1919–20, and the Germans in both world wars. So control over the area was of critical importance for the Soviet Union, and for Stalin.

At the end of the war, the Soviet army was in military control of Poland, Hungary, Czechoslovakia, Bulgaria, and Romania. Moscow began a gradual process of extending political dominance over these countries, in a procedure described by the Hungarian Communist Party chief as "salami tactics," meaning one slice at a time. The first round of parliamentary elections in most countries was generally free and fair, resulting in coalition governments including both communist and noncommunist parties. But by 1947, most of the noncommunist parties had been squeezed out, the news media and the police had been placed under control of the communists, and elections were increasingly rigged. A seizure of power by the Communist Party in Czechoslovakia in February 1948 signaled the end of democratic politics in Eastern Europe. The former British prime minister, Winston Churchill, had foreseen this division of Europe two years earlier, when in a speech at Westminster College in Missouri, he intoned that an "iron curtain" had descended across Europe "from Stettin in the Baltic to Trieste in the Adriatic."

THE ONSET OF THE COLD WAR

The US government complained about the erosion of democracy in Eastern Europe but was not prepared or inclined to do much about it in an area of peripheral strategic concern to the United States. But in two other areas—Germany and the combined regions of Greece and Turkey—the United States was prepared to take action, and in those two areas, the Cold War lines began to harden. In 1946 and 1947, Turkey was under pressure from the Soviet Union to return some territory that it had seized from Russia just after the communist revolution of 1917. Greece was mired in a civil war between the royalist government and communist insurgents who had won broad popular support for their resistance to the Nazis during the world war. Historically, both Greece and Turkey had looked to Britain to support them against their powerful northern neighbor. But Britain, weakened by the war and a postwar financial crisis, informed the US government that it could no longer assume these responsibilities. American president Harry Truman went to Congress with a request for funds to assist the two countries, but phrased the appeal in broad and universal terms; the money would be spent "to assist free peoples who are resisting attempted subjugation by armed minorities or by outside pressures."[1] This pledge to assist democracy everywhere, known as the **Truman Doctrine**, marked a sharp departure from traditional American isolationism and was a virtual declaration of leadership of the free world.

The Truman Doctrine was primarily a response to events in Greece and Turkey, but came at a time of heightened US-Soviet tensions over both the consolidation of communist rule in Eastern Europe and the administration of Germany. At the end of the war, Germany had been divided into four occupation zones (US, Soviet, British, and French) jointly administered by an Allied Control Commission. The capital city of Berlin, deep inside the Soviet zone, was also divided into four zones. From the start, Moscow and the Western allies differed over how to deal with Germany. In essence, Stalin wanted to keep Germany weak and prevent it from ever mounting another military threat against the Soviet Union. The US Truman administration, cognizant of the effects of reparations on Germany after World War I, was more intent on rebuilding Germany and integrating it into the world community. The disagreements paralyzed the Allied Control Commission, so the United States, Britain, and France went their own way, merging their three zones into one and then, in 1948, introducing a new currency in their zone without consulting the Russians. Moscow protested by blocking rail and road access from the Western zone of Germany to the Western zone of Berlin, one hundred miles inside the Soviet zone. President Truman briefly considered breaking the Berlin blockade by sending a column of US armored troops into Berlin. Almost certainly, this would have led to armed conflict with the Soviet Union, just three years after the conclusion of World War II. Instead, Truman resorted to an airlift of supplies to the three million residents of West Berlin. The **Berlin airlift** lasted almost a year, with one plane landing in West Berlin every minute until Moscow finally lifted the blockade. But by then, Europe was firmly divided. In 1949, elections in West Germany were held to constitute the Federal Republic of Germany, and a few months later, the Soviets set up their own state in East Germany, which they called the German Democratic Republic.

President Truman was convinced that Soviet pressure on Turkey, the communist insurgency in Greece, Moscow's salami tactics in Eastern Europe, and the Berlin crisis were all part of a broader Soviet plan to expand communism. A State Department official, George Kennan, had written an important article advocating a US policy of the "containment of Russian expansive tendencies." This doctrine of the containment of communism became the governing principle of American foreign policy for the next fifty years. Worried that the precarious political and economic conditions of some European countries provided a breeding ground for communist expansion, in 1947, the United States launched the **Marshall Plan**, which provided $17 billion for the reconstruction of Europe over five years. In 1949, the United States sponsored the creation of the **North Atlantic Treaty Organization** (**NATO**), which guaranteed US military protection for Western European countries under attack. This was the first peacetime military alliance for the United States since the time of the Revolutionary War and was yet another indication of the shift of power—political, military, and diplomatic—from Europe to the United States.

The Cold War soon shifted to Asia and became a global competition. In October 1949, Mao Zedong and his communists won power in China, fueling fears in the United States of a global "red tide" of communism. The next year, when communist North Korea attacked South Korea, President Truman viewed the situation as 1930s-style aggression, instigated this time by Moscow: "If the Russian totalitarian state was intending to follow in the path of the dictatorships of Hitler and Mussolini," he said, "they should be met head on in Korea."[2] US troops committed to Korea were soon fighting communist Chinese forces in the north, and the American commander, Douglas MacArthur, called for carrying the war into China

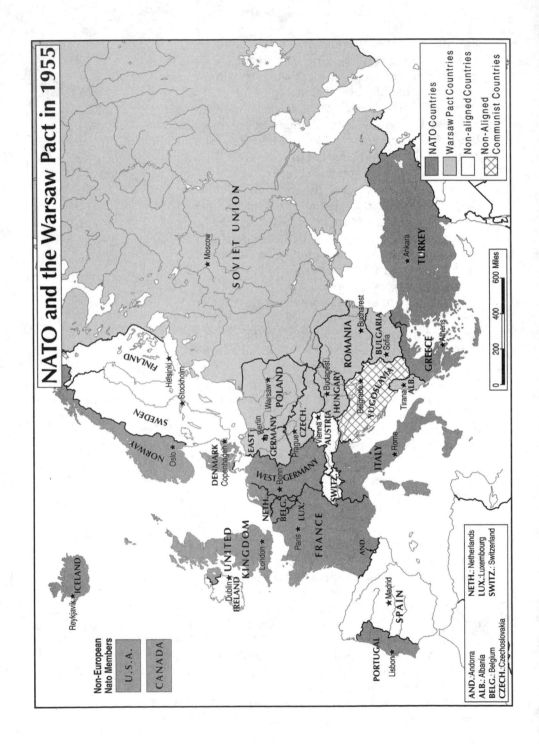

NATO and the Warsaw Pact in 1955

Non-European Nato Members

U.S.A.

CANADA

ICELAND
★ Reykjavik

IRELAND
★ Dublin

UNITED KINGDOM
★ London

NORWAY
★ Oslo

SWEDEN
★ Stockholm

FINLAND
★ Helsinki

DENMARK
★ Copenhagen

NETH.
BELG.
LUX.

WEST GERMANY
★ Bonn

EAST GERMANY
★ Berlin

POLAND
★ Warsaw

SOVIET UNION
★ Moscow

FRANCE
★ Paris

AND.

SWITZ.

CZECH.
★ Prague

AUSTRIA
★ Vienna

HUNGARY
★ Budapest

ROMANIA
★ Bucharest

PORTUGAL
★ Lisbon

SPAIN
★ Madrid

ITALY
★ Rome

YUGOSLAVIA
★ Belgrade

ALB.
★ Tirana

BULGARIA
★ Sofia

GREECE
★ Athens

TURKEY
★ Ankara

Legend:
- NATO Countries
- Warsaw Pact Countries
- Non-aligned Countries
- Non-Aligned Communist Countries

0   200   400   600 Miles

AND.: Andorra
ALB.: Albania
BELG.: Belgium
CZECH.: Czechoslovakia

NETH.: Netherlands
LUX.: Luxembourg
SWITZ.: Switzerland

Children of West Berlin greet arriving American planes during the Berlin airlift of 1948–49.
© *Imagno/Votava/The Image Works.*

(including using nuclear weapons). The Korean War stalemated, and an armistice was signed in 1953, but within another few years, the United States was committed to protecting another Asian country, South Vietnam, from the possibility of communist takeover.

There was another dimension to the Cold War—the nuclear arms race and the "balance of terror." The US monopoly on nuclear weapons was broken with the detonation of an atomic weapon by the Soviet Union in 1949. After that, both sides engaged in a competitive arms buildup such that, by the 1990s, each superpower had about twenty-five thousand nuclear weapons, including about eleven thousand on each side that were "strategic weapons" (i.e., those with intercontinental ranges). The strategic weapons were placed on Soviet or American territory or on submarines, but many intermediate and short-range ones were placed on European soil, on either side of the Iron Curtain. Britain and France, worried about being reduced to sideline spectators in world politics, also developed their own independent nuclear arsenals. If the Cold War had become hot—and nuclear—much of the destruction would have occurred in Europe.

The UN also became a casualty of the Cold War. The UN, largely an inspiration of Roosevelt, was meant to replace and improve upon the discredited

League of Nations.[3] In an effort to include all the major powers this time, each of the Big Five victorious allies—the United States, the Soviet Union, China, France, and Britain—were given permanent seats on the UN's governing Security Council, as well as veto power. In this way, any of the five could prevent action that they disagreed with. With the emergence of the Cold War, however, the United States and the Soviet Union could agree on hardly a single international issue, so UN action in settling international disputes was constantly frustrated by US or Soviet vetoes.

DECOLONIZATION

At the same time that Europe was recovering from World War II and being split in half by the Cold War, it was shedding its colonies. As we saw in chapter 8, most of the European empires had been acquired in the nineteenth century and had become an integral part of the European economies. With some exceptions, most of the European empires remained intact up through World War II. Germany had lost its colonies with its defeat in World War I; Italy (and Japan) lost theirs with their defeat in World War II. Even so, in 1945, large parts of the world's population and land masses were still under the control of Britain, France, Holland, Belgium, and Portugal. Britain's far-flung empire was 125 times as large as Britain itself. The Belgian empire was 78 times the size of Belgium; the Dutch empire 55 times the size of the home country; and the French empire, 19 times. Virtually all of these empires evaporated within about thirty years.

After the war, many factors worked against the continuation of European imperialism. Both the United States and the newly formed UN were opposed to old-style colonialism. When President Roosevelt and Prime Minister Churchill signed the Atlantic Charter in 1941, laying out their wartime goals and postwar plans, they acknowledged the "right of all peoples to choose the form of government under which they will live" and called for "sovereign rights and self-government restored to those who have been forcibly deprived of them." Perhaps this was aimed mostly at territories seized by Nazi Germany and imperial Japan, but it also held promise for the colonies of Churchill's Britain and for those of the other Allied powers.

Even if the Europeans wanted to keep their colonies, they were not really in a position to do so. All of these countries had been devastated and exhausted by the war; many were still issuing ration coupons to their citizens several years after the war's end. They no longer had the financial or military resources to enforce their rule in distant realms. Furthermore, a new breed of colonial elites, many of them educated in Europe, had learned the language of nationalism and democracy and were pressing their demands for independence. The disintegration of the European empires, and the emergence of dozens of new independent states from their ruins, revolutionized global politics and laid the basis for a transformed Europe.

For Britain, the largest empire in world history, the most important of these independence movements occurred in India—with a population of four hundred million, it was the "jewel in the crown" of the British Empire. Led by Jawaharlal Nehru and Mohandas Gandhi—the prophet of nonviolent resistance—India finally wrested independence from Britain in 1947. The struggle against Britain was largely peaceful, but independence came with horrible costs—an orgy of violence between Hindus and Muslims; the largest population movements in world history; and the creation of separate Hindu (India) and Muslim (Pakistan, and later Bangladesh) states out of British India. Gandhi was assassinated in 1948 by a Hindu extremist who opposed the Mahatma's efforts to keep Hindus and Muslims together in one country. India became the world's largest (and poorest) democracy, but ever since independence the subcontinent has been tormented by tensions and violence between religious communities, and between India and Pakistan—now both armed with nuclear weapons.

At the same time that Britain was negotiating India's independence, it was trying to disengage from its commitments in the Eastern Mediterranean. The most volatile of these areas was Palestine, part of the former Ottoman Empire that had been entrusted to Britain by the League of Nations after World War I. Most of the residents of Palestine were Arabs, although the interwar period had seen a steady stream of Jewish immigrants, mostly from Europe, hoping to establish a Jewish state in what they considered the Promised Land. Hundreds of thousands of Jews fled to Palestine during and after World War II, having escaped or survived the Holocaust. In 1947, the UN called for the division of Palestine into separate Jewish and Arab states, but the plan was rejected by the Arabs, and when Britain formally withdrew from the territory in 1948, Jewish leaders unilaterally proclaimed the establishment of Israel. Immediately, neighboring Arab states declared war on Israel, the first of a series of conflicts over the next thirty years. More than one million Palestinian Arabs fled or were expelled from Israel, becoming refugees in neighboring Jordan and other Arab states. Most Arab states still do not formally recognize the state of Israel, and the area has remained a seemingly intractable source of tension, violence, and conflict.

France's major colonial possessions were in Southeast Asia and North Africa. In the former, in what was called French Indochina, a national independence movement had emerged in Vietnam during World War II, under the leadership of a communist named Ho Chi Minh. At first, the conflict was mostly a guerrilla insurgency against the French, but as the Cold War developed, the local conflict became an international one, with conventional armies on each side supported and supplied by the United States and the Soviet Union. Despite the commitment of half a million troops to the conflict, the French suffered a major defeat at Dien Bien Phu in 1954. The government in Paris decided to cut its losses, close the books on Indochina, and withdraw its troops. The Geneva Accords later that year provided for a temporary division of Vietnam into a communist north and a noncommunist south, and free all-Vietnamese elections within two years. With the Cold War in full swing, though, Vietnam remained divided, the United States stepped in to replace the French, and the Vietnam war raged on for another twenty years, until the final victory of the communist North Vietnamese in 1975.

Just a few months after the devastating fall of Dien Bien Phu, France was confronted with another nationalist uprising in an even more important colony—Algeria. For France, this was a different kind of colony altogether than Vietnam. Algeria, after all, was just across the Mediterranean from France, and was the home of over a million French citizens. (Another half million lived in nearby Morocco and Tunisia.) Indeed, Algeria was considered part of France, as represented by the popular slogan "*Algérie, c'est la France.*" The recent loss of Vietnam made the French even more reluctant to abandon Algeria, and the conflict there persisted for a decade, roiling both the colony and France itself. The government in Paris fought off a military *coup d'état*; brought back into the presidency the World War II military hero Charles de Gaulle to settle the crisis; and ushered out the Fourth Republic with a new constitution, authored by de Gaulle, in 1958. Algeria was given independence in 1962.

De Gaulle was elected to prevent the loss of France's most important colony; Britain's Winston Churchill complained that he had not become prime minister "in order to preside over the liquidation of the British Empire." But under their auspices, their countries lost their most important colonial possessions—Algeria and India, respectively—and soon thereafter virtually all of their remaining colonies. Holland ceded independence to Indonesia in 1949. Beginning in 1957, with the independence of Ghana from Britain, one after another of Europe's African colonies became free. The Age of Imperialism, which happened so quickly with the Scramble for Africa in the last decades of the nineteenth century, collapsed almost as quickly in the first decades following World War II.

Independence and self-determination for the European colonies was a consequence and legacy of the evolution of liberty and democracy in Europe, with roots in the Enlightenment and the French Revolution. So these many new independent countries, constituting over half of the membership of the UN by the 1980s, were products of the ideals that had shaped modern Europe. The influence went both ways, however, because decolonization also had a big impact on Europe, as well as on the rest of the world.

For the Europeans after World War II, domestic economic growth came to be seen as more important than colonial trade. At the same time, the shedding of colonies reduced the imperial powers to the same standing as other European states, making cooperation among them less problematic and facilitating their integration into the Common Market (and eventually the European Union). All of the European countries retained strong ties with their former colonies, however, allowing a flood of immigrants into Europe. These two contrasting forces—of harmonization and integration on the one hand, and immigration and diversification on the other—would pose the major challenges facing Europe in the twenty-first century. These issues will be addressed in the concluding chapters of this book.

The multitude of newly independent countries came to be known as the "Third World," belonging neither to the First World of capitalist democracies, or the communist Second World. Indeed, the Third World became the central arena of Cold War rivalry between the United States and the Soviet Union, each striving to extend its global influence and limit that of its rival. Many Third World leaders refused to be drawn into this great power conflict, constituting the **"Non-Aligned Movement,"** which eventually grew to represent nearly two-thirds of the members of the UN.

POSTWAR WESTERN EUROPE

By 1949, Berlin was divided, Germany was divided, and Europe was divided—into East and West, communist and noncommunist. Both halves of the Continent faced enormous problems of postwar recovery. The wartime damage, both human and material, had been enormous, and virtually all countries suffered economic collapse and political instability. These problems were compounded by territorial changes and the largest population movements in history up to that time. The largest population transfers were caused by the shifting of Poland's borders about one hundred miles to the west, with the Soviet Union taking part of eastern Poland and compensating Poland with German territory to the west. Some nine million Germans were forced out of Poland's new western territories and into Germany, and some two to three million Poles migrated from the east (now part of Soviet Ukraine) into Poland, many of them moving into the homes and farms left behind by the fleeing Germans in the west. Millions of other Germans fled the Sudetenland part of Czechoslovakia into the Western or Soviet zones of Germany. The new German governments had to cope with all of these refugees, as well as with millions of other displaced persons, including the survivors of Nazi concentration camps.

Given the economic and social chaos of the immediate postwar period, the speed of recovery in Western Europe was remarkable. Almost every Western country quickly resumed democratic politics; only Spain and Portugal remained under dictatorships until the 1970s. Parliamentary elections in Britain in 1945 ousted Winston Churchill and the Conservative Party and voted in a Labour government committed to democratic socialism and the modern welfare state. France wrote yet another constitution and inaugurated the Fourth Republic, with socialists and communists winning the most seats in the first elections. The Italians abolished the monarchy and wrote a new constitution for a parliamentary republic. In that country, too, the Communist Party did well in elections, regularly winning the second-largest number of seats in Parliament but always excluded from any of the coalition governments. The strong showing of communist and socialist parties in these countries worried some people, given what was happening in Eastern Europe, but these parties were part of a democratic political process in England, France, Italy, and elsewhere and never threatened democratic institutions.

Economic recovery was also swift and sustained in Western Europe. Most countries had achieved prewar levels of industrial production by 1947, and US Marshall Plan funds helped stimulate the recovery. Over the next twenty-five years, the region experienced an "economic miracle" of unprecedented and uninterrupted economic growth, fueling rising living standards and widespread prosperity. Germany played a key role in this growth, becoming the leading industrial country in Western Europe by 1958. Economic policy was governed by the theories of the British economist John Maynard Keynes (1883–1946), who had published an influential book in 1936, *The General Theory of Employment, Interest and Money*. Keynes had argued that government planning and spending was often necessary to "prime the pump" of the capitalist economy, particularly in difficult economic times. In the 1950s and 1960s, European governments used their fiscal and monetary powers to promote investment, production, and employment and to control inflation. These policies, in combination with the strong role of democratic socialist parties on the Continent, contributed to the development of strong welfare states, with nearly full employment, social security, subsidized or free health care and education, and the redistribution of wealth through progressive tax systems. In some ways, by the 1970s, the nations of Western Europe had achieved the goals of Karl Marx, but without Marxism. Equality between men and women steadily expanded throughout the region, prompted by a new wave of feminism and increasingly reinforced by the European Union.

The combination of decolonization and Cold War tensions rendered the European states more dependent on each other and on the United States for both national security and trade. As noted above, the NATO alliance, signed in 1949 by the United States, Canada, Britain, and most Western European countries, obligated the United States to defend the European member states and provided a US "nuclear umbrella" over Europe. Washington's commitment was made real and visible to both Europe and Moscow by the permanent stationing of US troops in several European countries, including, eventually, three hundred thousand in Germany. These were seen as a "trip wire" that would trigger a larger (and perhaps nuclear) response from the United States if the Soviet Union ever attacked Western Europe.

Europe also embarked, after the war, on a major project of economic integration and community building. The first steps in this direction came from French foreign minister Robert Schuman, who in 1950 proposed an international organization to coordinate the iron and steel industries, particularly between France and Germany. Schuman's primary intent was to achieve reconciliation between these two countries after they had fought three wars against each other in the previous seventy-five years. He also saw it as "a first step in the federation of Europe." Out of this was born the **European Coal and Steel Community (ECSC)** in 1951, which was so successful at promoting trade and cooperation that its principles were extended to the entire economy in 1957 with the establishment of the **European Economic Community (EEC)**, which itself evolved into the **European Union**. Over the years, the membership of these organizations grew from the original six to twenty-eight, including many former communist states. (This will be discussed more fully in chapter 14.)

EASTERN EUROPE AFTER THE WAR

During and after World War II, eleven European countries with one hundred million people came under communist rule. Moscow seized Latvia, Lithuania, and Estonia during the war and incorporated them into the USSR. Yugoslavia and Albania (neither one adjacent to Soviet territory) adopted communism but pursued their own paths more or less independently of Moscow. Poland, East Germany, Czechoslovakia, Hungary, Bulgaria, and Romania were gradually converted into "people's democracies" with political leaders subservient to Moscow and Soviet-style political and economic institutions. A series of purges between 1948 and 1952 removed any Eastern European Communist Party leaders whom Moscow considered too nationalistic.

The policies of the communist regimes had both benevolent and oppressive elements. At first, the new governments seized most of the large landed estates and redistributed the property to ordinary peasants and farmers, a policy that fostered considerable goodwill toward the regimes. They also initiated socialist social policies of subsidized housing, health care, education, and guaranteed employment, which were also popular. On the other hand, the communist governments adopted the restrictive apparatus of the Soviet state: an increasingly powerful secret police; restrictions on independent organizations, media, and foreign travel; and censorship. Except in Poland, most churches were destroyed or shut down. In some countries, especially in the Baltic states and Poland, anti-communist guerrillas fought against the new regimes until the early 1950s, by which time they had been brutally suppressed.

Economically, each of the Eastern European states pursued the twin policies of rapid industrialization and **collectivization of agriculture** (the linchpins of Stalin's first five-year plan begun in the Soviet Union in 1928). Many farmers who had only recently been given land by the government resisted collectivization, but the consequences were not nearly as horrendous as they had been in the Soviet Union twenty years earlier. In economic policy, as in the Soviet Union, emphasis was placed on heavy industry (such as metallurgy and machine tools) at the expense of light industry and consumer goods. Government agencies planned investments, output, and distribution and fixed prices and wages. Virtually all workers in agriculture, industry, or service became employees of the state.

Soviet influence over the region was reinforced by a common foreign policy of **socialist internationalism** and a number of international organizations that tied the region together and ensured conformity. Partly in response to the US Marshall Plan, Moscow sponsored the **Council for Mutual Economic Assistance (CMEA or Comecon)** to coordinate trade among the European communist states and tie them more closely together economically. After West Germany joined NATO in 1955, the Soviets responded with the creation of an Eastern European military alliance, the Warsaw Treaty Organization (or the **Warsaw Pact**). The Soviet Union placed troops and nuclear weapons in Warsaw Pact states (especially East Germany), just as the United States did in NATO countries. With the establishment of these organizations, the Eastern European states became increasingly cut off from the rest of Europe. Churchill's statement about the Iron Curtain dividing Europe was even truer in 1955 than it had been in 1946.

From the end of the war through the 1960s, all of the Eastern European states experienced high degrees of economic growth and rapid social changes. All except Albania were transformed from primarily rural, agricultural societies to industrial, urban ones. Average annual growth rates of gross national product for the region were over 7 percent in the 1950s and over 5 percent in the 1960s, even faster than such growth rates in Western Europe. Literacy, health, and living standards improved dramatically for most people in the region.

Despite these accomplishments, there was much restiveness in Eastern Europe. The countries were under the thumb of Moscow and limited in their sovereignty, and their citizens were restricted in their freedoms of speech, press, assembly, religion, and travel. Almost from the beginning, there were demonstrations, riots, or strikes against communism or against the Soviet Union, but the army or the police put them all down, sometimes with assistance from Moscow. Not until 1985, with the accession of Mikhail Gorbachev to the leadership of the Soviet Union, did Moscow begin to loosen the reins of control in Eastern Europe. When Gorbachev did so, the whole system began to unravel. That is the story of chapter 13.

CONCLUSIONS: FROM COLD WAR TO *PERESTROIKA*

The end of World War II resulted in the division of Europe, the controlling presence of the United States and the Soviet Union, and the increasing domination of world politics by these two superpowers and ideological enemies. In some ways, this was a strange turn of events, when a close wartime alliance between these two countries had brought Nazi Germany to its knees. But a history of distrust and suspicion had existed between the United States and the Soviet Union dating from the beginning of the communist state, and hard-nosed realists like Winston Churchill had fully expected tensions to reemerge after the war. The United States had always been suspicious about the intentions of Lenin and Stalin and the universalist goals of communism. The United States refused to recognize the new communist state for sixteen years after the Russian Revolution, and during World War II American leaders like Senator Harry Truman, the future president, expressed the hope that the Nazis and the Soviets would kill each other off in their epic confrontation. Stalin and the Soviet leadership took note of such sentiments and found confirmation of US hostility in the country's long delay in opening a second front against the Germans in Europe, all through 1942 and 1943 until June 1944.

The division of Europe and Germany was a consequence of these emerging postwar tensions, and the metaphorical symbol of that division, Churchill's Iron Curtain, became concrete (literally) with the erection of the Berlin Wall in 1961. All across Europe, barbed-wire fences, guard posts, and minefields separated Eastern from Western Europe. Eastern European citizens required special permission from the authorities to travel to the West, and Westerners required visas issued by the Eastern European governments to travel or study in those countries.

Berlin Wall, 1961. East German border guards remove the debris after a truck successfully broke through the wall, which was built that year by the Soviet Union to prevent escape from Soviet-controlled East Berlin to Western-controlled West Berlin. The wall finally came down in November 1989 (see front cover). © ullstein/The Image Works.

On both sides of the Iron Curtain, countries recovered from the ravages of World War II, rebuilt their economies, modernized, and flourished economically. Some of the better-off Eastern European countries, such as East Germany and Czechoslovakia, had living standards that exceeded those of some of the poorer Western countries, such as Greece or Portugal. But by the 1970s, the Eastern European economies had begun to stagnate, burdened by the heavy hand of rigid central planning and cut off from much trade with the West. Increasingly, Eastern Europeans began to chafe at their lack of freedoms, the unavailability of consumer goods, and their subordination to the Soviet Union.

In the 1980s, the Gorbachev leadership in the Soviet Union began a series of reforms called **perestroika** and encouraged the Eastern European communist leaders to do the same. These reforms, sanctioned from above, opened the floodgates of revolution and within a few years led to the collapse of communist regimes first in Eastern Europe, then in the Soviet Union itself. The Cold War was over and the way was open, once again, for a united Europe.

13

🌰

1989: The Collapse of Communism and End of the Cold War

The year 1989 has become a symbol of revolution in much the same way that 1789 has, and if the fall of the Bastille in Paris epitomizes the French Revolution, the collapse of the Berlin Wall defines the fall of the Iron Curtain and the end of communism in Europe. If anything, the events of 1989 were even more startling and sweeping than those of two hundred years before. In the course of just six months, communist governments were swept out of power in all of Eastern Europe, and within a few years after that, out of the Soviet Union as well. After forty years of division, Germany was reunified and Eastern Europe began its march to the West. The Cold War was over.

The speed and scale of these changes are even more remarkable given the seeming rigidity and solidity of the **Soviet bloc** since World War II. Although resistance and dissent had occurred in Eastern Europe over the years, any significant challenges or changes were stymied or crushed by Moscow. After the early 1970s, however, the legitimacy of the Eastern European communist governments was increasingly eroded by economic stagnation and the growth of "civil society." When Mikhail Gorbachev became Soviet Party leader in 1985 and called for "restructuring" of the communist states, wittingly or unwittingly, he unleashed these forces for change. As reform spiraled into revolution, Gorbachev himself fell from power as the Soviet Union fell apart.

With the dissolution of the USSR, fifteen new independent states emerged, and as after the Napoleonic wars and the two world wars, the map of Europe was redrawn. In both Eastern Europe and most of the states of the former Soviet Union, governments were reconstituted as democracies and economic systems as capitalist. Many of these states tried to reorient themselves away from Russia and toward Western Europe, and almost all of them applied for membership in either NATO or the European Union. Europe was no longer divided.

BEFORE 1989: SOVIET HEGEMONY
AND THE BREZHNEV DOCTRINE

As we saw in chapter 12, after World War II, the Soviet Union established a tightly integrated and controlled alliance of communist states in Eastern Europe, which were referred to in the West as Soviet satellites, or the Soviet bloc. These states (East Germany, Poland, Czechoslovakia, Hungary, Bulgaria, and Romania) all had essentially a single dominant political party, the Communist Party, and a centrally planned and state-owned economy. Their foreign trade was mostly with each other and the Soviet Union, and they all belonged to the Moscow-dominated military alliance, the Warsaw Pact. Albania and Yugoslavia, neither of which bordered on the Soviet Union, also had communist systems but were not subservient to Moscow, though Albania was a member of the Warsaw Pact for a time.

While Joseph Stalin ruled the Soviet Union, there was little room for dissent, opposition, or differentiation in Eastern Europe: all of the governments there followed the Soviet model in lockstep. With Stalin's death in 1953, some relaxation of control occurred both within the Soviet Union and in Eastern Europe, and some countries were able to carve out niches of limited autonomy for themselves. Poland, for example, was allowed to maintain independent private farming in the countryside and to keep open its many Roman Catholic churches and seminaries. Romania, while keeping tight internal controls, was able to maintain a relatively independent foreign policy, although it remained a member of the Warsaw Pact.

There were, however, strict limits to how far the Eastern European states could stray from the Soviet path, and when it seemed to Moscow that communist rule or bloc solidarity was threatened, it would use intimidation or force to set things right. After the death of Stalin, for example, the new Soviet leader, Nikita Khrushchev, began a program of "de-Stalinization" of the Soviet Union, resulting in the release of many political prisoners, restrictions on the secret police, and relaxation of censorship. In Eastern Europe, these changes were taken as license for reform. In 1956, in Poland, workers' demonstrations and strikes forced a change in leadership in that country and the installation of a more national-minded Communist Party leader, who assured Moscow that the country would remain communist. That same year in Hungary, young people toppled the huge statue of Stalin in the center of Budapest, and a reformist leadership declared the country neutral and tried to withdraw

Hungary from the Warsaw Pact. This went beyond the permissible limits for the Kremlin[1] (the Soviet leadership), which ordered a military intervention to crush the rebellion. Thousands of Hungarians were killed, and several hundred thousand fled into exile.

The next serious challenge to Moscow's hegemony in Eastern Europe came from Czechoslovakia in 1968. There, a liberalizing Communist Party leader named Alexander Dubček spoke about creating "socialism with a human face." The Communist Party's reform program attacked the concentration of power in the party and proposed freedom of the press, assembly, and travel. The Soviet leadership, now under Leonid Brezhnev, cautioned the Czechoslovaks to rein in the reform, and when they were unable to do so, Moscow led an invasion of 750,000 Warsaw Pact troops to "normalize" the country. The **Prague Spring** came to an early end in the face of Soviet tanks. The Soviet leadership justified the invasion by, arguing that if socialism was in jeopardy in any communist state, this constituted a threat to all socialist states and thus required action by the entire socialist community. In essence, the **Brezhnev Doctrine**, as it was dubbed in the West, gave Moscow the right to intervene in any country in the bloc to prevent the deterioration of Communist Party control.

The Brezhnev Doctrine cast a pall over Eastern Europe for the next decade, but it did not deter the Poles from periodic bouts of strikes and unrest. Indeed, Poland had a tradition of revolt, often against the Russians, that dated back to the eighteenth-century era of the Partitions, when the Polish state was gobbled up by its three powerful neighbors, Russia, Prussia, and Austria. This tradition continued even after the consolidation of communist power, with demonstrations, strikes, or riots in 1956, 1968, 1970, and 1976.

The most powerful challenge to communist rule came in Poland in the summer of 1980, when workers went on strike to protest food price increases. At the huge Lenin Shipyards in the coastal city of Gdańsk (formerly the German city of Danzig), a shipyard electrician named Lech Wałęsa assumed leadership of the strike committee, which represented and coordinated strike activity at over two hundred enterprises. The workers forced the government to agree to their list of twenty-one demands, which included the formation of their own trade union, independent of the Communist Party. The workers named the union *Solidarność* (Solidarity).

Over the next sixteen months, some twelve million people (out of a total workforce of sixteen million) joined **Solidarity**. The position of Solidarity was strengthened further with the moral support of Pope John Paul II, the first Polish pope, who had been elected just two years before. With practically universal support in the country, the union became more and more powerful, and increasingly challenged the authority of the Communist Party. This raised concern in the Soviet leadership, which several times staged threatening military maneuvers along the Polish borders. Finally, under pressure from the Kremlin, in December 1981, the Polish government declared martial law, arrested Wałęsa and the rest of the Solidarity leadership, interned thousands of Solidarity activists, and banned the union.

This seemed to be yet another affirmation of the Brezhnev Doctrine. But in Poland, the situation and results were different from those in Hungary in 1956 or Czechoslovakia in 1968. In the first place, the Soviet army had not intervened directly, apparently fearing massive Polish national resistance to the use of Soviet troops. Second, the martial law abolition of Solidarity was not entirely effective. The union was reconstituted as an illegal underground organization and continued its activities in organizing strikes and demonstrations and publishing newsletters. Most important, however, was the simple legacy of Solidarity. One Solidarity adviser, Adam Michnik, observed that Solidarity had existed long enough to convince everyone that, after martial law, it was no longer possible to envision "socialism with a human face." "What remains," he wrote, "is communism with its teeth knocked out."[2]

Mass protests, like those of Solidarity in the 1980s, shook the regimes of Eastern Europe. But the roots of protest and dissent went back a decade or more in the region. As the economies and the regimes began to weaken in the 1970s, dissident groups became more active, visible, and popular. This was stimulated in part by the 1975 signing of the **Helsinki Accords** by the governments of the Soviet Union and Eastern Europe. These documents, the result of a long process of negotiations among thirty-five states in Europe plus the United States and Canada, contained a whole section on "respect for human rights and fundamental freedoms, including the freedom of thought, conscience, religion, or belief."

After the agreements were signed by their governments, dissident intellectuals in both the Soviet Union and Eastern Europe formed human rights monitoring groups to publicize their governments' violations of the human rights they had been guaranteed at Helsinki. Often, these were illegal underground publications (called *samizdat* in the Soviet Union), but some were published openly and defiantly, complete with the names and addresses of the signatories. In Czechoslovakia, for example, a group of intellectuals openly circulated a document titled **Charter 77**, which called on people to speak out on behalf of human rights guaranteed by Czechoslovak laws and the Helsinki Accords. The playwright Václav Havel became the spokesman for Charter 77; a dozen years later, Havel became one of the leaders of the revolution that brought down the communist government of Czechoslovakia. In Poland after 1976 there developed a large network of underground publishing houses producing newspapers, magazines, and books in thousands of copies.

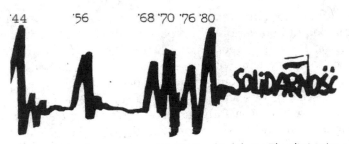

Poster of a cardiogram tracing the birth of Solidarity. The distinctive trademark resembles a surging crowd carrying the flag of Poland. Photo by David Mason.

GORBACHEV AND *PERESTROIKA*

Probably these popular protests and dissident activities would have gotten nowhere had it not been for a change of leadership in the Soviet Union. In 1982, Leonid Brezhnev died at the age of seventy-six after eighteen years as leader of the Communist Party of the Soviet Union. His next two successors, also elderly, died within a few years, and in 1985, Mikhail Gorbachev was chosen Communist Party leader. At the age of fifty-four, Gorbachev was by far the youngest member of the Soviet leadership, the first party leader born after the Russian Revolution, and the first to begin his political career after the death of Stalin. He was also educated (with a law degree), articulate, and charismatic. Almost immediately, he began to push for a whole series of increasingly radical reforms, both economic and political.

The core of the reform program was what Gorbachev called *perestroika*, or "economic restructuring." After years of rapid economic growth in the 1950s and 1960s, the Soviet economy had been growing at only about 2 percent annually for a decade. The rigid system of state control and central planning no longer functioned well in a complex and global economy.[3] Internal problems were compounded in the 1980s by a sharp decline in world prices for petroleum, a major source of export earnings for the Soviet Union. Furthermore, the long and costly Cold War arms race with the United States was an increasing drain on economic resources. These economic problems had a deleterious effect on living standards in the USSR. Even the official press admitted that the Soviet Union ranked between fiftieth and sixtieth of the world's countries in per capita consumption of goods and services. Gorbachev recognized that the legitimacy and stability of the Soviet regime (and other communist regimes) was increasingly dependent on economic success and consumer satisfaction and that a more efficient economy required commitment, hard work, and support from the population. As he himself put it, "A house can be put in order only by a person who feels he is the owner."[4]

Perestroika, then, involved making a number of liberalizing changes to the economic system without ever abandoning socialism. Central planning was scaled back, allowing more decision making at the factory level. Small-scale private and cooperative firms were allowed to operate independently of government planning. The government allowed some limited role for the free market in agriculture as well.

In his effort to revitalize the Soviet system, Gorbachev linked *perestroika* with **glasnost**, meaning "openness" or "publicity," and meant to open Soviet society to a critical evaluation of its past and present problems. Censorship was relaxed, and previously taboo subjects began to receive coverage: joblessness, drug abuse, prostitution, crime, urban blight, homelessness, and so forth. The campaign for *glasnost* was accompanied by democratization of the political system, which included the introduction of multicandidate (although not multiparty) competition in elections, the sanctioning of independent groups and associations, improved relations with the Russian Orthodox Church, and a reduction in the dominating role of the Communist Party. These changes did not create Western-style democracy in the Soviet Union, but they were steps in that direction.

A final, critical element of Gorbachev's reforms was "new thinking" in foreign policy. Here, too, the basis of change was economic. If Moscow wanted to develop an economy that was more efficient and more oriented toward consumer goods, it needed to expand trade, attract technology, reduce military spending, and cut back on aid to other countries. All of this required a more relaxed international atmosphere and, in particular, an improved relationship with the United States. So within a few years, Gorbachev floated a number of major arms-control proposals, reduced Soviet defense spending, pulled back some troops stationed in Eastern Europe, and began to disengage from Afghanistan (where the Soviets had been fighting Islamic *mujahidin* since 1979).

As Soviet policies toward the rest of the world changed, so did the Kremlin's orientation toward Eastern Europe, the region of primary economic, strategic, and ideological importance to Moscow. Hoping to make the Eastern European economies more efficient and less dependent on the Soviet Union, Gorbachev made a series of visits to the Eastern European capitals to prod those countries toward their own *perestroika*. He also subtly backed away from the principles of the Brezhnev Doctrine, stressing "the right of every people to choose the paths and forms of its own development."[5] All of this strengthened the hands of reformers in the region and led to increasing demands for change. This time, it seemed, Moscow would not block reform in Eastern Europe.

THE REVOLUTIONS OF 1989

The first test of Moscow's new thinking came, once again, from Poland. Since the martial law crackdown on Solidarity in 1981, Poland had muddled along in political stalemate and economic stagnation. The government had lifted martial law in 1983 and released Lech Wałęsa, but he remained officially a "nonperson." In 1988, a new round of price hikes sparked worker protests and strikes. At first, the strikers' demands were largely economic, but soon they expanded to include calls for political change, including the legalization of Solidarity. The government turned to Wałęsa to help end the strikes, leading to a series of roundtable negotiations among representatives of the government, the Catholic Church, and Solidarity.

The negotiations were concluded in April 1989, with a path-breaking set of agreements that provided for the reinstatement of Solidarity and for parliamentary elections in which Solidarity could put up candidates against the communist incumbents. At the signing ceremony of this pact, Wałęsa proclaimed, "This is the beginning of democracy and a free Poland."[6] The elections were scheduled for early June, just two months after the roundtable agreements. The Solidarity-led opposition was at an incredible disadvantage, trying in that short time to transform itself from illegal underground to legal electoral contestant. Nevertheless, in June, the opposition staged a stunning victory, winning almost every seat it was allowed to contest.

With this unexpected turn of events, the Communist Party no longer commanded a majority in the parliament. In August, a coalition government was formed under Tadeusz Mazowiecki, a journalist, Catholic activist, and Solidarity supporter. For the first time since 1948, a noncommunist government held power in Eastern Europe. This was a blunt challenge to the principles of the Brezhnev Doctrine, but all through these events, the Kremlin looked on quietly and even with approval. That summer, a Gorbachev spokesman jokingly referred to Moscow's new "Sinatra Doctrine." This referred to Frank Sinatra's song "My Way" and implied that the Soviet satellites would now be allowed to go their own way. The next year, Lech Wałęsa was elected president of Poland. The Brezhnev Doctrine was dead.

The Polish roundtable negotiations and elections opened the floodgates of reform in the rest of the Soviet bloc. In Hungary, the government and the opposition entered into Polish-style negotiations on the future of the country. Within a few months, they had agreed on constitutional reform, a multiparty system, and free parliamentary elections in 1990. By the fall of 1989, the Hungarian Communist Party was dissolved, and the word "People's" had been dropped from the name "Hungarian People's Republic." Hungary opened its borders with the West, with a ceremonial cutting of the barbed wire barrier on the Austrian border. Hungary then became a funnel through which thousands of Eastern Europeans traveled on their way to the West. East Germans, in particular, now had a way around the Berlin Wall, and tens of thousands fled to the West.

In East Germany, a hard-line communist leadership under Erich Honecker had resisted Soviet-style reforms. But tensions came to a head in October 1989, as a result of two circumstances: the popular exodus through Hungary and other countries, which had reached almost two hundred thousand people by then, and the visit to Berlin by Gorbachev. The Honecker government had at first allowed some East Germans to travel to West Germany through other countries but then clamped down. The new restrictions led to protests and demonstrations in East Berlin, Dresden, Leipzig, and other cities. At this time, Gorbachev came to East Berlin to participate in the country's fortieth-anniversary celebrations. Wherever he went, he was greeted by chants of "Gorby! Gorby!" and the police had to break up several demonstrations and protests.

After his departure, the demonstrations grew larger and more political, reaching three hundred thousand in Leipzig and half a million in East Berlin. Demands were made for free emigration, the resignation of Honecker, and the legalization of a political opposition. In the first few days of November, the entire government resigned, then the Communist Party's leadership did the same. As the government weakened and travel restrictions were eased, people once again poured out of the country. Finally, on November 9, 1989, the government ended all travel restrictions, and the Berlin Wall was opened. Young people stormed the wall, chopped at it with pickaxes, and celebrated with champagne (see photo on front cover).

That day marked the beginning of the end for East Germany. Over the next months, the Communist Party made an effort to reform and democratize itself, as was happening in Hungary and Poland. The country's parliament voted to end the communists' leading role and promised free elections in the spring of 1990. But by then, a flood tide was under way, from both East and West, for the unification of the two Germanys. East Germany disappeared on October 3, 1990, absorbed into a reunified Germany less than a year after the collapse of the Berlin Wall.

The turmoil in East Germany in October and November 1989 spilled over into neighboring Czechoslovakia. As huge demonstrations in the capital city, Prague, demanded political change, Václav Havel and members of Charter 77, as well as of other opposition groups, put together the Civic Forum to coordinate the protests and to demand the resignation of the Communist Party leadership. On November 24, after 350,000 people had gathered in Prague's Wenceslas Square to cheer Alexander Dubček (the hero of 1968) and Václav Havel, the entire party leadership resigned. A new leadership agreed to the formation of a coalition government, free elections, and freer travel to the West. The communists had bowed out

Playwright, dissident, and future president Václav Havel addresses enormous crowds during the Velvet Revolution in Prague, November 1989. Courtesy of the Czech News Agency, CTK.

without a fight, and Czechoslovaks exulted over their **Velvet Revolution**. As Havel claimed, with only slight exaggeration, the revolution had taken ten years in Poland, ten months in Hungary, ten weeks in East Germany, but only ten days in Czechoslovakia. In December 1989, Václav Havel became president of Czechoslovakia.

In the course of just six months, from June through December 1989, communist governments fell in Poland, Hungary, East Germany, Czechoslovakia, Bulgaria, and Romania. Only in Romania did the revolution turn violent. There, over the course of just ten days, more than a thousand people were killed in the uprising, culminating in the execution of communist dictator Nicolae Ceaușescu and his wife, on Christmas Day. Remarkably, with that lone exception, all other East European revolutions occurred peacefully.

Never before in history had so many countries undergone revolutionary changes in such a short time, and with little violence. Some were managed by Reformist Party leadership, as in Hungary; some by "people power," as in East Germany and Czechoslovakia; and some by a combination of the two, as in Poland and Bulgaria. In every case, though, the ease and rapidity of change was breathtaking. Regimes that were considered well entrenched and well protected simply tumbled, one after another, into the "dustbin of history" (a phrase Marx had used to describe the fate of capitalist states). Within two years, communism collapsed in the Soviet Union itself.

BOX 13.1
Václav Havel, Frank Zappa, and the Velvet Revolution

In the Soviet Union and Eastern Europe, as in tsarist Russia in the nineteenth century, the ban on opposition parties or organizations meant that writers, artists, and intellectuals played an important political role. One of the most prominent dissident intellectuals in Eastern Europe was the playwright Václav Havel. In his twenties, he took a job as a stagehand at Prague's ABC Theater and began writing plays himself. During the more open period of the Prague Spring in 1968, he traveled to the United States, where he identified with the 1960s counterculture, especially rock music. After the Soviet intervention put an end to the Czechoslovak reforms in August 1968, the new hard-line government in Prague banned Havel's plays, arrested him several times, and jailed him twice.

In 1977, the government arrested and tried a popular Czechoslovak rock band called The Plastic People of the Universe, named after lyrics in a song by American rocker Frank Zappa. In protest of the trial, a number of Czechoslovak artists and intellectuals signed a manifesto for artistic and political freedom, which they called Charter 77. This became a kind of floating intellectual protest organization, with Havel as the spokesman. Havel formulated his ideas about resistance to tyranny in an important 1969 essay, "The Power of the Powerless," which later became a book. He argued there that a totalitarian political system is built on lies and that people allow the system to exist by accepting the lies and living within them. The only moral solution to and way out of totalitarianism is for individuals to reject the lies and "to live within the truth."

Havel's essay, published illegally in Czechoslovakia and other Eastern European countries, was widely influential and became, in essence, a blueprint for what happened in 1989. With the fall of communism in Czechoslovakia's Velvet Revolution, Václav Havel became the president of the country (and remained so until 2003). As president, he brought Frank Zappa to Czechoslovakia, told him his music had helped inspire their revolution, and offered him a job as special ambassador to the West for trade, culture, and tourism. American Secretary of State James Baker nixed the idea.

THE DISINTEGRATION OF THE
SOVIET UNION AND YUGOSLAVIA

Nationalism and liberalism played a big part in bringing democracy and sovereignty to the Eastern European states in 1989, and they also contributed to the disintegration of the two multinational states of the region, the Soviet Union and Yugoslavia. In the Soviet Union, the changes that Gorbachev had unleashed in Eastern Europe came boomeranging back to the country where they started. The USSR was a union of fifteen republics, each representing a different nationality, many of which were brought forcibly into the Russian Empire before 1917 or into the Soviet Union afterward. As centralizing controls were weakened during the Gorbachev era, nationalism flourished in all of them. When the Eastern European states broke away from communism and the Soviet bloc in 1989, many of the Soviet republics saw similar opportunities. In the course of 1990 and 1991, every one of the fifteen republics declared independence, although Moscow did not recognize those declarations.

In the spring and summer of 1991, Gorbachev and the leaders of a number of the republics, including Boris Yeltsin of the Russian Republic, attempted to hammer out a formula to create a more decentralized union with greater autonomy for each of the republics. Shortly before the treaty was to be signed in August, though, a hard-line group representing the Communist Party, the army, and the security agencies attempted to oust Gorbachev from power. Russian president Boris Yeltsin managed to rally opposition to the coup and face down the plotters. But in the aftermath of the coup attempt, the country's fragmentation accelerated. At the end of the year, Yeltsin and the presidents of Ukraine and Belarus signed a treaty formally dissolving the USSR. Gorbachev resigned and retired. After seventy-two years, the Soviet Union was no more.

Yugoslavia, like the USSR, was a multinational federal state held together by a single political party, the League of Yugoslav Communists. With a total population of only twenty-four million, it was an extraordinarily heterogeneous country with no majority population. The Serbs were the largest group, but they constituted only about a third of the total. As communism disintegrated in Eastern Europe and the Soviet Union, Yugoslavia also began to fall apart. Elections in Yugoslavia's republics in 1990 brought nonsocialist and independence-minded governments to power in Slovenia, Croatia, Bosnia-Herzegovina, and Macedonia. But the government of Serbia, under President Slobodan Milošević, remained committed to maintaining the integrity of the state under predominantly Serbian influence.

Serbia clashed at first with both Slovenia and Croatia, but the biggest problem came in Bosnia, where about 43 percent of the population was Muslim (from the days of Ottoman influence in the region) and a third was Serbian. With the declaration of independence by the Bosnian government, Serbian guerrillas, backed by Serbia and the Yugoslav army, began seizing Bosnian territory for the creation of a Serbian state. This led to a brutal and horrifying civil war that caused almost a quarter of a million deaths, the worst violence in Europe since World War II. Finally, after a two-week bombing campaign by North American Treaty Organization (NATO) forces against Serb positions, the parties were brought to the negotiating table in Dayton, Ohio. The Dayton Accords of 1995 provided for a single

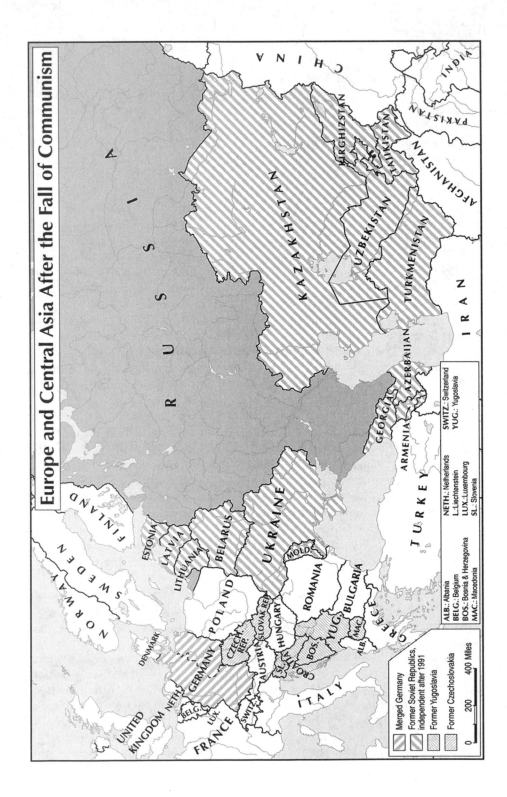

Europe and Central Asia After the Fall of Communism

CHINA

INDIA

PAKISTAN

AFGHANISTAN

KYRGHIZSTAN

TAJIKISTAN

UZBEKISTAN

TURKMENISTAN

KAZAKHSTAN

IRAN

RUSSIA

GEORGIA

ARMENIA

AZERBAIJAN

TURKEY

FINLAND

NORWAY

SWEDEN

ESTONIA

LATVIA

LITHUANIA

BELARUS

UKRAINE

MOLD.

DENMARK

UNITED KINGDOM

NETH.

BELG.

LUX.

FRANCE

SWITZ.

GERMANY

POLAND

CZECH. REP.

AUSTRIA

SLOVAK. REP.

HUNGARY

SLO.

CRO.

ITALY

ROMANIA

BULGARIA

BOS.

YUG.

MAC.

ALB.

GREECE

ALB.: Albania
BELG.: Belgium
BOS.: Bosnia & Herzegovina
MAC.: Macedonia

NETH.: Netherlands
L.:Liechtenstein
LUX.:Luxembourg
SL.: Slovenia

SWITZ.: Switzerland
YUG.: Yugoslavia

Merged Germany

Former Soviet Republics,
independent after 1991

Former Yugoslavia

Former Czechoslovakia

0   200   400 Miles

Bosnian state divided into two roughly equal entities: a Muslim-Croat federation and a Serb republic. A NATO peacekeeping force of nearly sixty thousand troops, including about twenty thousand Americans, monitored the cease-fire and supervised implementation of the accord.

Other problems of nationalism and ethnic conflict were unleashed with the collapse of the centralizing power of communism. Czechoslovakia, three years after the Velvet Revolution, was peacefully dissolved and replaced by two separate states: the Czech Republic and Slovakia. Russia, after the breakup of the Soviet Union, was itself a federation of many nationalities and faced numerous separatist insurgencies, especially in the North Caucasus region along Russia's southern border. The most prolonged and violent of these was in the Muslim region of Chechnya, where two grueling wars convulsed the area for fifteen years (1994–2009) and cost tens of thousands of lives, both military and civilian.

In Yugoslavia, another round of conflict erupted between Serbs and Albanian Muslims in the region of Kosovo, requiring yet another military intervention by NATO (primarily US) forces. Yugoslavia finally disappeared altogether, fragmented into six small sovereign countries that had been its constituent republics, in much the same way that the Soviet Union had earlier collapsed. Nationalism, which had played a positive role in delivering Eastern Europe from the Soviet bloc, also had its negative side, expressed in ethnic rivalry, hostility, and conflict.

With all these changes, the borders of Eastern Europe were redrawn in a manner even more thoroughgoing than after World War I, with the emergence of a panoply of new states. From the former USSR, all fifteen constituent republics became sovereign and independent countries. Six new states, including Croatia, Slovenia, Bosnia, and Serbia, emerged from Yugoslavia. Germany's reunification made it the most populous and economically powerful country in Europe. All of these new countries, as well as the newly independent ones of Eastern Europe, wrestled with questions of identity and their relationships with the rest of Europe.

TRANSITION FROM COMMUNISM TO MARKET DEMOCRACY

The new postcommunist governments in Eastern Europe and the former Soviet Union faced a daunting complex of tasks: the re-creation of democratic politics, the construction of market economies, and a reorientation of foreign policy toward the West. These changes required a fundamental transformation of each country's social and economic systems and even a psychological reorientation for much of the population. In many respects, these changes turned out to be more wrenching and traumatic than the relatively quick and painless political revolutions.

Nevertheless, most of the Eastern European states made remarkably speedy progress toward both democracy and capitalism. Within a few years, most had been through several sets of free elections, had adopted new constitutions, and had established representative legislatures, competitive party politics, the rule of law, and a free press. Some of them had even voted back into power, in free elections, representatives of the former communist parties!

In the economic realm, the task was not so smooth or easy. Dismantling the old system of central planning and full employment disrupted almost everyone's life. Building a market economy based on private ownership, entrepreneurship, and investments would also take time in countries without such experience or traditions and without any capital. The tasks of economic restructuring included price deregulation, currency rationalization, the elimination of government subsidies to consumers and producers, the creation of a modern banking system and a stock market, and a large-scale program for the privatization of state enterprises and farmland.

In both Eastern Europe and the former Soviet Union, all countries experienced sharp economic declines in the early years of the transition, with plummeting output, surges in unemployment, and skyrocketing inflation. Russia's problems were more severe than most, with an economic depression that rivaled that of the Great Depression in the United States and Germany during the 1930s. But by about 1994, most countries had begun to recover, the private sector was taking hold, and consumer goods and services were more available. They were increasingly looking like typical Western consumer societies.

The dawn of capitalism, though, brought with it the usual share of problems. Unemployment, which had been nearly nonexistent in the communist era, reached near double-digit rates in many countries at the end of the 1990s. The number of people in the region living in poverty increased tenfold between 1989 and 1996. Increases in unemployment and poverty contributed to worsening health indicators, especially in the countries of the former Soviet Union, where mortality and morbidity rates were without peacetime precedent. There were also big increases in inequality. The growing gap between rich and poor was particularly galling for many citizens because many of the *nouveau riche* were their former oppressors, members of the old Communist Party apparatus. In many postcommunist countries in the 1990s, large percentages of the populations expressed the view (in public opinion surveys) that they had been better off in the communist era than they were in the democratic one.

Nevertheless, most people in the postcommunist states were glad to be free of the restrictions and privations of the communist era and welcomed the return of "normal lives" and the chance to rejoin Europe. Most Eastern

European countries reoriented their trade from East to West, and many citizens of the region took advantage of new opportunities to travel to or work in Western Europe. With the dissolution of the Warsaw Pact, most former members of that alliance rushed to affiliate with NATO—an organization originally set up to oppose communism—and by 2009, twelve of the twenty-eight members of NATO were postcommunist countries. The former communist states were even more anxious to join the European Union (EU), for both symbolic and economic reasons. Eight of them joined the EU in its 2004 expansion of membership, and three more after that (more on this in the following chapter).

Twenty years after the 1989 revolutions, almost all of the former communist states had successfully navigated the path to democratic politics and capitalist economics. What had been "Eastern Europe" was thoroughly heterogeneous, with some people very wealthy and others quite poor, but not too different in that respect from "Western Europe." Slovenia and the Czech Republic, for example, had overtaken the living standards in Portugal, the poorest country in the Western camp. Some of the ex-communist countries had better credit ratings, and less corruption, than some of the older EU members. And the opening up of national borders led to a flood of immigrants from east to west Europe, boosting economic growth but also compounding issues of immigration prompted by decolonization a generation earlier.

CONCLUSIONS: THE IMPACT OF 1989

The causes of the 1989–91 revolutions, like those of 1789, 1848, and 1917, were both systemic and immediate. In the long term, the Soviet and Eastern European governments had suffered declining economies; growing popular dissatisfaction, political dissent, and nationalism; and declining legitimacy. Given the apparatus of repression possessed by the communist governments, the system could probably have limped along even with these disabilities but for the appearance of Gorbachev, *glasnost*, and *perestroika*. *Perestroika* encouraged change and reform, and *glasnost* uncorked the genie of public opinion. Once the masses took to the streets, political changes could not be stopped without the application of force. Fortunately, Gorbachev would not countenance the use of force. For this, he won the 1990 Nobel Peace Prize.

The magnitude and speed of the changes in this revolution were unprecedented: in the course of only two years, nine authoritarian governments collapsed, and twice that many new states were born out of the rubble. In some ways, the breakup of the multinational states of the Soviet Union and Yugoslavia and the reunification of Germany were a culmination of the post–World War I process of creating nation-states, the goal enunciated at that time so forcefully by President Woodrow Wilson in his Fourteen Points. But just as in that earlier time, when nationalism proved to be double-edged, in the 1990s it showed its intolerant and violent side in Bosnia, Croatia, Kosovo, Chechnya, and elsewhere.

Mostly, however, the anticommunist revolutions were peaceful, and this was another remarkable aspect of 1989. Past revolutions, even ones that failed, had been violent to one degree or another. In Eastern Europe, one country after another relied on "people power" to bring down their governments without resort to arms. It seemed that even staunchly authoritarian governments could not stand in the face of popular disaffection publicly expressed. This form of regime change became a model for other peoples and countries as well, most notably in South Africa, which began its own form of *perestroika* in 1989, leading to black majority-rule government.

The revolutions of 1989 did not simply destroy governments; they also ended an ideology. Although communism may have come from within Russia in 1917, it was imposed on Eastern Europe from without in the years after World War II, and it never did take very well. Stalin once observed that "communism fits Poland like a saddle fits a cow." Although many Eastern Europeans welcomed the communist governments at first, this support waned over the years. By the 1980s, although many people favored socialism, hardly any supported Soviet-style communism. With the overthrow of communist governments, the communist ideology also faded.

The end of communism in Europe also ended the Cold War. What had begun in Berlin ended there. The conflict between capitalism and communism had been an important factor in European and world affairs since the Russian Revolution of 1917 and had dominated international politics since World War II. The ideological element in international politics faded away, at least temporarily. One US State Department official, Francis Fukuyama, wrote an essay and a book titled *The End of History*, in which he proclaimed "the end of mankind's ideological evolution and the universalization of Western liberal democracy as the final form of human government."[7] This assessment was overly simplistic and optimistic, but in the United States, it reflected the widespread view that the United States had won the Cold War.

There is no doubt, though, that the rise of liberal democracy in Eastern Europe offered the best chance yet for a Europe "united and free." From the Baltic states through Poland, the Czech Republic, and Hungary, to Slovenia and Croatia, governments were committed to democracy, market economies, and membership in the European Community. The "iron curtain" had lifted, and if there was still a division in Europe, it was much farther to the east.

14

❧❧

The European Union:
Europe United and Free?

The collapse of communism in Europe brought a flood of new applicants to the European Union (EU) and raised the possibility of a truly integrated, perhaps even united, Europe. The EU is the latest incarnation of what is sometimes called the **Common Market**, which started out as a customs union of six countries in the 1950s.[1] Over the decades, the organization grew in membership and scope, creating a virtual "Europe without borders" with a common currency, the **euro**, and a common commitment to democratic politics, human rights, and a market economy.

Just as the EU was planning for further and deeper integration, communism began to fall apart in Eastern Europe and virtually all of the European postcommunist states applied for membership. With the entry of thirteen new countries since 2004, including eleven postcommunist states, the EU now has twenty-eight members and constitutes a major force in the world economy and international politics.

ORIGINS OF THE COMMON MARKET

The first ideas and plans for the European Common Market came in the aftermath of World War II, although proposals for some kind of united Europe date back to the eighteenth century. Even before the French Revolution, Jean-Jacques Rousseau proclaimed, somewhat prematurely perhaps, that "there are no longer Frenchmen, Germans, and Spaniards, or even English, but only Europeans."[2] So the idea of a united Europe, at least, is an old one.

The first real impetus for European unification, though, came after the wreckage of World War II. In 1946, in the same year that he delivered his "Iron Curtain" speech, Winston Churchill appealed for "a kind of United States of Europe," beginning with a partnership between France and Germany, countries that had fought three wars with each other in the course of seventy-five years. (Churchill, however, saw no place for his own country in such a union.) Delegates from ten European countries met in Strasbourg, France (right on the border with Germany), to discuss something along these lines. Out of this came the Council of Europe, with the hopes that this might eventually become a legislature for a federated Europe. The council relied mostly on debate and diplomacy, had no real powers, and never became an important political force.

A far more ambitious proposal came from two cosmopolitan Frenchmen, Jean Monnet (1888–1979) and Robert Schuman (1886–1963). Monnet was a visionary economist and administrator (if those terms don't constitute an oxymoron!), who in the 1920s served as deputy secretary general of the League of Nations. Schuman, a disciple of Monnet, was born in the contested region of Alsace-Lorraine and was a diplomat and the French foreign minister from 1948 to 1950. Both of them were looking for ways to change the fateful dynamic of French-German relations and to integrate Germany more closely with the rest of Europe.

Monnet had in mind the economic integration of the two countries. By getting France and Germany to cooperate in the economic sphere, they would build up a web of interdependence that would spill over into the political sphere. Eventually, this cooperation and interdependence would render war between them politically unthinkable and economically impossible. In a process he called **functionalism**, he envisaged a step-by-step transfer of certain economic or political functions, or "spheres of activity," from national to **supranational** control, above the level of the nation-state. Concentrating first on nonpolitical spheres of cooperation, he thought, would be easier than trying for political rapprochement right away.

The French foreign minister, Robert Schuman, took these ideas and, with support from sympathetic political leaders in Germany, Italy, and elsewhere, put them into concrete form in the Schuman Plan of 1950. Its primary goal was to coordinate coal and steel production, much of which was located in the Ruhr valley, the Saarland, and Alsace-Lorraine, the very areas that had been so hotly contested in the wars of the past century. This initial focus on coal and steel was limited; Schuman saw it as "a first step in the federation of Europe."[3] Out of the Schuman Plan emerged the European Coal and Steel Community (ECSC), which began operation in 1952, with Jean Monnet as the first ECSC president.

The ECSC consisted of six states: France, Germany, Italy, and the three "Benelux" countries of Belgium, Netherlands, and Luxembourg, which had already formed their own customs union a few years earlier. By the time of the formation of the ECSC, of course, Europe was already firmly divided by the Iron Curtain and the North Atlantic Treaty Organization (NATO), so there was no question then of extending the plan into Eastern Europe. In any case, for France at that time, the biggest perceived threat was Germany, not communism. And most of the coal and steel resources of Europe were located in the territory of these six member states.

Although the inspiration for the ECSC was noble and idealistic, the goals and the operation of the organization itself were quite prosaic. The main purpose of the community was to stimulate production and trade in coal and steel, primarily by the elimination of barriers to trade. For those who are not economics majors, this may require a short explanation. Governments often protect industries within their borders by restricting cheaper imports from abroad. They do this primarily through tariffs, which are taxes on imports, and through **quotas**, which are limits on the quantities of goods imported from particular countries. For example, if US automobile manufacturers (e.g., Ford or General Motors) are losing out to cheaper and/or better imported cars from Japan (e.g., Honda and Toyota), the US government can help protect US industries by imposing tariffs and quotas on Japanese automobiles coming into the United States. These tariffs will make the retail cost of Japanese cars more expensive in the United States and thus reduce their competitive advantage. Quotas will restrict the number of Toyotas and Hondas that can be imported into the United States, thus preventing them from flooding the US market. For the United States, the main advantage of such restrictions is that it helps US manufacturers avoid declining sales and the possibility of having to lay off workers or declare bankruptcy. The main disadvantage is that, for American consumers, automobiles will be more expensive. The idea behind a customs union or free trade area is to eliminate tariffs and quotas affecting goods exchanged among participating countries so that products will be less expensive for consumers in those countries. Usually, it results in the less efficient producers going out of business because they lose government protection. But in theory at least, free trade among those countries should stimulate sales, production, and growth overall.

With the ECSC, the aim was to eliminate such trade barriers and thereby stimulate efficient production of coal and steel, which were backbones of the industrial economies of Europe. It was thought that increased efficiency in these areas could drive overall economic recovery and development. To facilitate this process, the coal and steel industries of the six member states were put under supranational control in an institution called the High Authority, with its headquarters in Luxembourg. The High Authority included representatives from each of the six countries, although decision making was partly by majority vote, which meant that some decisions could go against the interests of one or more countries; this was the supranational element of the ECSC. Besides supervising production, marketing, and prices, the High Authority also assisted weaker manufacturers in modernizing, readapting, or converting.

FROM COMMON MARKET TO EU

The ECSC was so successful in both economic and political terms that its achievements began to spill over, just as Jean Monnet had predicted, into broader areas and into more countries. Within a few years, "the Six" began discussing an expansion of the principles of the ECSC to the whole economy. In 1957, they signed the Treaty of Rome, creating the European Economic Community (EEC), which came to be known as the Common Market. The goal of the EEC was to eliminate tariffs among the six countries on all products, not just coal and steel, and to create a common external tariff for all products coming into the EEC from other countries. It also aimed at the free movement of capital and labor within the community and a harmonization of the social and economic policies of all six countries. A long-term goal was full economic and political integration. In support of the expanded activities and goals of the new organization, four new institutions were established: the Council of Ministers and the European Commission (with a permanent secretariat) located in Brussels; the European Court of Justice in Luxembourg; and the European Parliament in Strasbourg.[4] A European bureaucracy was being born, complete with "Eurocrats," and "Brussels" became shorthand for the institutions of this new Europe.

The EEC was also a roaring success, drawing the Six closer together, especially West Germany and France, and stimulating economic growth. West Germany, France, and Italy all experienced "economic miracles" in the 1950s and early 1960s, growing into solid middle-class welfare states. Their growth fueled development in the rest of the community. Trade among the six member countries grew twice as fast as trade with countries outside the zone. By 1968, the last internal tariffs were removed years ahead of schedule. The institutions of the ECSC, EEC, and Euratom (the European Atomic Energy Agency) were merged into the renamed European Community (EC) in 1967.

By this time, the success of the community was attracting interest from other countries besides the original six. At the beginning, Britain had refrained from joining for a number of reasons: its ties to colonies and former colonies in the British Commonwealth, its special relationship with the United States and its commitment to US-dominated NATO, and its reluctance to embrace the supranational elements of the European institutions. By the 1960s, though, the British government was reconsidering: EEC economic growth far exceeded that of the United Kingdom. London sought EEC membership twice in the 1960s, but both times the application was vetoed by the French president, Charles de Gaulle, who was wary of Britain's close ties to the United States and worried that Britain would try to dominate Europe. It was not until after de Gaulle left office that the United Kingdom finally entered the EC on its third try, in 1973, along with Denmark and Ireland.

In the 1980s, a tougher challenge for the EC arose with the application for membership by Greece, Spain, and Portugal, all countries that were considerably poorer than the existing members and ones with recent authoritarian pasts as well. As membership expanded from the core countries, the EC set both economic criteria, in terms of a free market economy, and political ones, including democratic politics and respect for human rights. After extended negotiations and preparations, though, these three countries joined as well. In 1995, three additional countries joined: Finland, Sweden, and Austria. These were all countries that had maintained a modicum, at least, of neutrality during the Cold War, and none of them were members of NATO. But they too wanted to climb onto the bandwagon of the expanding European Community. The original six were now fifteen countries with a combined population of 375 million.

As membership in the community was growing, so too were plans for even deeper integration of the member states. In an important symbolic step, the EC adopted a flag, twelve gold stars on a deep blue field. In 1986, with the Single Europe Act, they agreed to create a Europe without borders by 1992. At a pivotal meeting in the Dutch city of Maastricht in 1991, leaders of the twelve EC countries confirmed this direction, changing the name of the EC to the European Union, adopting the new Treaty of the European Union (also called the Maastricht Treaty), and committing themselves to common production standards, uniform tax rates, common EU citizenship, a common foreign and security policy, and a single European currency.

With the formal birth of the EU in 1993, the countries of Europe became ever more closely tied together. As individual countries moved to synchronize their economic and social policies, EU regulations began to supplement, supersede, and "harmonize" national legislation. In the early 1990s, for example, more laws affecting France were adopted by the community than by the French government itself. Britain, which did not have a formal, written constitution or bill of rights, simply incorporated the European Convention on Human Rights into English law. As well,

BOX 14.1
Beethoven's *Ode to Joy* and the European Union

In 1985, the European Council adopted Beethoven's stirring melody *Ode to Joy* as the anthem of the European Union (EU). The melody is from the last movement of Beethoven's Ninth Symphony (composed in 1823), which features four solo voices and a large chorus with the orchestra. Beethoven wrote the music for a 1785 poem, "To Joy" (*An die Freude*), by the German Friedrich Schiller. The poem expresses an idealistic vision of peace, harmony, and universal brotherhood, which Beethoven accentuates with his addition of the line "*alle Menschen werden Brüder*" (all men will become brothers). The EU actually adopted the music only, not the lyrics, as the anthem because of the many different languages of the EU, although the idea of common humanity is clearly understood. As the EU's official website puts it, "In the universal language of music, this anthem expresses the European ideals of freedom, peace, and solidarity."

policymakers and bureaucrats from Lisbon to Helsinki had to wrestle with matters as weighty as agricultural price supports or as minute as the obligatory dimensions of the European condom (the Italians apparently lobbied for smaller)[5] or whether British beer could be served in traditional pints rather than European liters. Somehow, this seems to have vindicated Jean Monnet: countries that bicker over beer and condoms are unlikely soon to engage in armed military conflict.

These developments obviously also involve a ceding of some national autonomy. The biggest challenge for the EU so far, and the one most laden with symbolism, was the introduction of a common European currency, the euro, in 2002. This was a contentious issue from the beginning. Many countries were unwilling to let go of currencies (like the French franc and the British pound) considered part of their national identities, and many governments were worried about losing control over their economies once they lost control over the value, volume, and flow of money. In the end, Britain, Sweden, and Denmark decided not to adopt the euro, but on January 1, 2002, the new currency was introduced in the other twelve countries. In a massive logistical operation, 14.5 billion banknotes and 50 billion coins were distributed across the Continent to some 300 million people. Despite prophecies of major snafus (e.g., could vending machines handle the new coins?) and economic chaos, the transition was remarkably smooth, and within a year the euro had completely replaced the lira, franc, mark, and peseta. Tourists no longer had to exchange money when traveling from one EU country to another, and banks and businesses did not have to worry about shifting exchange rates between their national currencies. By 2014, eighteen EU countries

The euro coin has a "common" side in all countries, showing a map of Europe and symbolizing the unity of the European Union. The reverse side shows country-specific designs, surrounded by the twelve stars of the European Union. The French euro coin has the motto "Liberté, Égalité, Fraternité," whereas the Italian shows the Vitruvian Man by Leonardo da Vinci.

were in the "**eurozone**," and euros were pervasive even in noneuro countries like England, causing yet another kind of spillover.

EXPANSION TO EASTERN EUROPE

This intensive "deepening" of the EU was accompanied by a renewed debate within the community about its "widening," with the emergence from communism of a dozen new democratic, market-oriented states in Eastern Europe. Virtually all the postcommunist European governments applied for membership in both NATO and the EU, seeing membership in these

The European Union

Western organizations as a source of security (primarily against Russia) and economic assistance, but also as a symbol of their return to Europe.

For existing EU members, the expansion posed a dilemma. Creating a Europe without borders, as the Maastricht Treaty called for, was difficult enough for fifteen countries, ranging from relatively poor countries like Portugal and Greece to prosperous ones like Germany and Sweden. The Eastern European candidate countries had standards of living less than half the EU average, and many of them were still wrestling with the establishment of democratic customs and institutions.[6] An expansion eastward was going to be costly for the EU, which provides "structural

A cartoon appearing in the Polish weekly Nie, *in 1992, celebrates Poland's "return" to Europe. Permission to reproduce granted by the artist, Andrzej Sejan.*

adjustment" funds for poorer countries and regions to bring them closer to the EU average. All of these Eastern European states would qualify for such support. In addition, with many new member states, changes would have to be made in the whole process of decision making and voting in the European Commission and other EU institutions.

Despite these potential problems, the existing fifteen EU members agreed to bring ten new countries into the organization in 2004, two more in 2007, and another in 2013: these were the three former Baltic republics of the USSR (Estonia, Latvia, and Lithuania); eight postcommunist Eastern European states (the Czech Republic, Slovakia, Hungary, Poland, Slovenia, Romania, Bulgaria, and Croatia); and the two island nations of Cyprus and Malta.

THE EUROPEAN SUPERPOWER?

The EU is a new kind of international alliance, aimed at employing "**soft power**" rather than military power to shape and influence the region. Facilitating this aim, it has become an economic powerhouse. The EU, now with twenty-eight member states, has a combined population of over five hundred million (only China and India are larger) and an economy bigger than that of the United States. This new "European Superpower" has become "the biggest and richest capitalist marketplace in the world."[7] The EU accounts for about a fifth of the world's **gross domestic product** (GDP) and contains about half of the industrial world's consumer population. It is also, by far, the world's biggest trading power and has become the world's biggest magnet and biggest source for investments.

Europe's economic heft is complemented by the world's best living standards and most developed system of social welfare. Many EU countries have less poverty, more equality, cheaper and better health care, and better-educated students than the United States. Most have much more generous unemployment assistance, parental leave programs, and child allowance benefits than does the United States. The various EU treaties provide the world's strongest guarantees of gender equity. The European system of social welfare has come to be known as the "European social model" and is a source of envy and imitation all over the world.

Indeed, Europe's size, economic strength, and social welfare have contributed to Europe's reemergence as an imposing force in the world economy and international politics. The titles of recent books show which way the wind is blowing: *The United States of Europe: The New Superpower and the End of American Supremacy* by journalist T. R. Reid; *The European Superpower* by political scientist John McCormick; and *The Next Superpower?* by former US ambassador to the EU Rockwell Schnabel. My own book, *The End of the American Century*, sees a united Europe, along with China, as two major contenders for global predominance following the decline of the United States. In 2012, the EU was awarded the Nobel Peace Prize for its contributions "over six decades . . . to the advancement of peace and reconciliation, democracy and human rights in Europe."

GROWING PAINS

To be sure, the expansion and development of the EU have entailed growing pains. At the same time that the union was expanding, it was trying to finalize a new constitution that would integrate new members and strengthen the supranational political institutions of the organization. But at the last moment, voters in France and Holland rejected the constitution, temporarily halting the integrationist trend. Some French and Dutch voters were worried about surrendering national sovereignty to the EU; others were concerned about potential negative impacts of expansion and globalization.

Most of the principles of the constitution were revived, however, in a less grandiose document called the Lisbon Treaty, which was finally approved by all member states in 2009. The treaty aimed to give the EU a stronger international role and to update the voting and decision-making procedures for its larger membership. It creates a full-time presidency and foreign minister, supported by a network of EU diplomats around the world. A new voting system reflects a country's population size, and the directly elected European Parliament is given more power. With expanded membership encompassing most of Europe, the Lisbon Treaty was yet another step on the path to a single, united Europe.

The initial defeat of the EU constitution highlighted the tension between the processes of "broadening" and "deepening" that bedeviled the organization. The expansion of membership to countries that were generally poorer and less experienced with both democracy and capitalism made it more difficult to harmonize policies across all twenty-eight member states. Most of the new members were not sufficiently prepared economically to adopt the euro.

The EU's policy of free movement of labor across borders was strained to the breaking point when hundreds of thousands of east Europeans flooded into wealthier EU countries seeking jobs. Immigration from one EU country to another increased by 10 percent a year from 2002 to 2006. When I visited Ireland in 2005, for example, almost all service workers we encountered—waiters in restaurants, clerks in stores, dockhands on ferries—were Polish, Czech, or Romanian rather than Irish. In 2006 alone, nearly three hundred thousand Poles migrated to other EU countries. This flood of immigrants helped fuel economic growth in the host countries but also caused ethnic tension and fanned anti-immigration sentiment in some countries.

Immigration from new EU countries into "old" ones came on top of a longer-term trend of immigration from the former European colonies into the "old" colonial states. Almost every country in Europe was becoming more ethnically heterogeneous, so issues of immigration, integration, and ethnicity were increasingly entering the political process. The most contentious of these involved the status of Muslims living in European countries. Their numbers were growing quickly all over Europe, but especially in France (whose former colonies in Africa were mostly Muslim), where Muslims now made up about 10 percent of the total population.

France's rigorously secular culture, dating from the time of the French Revolution, often runs up against public manifestations of religiosity. In 2004, the government banned the wearing of overtly religious garb or symbols in public schools, including the headscarf (or *hijab*) that many Muslim women wear. This caused a furor both in France and worldwide, which, however, effected no change in the policy. Indeed, six years later, the French cabinet voted a total ban on the Muslim full-face veil (the *niqab*) from public spaces. Subsequently, varying restrictions on Muslim veils were adopted in Belgium, Austria, Germany, and Bulgaria. "Identity politics" were pulling against the broader trends of globalization and integration in Europe, as elsewhere in the world.

The global economic and financial crisis beginning in 2008 put other strains on the EU, especially on the poorer countries of the south like Spain, Portugal, Italy, and, most critically, Greece. By 2010 Greece's national debt was more than four times that allowed by EU rules, and its budget and financial crisis threatened to destabilize Greece, disrupt the European economies, and undermine the euro. As the Greek government wrestled with its debts, it announced cuts in social services and government programs, sparking widespread and sometimes violent protests throughout the country. There was serious discussion within Greece about taking the country out of the eurozone, raising questions about just how a country could abandon the euro once it had been adopted—and the possible effects on the rest of Europe. British foreign secretary William Hague (a Eurosceptic) called the euro "a burning building with no exits." All the benefits of the eurozone also brought with them the prospect of recessionary contagion or worse from one country to another.

Indeed, Ireland, Portugal, Spain, and Italy were also experiencing serious budget and debt crises of their own. The EU response was decisive and muscular, with bailout packages for all four countries in 2010–11 and multiple bailouts for Greece totaling over 240 billion euros. In 2012 the EU established a new institution, the European Stability Mechanism, as a permanent bailout fund for beleaguered EU economies. As a condition for EU assistance, all the countries receiving assistance adopted budget cuts and other austerity measures, which, however, did little to alleviate the huge unemployment rates in most of these countries. At the height of the crisis, about a quarter of the population was jobless in both Greece and Spain.

Despite the continuing pain of recession and austerity, by 2014 the immediate crises seemed to have passed, in both Greece and the other countries. Debt levels were reduced somewhat, and most economies, including that of Greece, showed positive, albeit small, economic growth beginning that year. The euro was no longer in danger of disappearing. The EU responses, with the bailouts, were strikingly similar to the US government's rescue of its own collapsing financial sector in 2008–9. The financial crisis in Europe raised questions once again about the viability of an expanded and strengthened EU and a common currency. But the forceful response by the European Central Bank also showed the strength of the institutions of the EU, including the euro. Indeed, in 2015 Lithuania adopted the euro as its currency, which expanded the eurozone to nineteen countries.

BREAKING POINT? IMMIGRATION CRISIS AND BREXIT

The recovery from the economic crisis was shortly followed by two other stunning and wrenching developments: a massive flood of Arab refugees and the British decision to exit the EU. Both posed serious challenges to the viability of the organization.

The earlier acceleration of legal migration from within the EU (mostly from eastern to western Europe) was soon dwarfed by an even bigger influx of refugees and illegal immigrants from outside the union, especially from Arab and African countries. Most of them were Muslims. The crisis peaked in 2015 and 2016, with over a million asylum seekers arriving in the EU each year—twice as many as any previous year. The vast majority were from the war-torn countries of Syria, Afghanistan, and Iraq, and most were arriving by boats across the Mediterranean, landing in Greece and Italy. Most were processed by border officials as immigrants or asylum seekers, but hundreds of thousands entered illegally, often covertly. Because of the EU's "open borders" policy, it was relatively easy for many of them to make their way northward into Europe. The biggest destination was Germany.

This flood of immigrants posed multiple problems for the peoples and governments of the EU: economic, political, and moral. Processing, accommodating, and resettling these vast numbers of people was hugely expensive of course, and the burden fell especially heavily on Greece and Italy, already suffering their own economic crises. In 2015, the EU ministers attempted to spread the burden by voting to relocate some 160,000

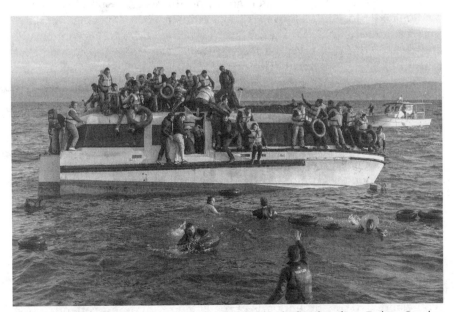

Syrian and Iraqi refugees arriving on the Greek island of Lesbos from Turkey, October 2015. Some one million refugees and migrants crossed the Aegean Sea to Greece in 2015. Courtesy of Ggia/CC-BY-SA-4.0.

refugees from Greece and Italy to other countries, through a system of quotas. But some countries refused to accept the transfers. The economic problem fed the political: economic decline in Europe after 2008 fueled anti-immigration sentiments all over the continent, often combined with nationalist and anti-EU feelings. And then the moral issue: how could prosperous Europe turn away these desperate refugees, often fleeing life-and-death situations? Furthermore, thousands of refugees were drowning in their attempts to cross the Mediterranean to Europe. This issue was brought home to millions with the photograph of a Syrian toddler, Alan Kurdi, dead on a Mediterranean beach.

In the midst of dealing with this crisis, the EU was suddenly faced with a stunning development at the other end of the continent: a vote by Britain to withdraw from the European Union. This idea, nicknamed **Brexit** (merging the words "Britain" and "exit") had been advanced for years by a relatively small political party in Britain, which had argued that the EU imposed too many rules on British businesses, inserted European-made laws on the British legal system, and cost London billions in subsidies to poorer EU countries. This was a nationalist and inward-looking response to the inter-nationalization and globalization represented by the EU, and never seemed to have that much support within the United Kingdom. But the advocates of Brexit were also worried about excessive immigration into the country, and the European immigration crisis inflamed those sentiments.

The government of Prime Minister David Cameron, which opposed Brexit, called for a popular referendum on the issue, assuming it would be defeated. Most polls showed a substantial majority favoring "remain." The result of the June 2016 referendum stunned almost everyone, inside and outside of Britain. With a large turnout, the "leave" vote won by a margin of 52 to 48 percent. The prime minister promptly resigned, succeeded by Theresa May, the former home secretary, who herself had opposed Brexit but pledged to carry out what the people had chosen. "Brexit means Brexit," she said.

The EU's Treaty of Lisbon (essentially the EU constitution) contained a provision (Article 50) for a two-year process for a member to exit the union, and London triggered this process in March 2017. It was not going to be easy, though. Britain had been a member since 1973, so there were forty-three years of treaties and agreements on thousands of subjects that needed renegotiating. The single market, completed in 1992, allowed free movement of goods, services, money, and people across the twenty-eight member states. All of that was now in limbo, affecting especially millions of UK citizens living on the continent and Europeans in the United Kingdom. Furthermore, while British citizens overall had narrowly approved Brexit, the referendum was soundly defeated in both Scotland and Northern Ireland, two constituent parts of the United Kingdom. Scotland at first

British newspapers reporting on the resignation of Prime Minister David Cameron after the Brexit vote in June 2015. iStock/lenscap67.

threatened to (somehow) stay in the EU, even if the United Kingdom left. And since the Republic of Ireland remained in the EU, that posed problems for the border between Northern Ireland (part of the United Kingdom) and the Republic (a sovereign state separate from the United Kingdom).

The Brexit vote, like the election of President Trump in the United States later in the year, signaled the discomfort many people felt about the challenges and disruptions caused by globalization and the growing permeability of national boundaries. Immigration, and terrifying incidents of terrorism, heightened these concerns. Increasing anxiety about national identity and threats to "European culture" fueled the rise of populist, nationalist, and antiestablishment political parties all over Europe, raising concerns about the future of the EU, and even of democratic institutions. But the roots of democracy in Europe were deep, and the web of cooperation wide, fortified by sixty years of experience.

WHAT IS EUROPE?

The collapse of the Berlin Wall, the reunification of Europe, and the expansion of the EU raised new questions about just what constitutes Europe. Is it defined only by geography (and if so, where?) or also by history, traditions, culture, or religion? These issues became concrete and highly political in the debate over expansion. For example, can Turkey really be considered part of Europe as an Islamic (though secular) state that is only partly in Europe and mostly in Asia Minor? And what about Russia? If

Poland, Bulgaria, and the Baltic republics can be part of the EU, could Russia too? Indeed, of the twenty-eight EU member states, none are Muslim and only four, Cyprus, Greece, Romania, and Bulgaria, are Orthodox Christian. The rest are all Western Christian, so is this the unifying element of the new Europe? The crisis in Ukraine in 2014, occasioned in part by Ukraine's differences with Russia over its orientation toward Europe, made this theoretical question very real, political, and violent. (This issue will be addressed in the following chapter.)

The issue of Europe's identity became part of the 2003–4 debate over a new EU constitution. The biggest controversy was over references to religion, reflecting a tension that dates all the way back to the Enlightenment. An early draft of the preamble referred to the Christian and Jewish heritage of European society, but countries with strict separation of church and state, such as France and Belgium, objected to this language, and it was later excluded. The drafters of the constitution had also suggested references to the legacy of Greco-Roman civilization and the Enlightenment. But some of the more religious countries, like Ireland, Spain, and Poland, objected to the secular implications of that. As the official Vatican newspaper, *L'Osservatore Romano*, proclaimed in a headline, "Either Europe is Christian or it is not Europe."[8]

In the end, references to both Christianity and to the Enlightenment were left out of the draft constitution and out of the Lisbon Treaty that replaced it. The Lisbon Treaty, implemented in 2009, instead refers to "the cultural, religious, and humanist inheritance of Europe" from which have developed "the universal values of the inviolable and inalienable rights of the human person, freedom, democracy, equality, and the rule of law." Although not directly mentioning the Enlightenment, this language and these principles trace back to that era and reflect the enduring legacy of the Enlightenment in European society. On these principles, at least, almost all Europeans could agree.

Although the issue of religious identity was finally skirted in the treaties, it promised to be one of the more divisive issues in the new, united Europe, just as it had been a source of conflict and division in the eighteenth

---

BOX 14.2
The Values of the European Union

"The Union is founded on the values of respect for human dignity, freedom, democracy, equality, the rule of law and respect for human rights, including the rights of persons belonging to minorities. These values are common to the Member States in a society in which pluralism, non-discrimination, tolerance, justice, solidarity and equality between women and men prevail."

—Article 2 of the Lisbon Treaty (2009)

century. Enlightenment ideas of rationalism, secularism, and human rights had come to dominate Western Europe more so than any other place on the planet. Although a majority of people in most European countries believe in God, only one in five says religion is "very important" to him or her, and only small minorities of the European populations regularly attend religious services. In France, which is predominantly Catholic but very secular, only one in twenty people attends a religious service every week, compared to about one in three in the United States.[9] This has caused some tension among EU members and also between Europe and the United States. Some of the new Eastern European members of the EU, especially overwhelmingly Catholic ones like Poland and Lithuania, are discomfited by the fervent secularism of Western Europe, as demonstrated in the debate over the EU constitution. This has caused problems in trying to harmonize social policies across the twenty-eight members of the community, especially on religiously sensitive issues like divorce, euthanasia, and abortion. The widening of Europe has reopened these issues that have mostly been settled in the western part of the Continent.

Religion has also sharpened the divide between Europe and the United States. As noted above, Europeans in both the east and west are far more secularized than Americans, and religion plays a much stronger role in political life in the United States than it does in Europe. From the European point of view, Americans are more likely to think in terms of good and evil or right and wrong, which many Europeans see as reckless and dangerous. After the terrorist attacks of September 11, 2001, most European citizens and leaders alike were uncomfortable when US president George W. Bush so frequently invoked morality and religion in talking about the war on terrorism. His decision to attack Iraq in 2003 seemed more a matter of missionary zeal than hard evidence of weapons of mass destruction or Iraqi links to terrorism. Thus, European members of the United Nations Security Council, especially Germany and France, were reluctant to endorse the war, leading to the chilliest relations between the United States and Europe in a century. Bush's secretary of defense, Donald Rumsfeld, brushed aside these objections from what he called "old Europe" and implied that the future lay with the new democracies of Eastern Europe. This snub was not received well in Berlin and Paris.

The tensions between the United States and Europe reflected a growing independence and assertiveness on the part of the European countries and a certain measure of the success of the European project. In the dispute about the Iraq war, Germany and France were allies against the United States rather than adversaries of each other as they had been in World War II. The ECSC, the EEC, and the EU had brought these two countries together, as well as much of the rest of Europe, not only in a web of economic exchange but in a community of shared values that included democracy, market economics, social welfare, human rights, and peace.

Conclusion

Europe in the Twenty-First Century

In the two centuries following the French Revolution, Europe was transformed from a factionalized collection of feudal, hierarchical, Christian
monarchies into an affluent community of peaceful, democratic, secular,
and capitalist states. Along the way, these changes were shaped by up-
heavals of revolution and war. The Enlightenment and the French Revolution of 1789 first raised ideas of individualism, human rights, and popular
sovereignty. The Napoleonic Wars and the People's Spring of 1848 spread
these notions across Europe, planting the seeds of liberalism and nationalism. The Industrial Revolution, based on the emergent principles of capitalism, brought expanded prosperity but also new forms of exploitation
and inequality. Marxism was a reaction to the excesses of capitalism and
led in two directions: toward socialism and social democracy in much of
Western Europe, and toward communist revolution in Russia. The Darwinian revolution transformed both science and religion and changed the
way we think about human beings and their place on the planet.

By 1900, then, most of the ideas and movements that have shaped
contemporary Europe were in place. But so many radical changes in the
nineteenth century had unleashed forces that could not be contained in
the old system. Nationalism was shaking the foundations of the European
empires at the same time that it was forging powerful new states like Germany. These forces erupted in the cataclysm of the two world wars, with
the first leading almost inexorably to the second. These wars were different from any that had gone before, with new military technologies and
mass armies causing unprecedented death and destruction. For the first
time in warfare, civilians became deliberate, even primary, targets, with

massive aerial bombardments of London, Berlin, Tokyo, and Hiroshima. During the war and before, totalitarian dictatorships in Russia, Germany, and Italy brought misery and terror even to their own populations.

The world wars also brought two new players into the game of European politics: the United States and the Soviet Union. The conflicting interests and ideologies of these two powers were muted in the years between the two world wars, as the United States retreated into isolation and the new communist state wrestled with war, civil war, collectivization, and famine. With the defeat and occupation of Germany at the end of World War II, though, these two states emerged as global superpowers and dominating forces in Europe. At the same time, the major European powers were recovering from wartime devastation and shedding their empires.

The Cold War began in Europe, and it divided Europe for the next half century. Eastern Europe became more integrated under the hegemony of the Soviet Union, and Western Europe moved toward economic and political union, but the two halves of the continent moved apart from each other, separated by Churchill's "Iron Curtain." The next great revolutions, the peaceful ones of 1989–91, brought an end to communism in Europe, to the Cold War, and to the division of Europe. Under the banner of the expanding European Union (EU), Europe finally had the chance to be united, free, prosperous, and at peace.

To be sure, Europe continued to be faced with conflicting tendencies toward integration and fragmentation, toward globalism on the one hand and ethnic separatism on the other. As we've seen, while the European community steadily grew in numbers and powers, many people were uncomfortable with the growing influence of the EU, the restrictions on national sovereignty, and the threats and disruptions caused by immigration and open borders. The immigration crisis of 2015 and a spate of shocking terrorist attacks after 2014, in the United Kingdom, France, Belgium, Germany, and Spain, intensified those concerns. The 2016 "Brexit" vote was a striking manifestation of them.

Furthermore, at the same time that Europe was becoming bigger and more heterogeneous, there were places in the continent where peoples were pulling away from national states in favor of smaller and more homogeneous ones. In Great Britain, sentiment for Scottish independence led the British Parliament to approve a referendum on that issue in Scotland, which had been part of Britain for more than three hundred years. Polls leading up to the September 2014 referendum in Scotland showed it to be a very close call, but the breakup of the United Kingdom was averted with a vote of 55 percent against independence. The 2016 Brexit vote, which most Scots opposed, led to calls for a second referendum on independence, including (initially) by the first minister of Scotland, Nicola Sturgeon.

Spain faced a similar separatist challenge from Catalonia, a province in the northeast corner of the country with Barcelona as its capital, and its own language (Catalan). A separatist movement there gained strength steadily and in 2017, the region's government scheduled a popular referendum on independence from Spain, even though the national government in Madrid declared the vote unconstitutional and illegal. In the vote on October 1, over 90 percent voted in favor of independence, and a few weeks later, the Catalan Parliament declared independence from Spain. The prime minister of Spain, Mariano Rajoy, promptly fired the Catalan president and his cabinet, dissolved the Catalan Parliament, and scheduled new elections in the region for December. The Catalan president, Carles Puigdemont, fled the country, seeking refuge in Brussels, the capital of the EU, which he hoped would be sympathetic to his cause. But the European Commission issued a statement declaring the independence referendum illegal. In the December elections, the secessionists won again, leaving the situation even more chaotic and unsettled, and demonstrating anew the strength of "identity politics" in contemporary Europe.

RUSSIA'S PLACE IN EUROPE AND THE CRISIS IN UKRAINE

Despite all these challenges, the "unification" of Europe after World War II was an amazing accomplishment, as was the emergence of the EU as a global political and economic power. A united and stable Europe, though, raised new questions about the status and role of both Russia and the United States. Russia's place in Europe had always been somewhat conflicted and ambivalent, within the country and outside it. In the nineteenth century, as we saw in chapter 10, the debate between "Westernizers" and "Slavophiles" was a major source of intellectual and political ferment. This ambivalence has haunted Russia ever since. On the one hand, Russia historically had claimed to be the Third Rome, had played a major role in the Concert of Europe and the defeat of Napoleon, and had been a deciding factor in the beginning of World War I and the ending of World War II. In the 1980s, Soviet leader Gorbachev called for "a common European home . . . from the Atlantic to the Urals." In 2003 Russian President Putin asserted that "by their mentality and culture, the people of Russia are Europeans."[1]

On the other hand, Russia was always somewhat apart from Europe both geographically and culturally, and with the communist revolution of 1917, the country deliberately distanced itself from the "bourgeois West." After the collapse of communism in the 1990s, Russia under Presidents Boris Yeltsin and Vladimir Putin remained wary of the eastward march of the North Atlantic Treaty Organization (NATO) and the EU. Russia's commitment to democratic politics and market economics seemed far less certain than in western Europe, or even in the other postcommunist states. It was clear that the eastern European countries' enthusiasm to join NATO and the EU was partly as protection against Russia. So in many respects, Europe seemed to be edging away from Russia.

This whole issue was exhibited with the explosive events in Ukraine in 2014. In that country, a popular insurrection ousted a pro-Russian Ukrainian president, and Russia, in response, annexed Crimea, which was part of Ukraine. Ukraine is right along the fault line between Europe and Russia ("Ukraine" literally means "on the border"), so it epitomizes the difficulties of defining and resolving just how far "Europe" extends to the east.

Ukraine had been one of the constituent republics of the Soviet Union before the latter's dissolution at the end of 1991. The Ukrainian language and culture are close cousins of Russian, but they remain distinct, and Ukrainians have had a strong sense of ethnic and national identity for centuries. Ukrainians constituted about three-quarters of the population of Ukraine, but Russians were a strong minority, making up almost 40 percent of the eastern regions along the border with Russia and well over half of the population in the Crimean Peninsula. Crimea itself had been part of both the Russian Empire and the Russian Republic of the Soviet Union and contained an important Soviet naval base on the Black Sea at Sevastopol. In an odd geopolitical maneuver in 1954, the Soviet leadership transferred Crimea from the Russian Republic to the Ukrainian Republic, though at the time this hardly seemed significant since both were part of the Soviet Union (the USSR).

After independence in 1991, Ukraine, like many of the former republics of the Soviet Union, began seeking closer ties to the West, including both NATO and the EU. In an agreement signed by both Russia and the United States (the Budapest Memorandum), Ukraine gave up its nuclear weapons in exchange for guarantees of its security and territorial integrity. When Victor Yanukovych was elected president of Ukraine in 2010, though, he terminated negotiations toward NATO membership and at the end of 2013 pulled out of an association agreement with the EU in favor of loans and other concessions from Russia. This decision sparked huge protest demonstrations in Kiev, the capital, and elsewhere, and the killing by the police of at least a hundred protesters. Yanukovych fled Kiev, and the Ukrainian Parliament promptly deposed him and formed a new government that was quickly recognized by the United States and the EU but declared illegal by Moscow. Within a few days, Russian forces began taking over Crimea, and in March 2014 it was formally annexed into the Russian Federation. The United States, the EU, and the

United Nations all vigorously objected to this action, and none of them have recognized Russia's claim to Crimea.

Soon thereafter, pro-Russian rebels fanned out across two provinces in eastern Ukraine, seizing public buildings, ousting local officials, and blockading highways. Ukrainian president Petro Poroshenko sent troops to the region to try to end the rebellion, but Putin's Russia reciprocated by supplying manpower, funding, and material to the separatist rebels. Despite numerous cease-fires, the fighting in Ukraine persisted, claiming at least ten thousand lives by 2017, and forcing some 1.5 million from their homes.

This whole conflict—the most violent and fearsome in Europe since the 1990s civil war in Yugoslavia—illustrates many of the themes raised in this book: the tension between nationalism and globalism; the two-sided tendency of nationalism to both unite and divide; and the question of the geographic extent and identity of "Europe." The crisis in Ukraine was sparked precisely because Ukrainians wanted to move closer to Europe, and Russia objected to that. Perhaps this crisis has settled the issue, though, of whether Russia is part of Europe or not. In the spring of 2014, in the midst of the conflict in eastern Ukraine, Russian president Putin directed a committee to develop a new "state policy in culture" which would emphasize that "Russia is not Europe."[2]

EUROPE'S EVOLVING RELATIONSHIP WITH THE UNITED STATES

At the same time as Europe's ties with Russia were growing more strained, Europe's relationship with the United States was becoming more ambivalent, too. The United States, like Russia, has a checkered history of relations with Europe. Although enormous cultural, religious, economic, and political influences crisscrossed the Atlantic, the United States maintained its isolationist distance from Europe up until World War I. But during the twentieth century, the United States played a decisive role in Europe, twice intervening to end world wars, rebuilding Western Europe after World War II, and intervening militarily in the Balkans in the 1990s. Even during the postwar North Atlantic alliance, though, some tensions existed between the United States and Europe, with the French in particular resenting US political, economic, and cultural hegemony on the continent.

The end of the Cold War brought a new configuration of power in world politics and in Europe. The United States was now the sole superpower, and with this came a certain triumphalism in the United States and a tendency toward arrogance and unilateralism. The United States backed away from several international treaties considered important by the Europeans (like the Kyoto Protocol on carbon emissions and the International Criminal Court). The terrorist attacks of September 11, 2001, brought widespread sympathy for the United States from Europe, but the Bush administration lost most of that support two years later by ignoring the United Nations and brushing aside French, German, and Russian objections in its decision to make war against Iraq. Massive protest demonstrations against the war in almost every European capital even threatened to bring down governments (like those in Britain and Spain) that had supported the US war. A few months after the war began, a survey of people in the fifteen EU countries revealed that over half of them believed the United States constituted a threat to world peace.[3] It seemed that Europe was also growing apart somewhat from the United States.

The election of Barack Obama as US president sparked an immediate upturn in European views of the United States and in US-European relations, due to Obama's more internationalist and conciliatory approach to other countries. However, the advent of the Obama administration coincided with a collapse in the US financial sector and the worst economic downturn since the Great Depression. America's global reputation, already battered by the war in Iraq, suffered further and seemed to open the way for the emergence of new global powers, among them China and the EU.

The US reputation and influence in Europe was battered with the advent to the US presidency of Donald Trump. Trump belittled both NATO and the EU, threatened to walk away from the Iran nuclear deal (which had been negotiated with EU support), and pulled the United States out of the historic 2015 Paris Agreement on climate change, which was considered an urgent priority by European citizens and governments alike. (The United States is now the only country in the world that is not part of the Agreement.) He frequently mocked European leaders and their countries. His words and actions were not received well in Europe. Global opinion surveys in 2017 showed a precipitous decline in positive views of the new US president, and of the United States itself, with especially sharp drops among Europeans.[4] President Trump's nationalist and unilateralist rhetoric and actions led some European leaders to call for a distancing from the United States and a more independent and assertive foreign policy of their own. German chancellor Angela Merkel called for Germans to be ready to "fight for our future on our own, for our destiny as Europeans."[5]

In some ways, Trump may have been pushing Europe in a direction in which it was already heading. In a world in which "soft power" was becoming more important than hard military power, the EU had the world's biggest economy and was, by far, the world's biggest trading power. It was a global economic powerhouse. It increasingly seemed willing to assume some of the power and authority that usually accompanies economic strength.

The distancing of Europe from both Russia and the United States was a function of both the decline of those Cold War superpowers and the increasing strength and confidence of Europe. Western Europe had weaned itself from the predominant influence of the United States, eastern Europe had thrown off Soviet domination, and together they were demonstrating their autonomy and self-sufficiency. For much of the modern era, the peoples of Europe had been oppressed by kings or tyrants, devastated by wars or revolutions, or dominated by outside powers. For the first time in their history, they had the liberty presaged by the French Revolution, the equality offered by socialism, and the solidarity promised by a united Europe.

Glossary

absolute monarchy. A monarchy with unrestrained power, as in most of Europe in the eighteenth and nineteenth centuries.

ancien régime. The old regime political and social system in France before the French Revolution of 1789, characterized by an absolute monarchy, mercantilism, and a rigid and hierarchical social structure.

apartheid. The policy of racial segregation practiced by the government of South Africa before black majority-rule government was achieved in 1994.

autocracy. A system of government by one person with absolute power. This can take many forms, including absolute monarchy, dictatorship, and totalitarianism.

Balkans. The Balkan peninsula in southeastern Europe comprising Albania, Bulgaria, Greece, Romania, and parts of former Yugoslavia.

Berlin airlift. The yearlong airlift of supplies by the United States to West Berlin, begun in 1948 after the Soviet Union blocked access to West Berlin from Western Germany; a key element in the beginning of the Cold War.

Berlin Wall. A wall built in 1961 by the Soviet Union dividing Soviet-controlled East Berlin from Western-controlled West Berlin, to prohibit Easterners from fleeing to the West through West Berlin. Dismantled in November 1989.

blitzkrieg. German phrase for "lightning war," meaning to overwhelm the enemy quickly; used by Hitler's troops at the beginning of World War II.

Bolsheviks. The faction of the Russian Social Democratic Labor Party, led by Vladimir Lenin, that seized power in the 1917 revolution and became the Communist Party of the Soviet Union.

bourgeoisie. French word for "town-dweller" used by Marx to describe the middle classes in capitalist society.

Brexit. An abbreviation for "British exit" referring to the decision of the United Kingdom to leave the European Union after the 2016 referendum.

Brezhnev Doctrine. A policy enunciated by Soviet Communist Party leader Leonid Brezhnev that justified Soviet military intervention in neighboring socialist states (e.g., Czechoslovakia in 1968) that had strayed too far from the Soviet model.

cahiers de doléances. The list of grievances drawn up by voters in the elections to the Estates General in France in 1789; politicized the population at the beginning of the Revolution.

Charter 77. The document signed in 1977 by a group of Czechoslovak intellectuals (including Václav Havel) that called on the government to respect human rights guaranteed in the Helsinki Agreements. Came to refer to the human rights movement in that country.

civic nationalism. Nationalism promoted "from above" by leaders like Bismarck and Cavour, as distinguished from popular nationalism initiated "from below."

class consciousness. A term Karl Marx used to describe the development of a revolutionary frame of mind among workers (the proletariat) in capitalist societies.

CMEA. *See* Council for Mutual Economic Assistance.

Cold War. The term used to describe the warlike state of tension between the Soviet Union and the United States from the end of World War II until the collapse of communism in 1989–91.

collective security. The organizing principle behind the League of Nations and the United Nations, which held that aggression against one country would be treated as aggression against all countries and therefore should be resisted by the common action of all.

collectivization of agriculture. The forcible merger of individual peasant farms into collective farms in communist countries, first begun by Soviet party leader Stalin in 1929.

colonialism. The practice of one country extending control over another by establishing a colony and sending settlers there.

Comecon. *See* Council for Mutual Economic Assistance.

Common Market. An area free of barriers to trade (such as tariffs or quotas); term used to describe the early versions of the European Union.

communism. A political theory advocating a society in which all property is publicly owned, social classes and the state disappear, and everyone receives his or her basic needs; elaborated by Karl Marx in *The Communist Manifesto* and pursued by Lenin and the Communist Party in the Soviet Union.

Communist Manifesto, The. An 1848 pamphlet written by Marx and Engels calling for the overthrow of capitalism and the establishment of communism.

Concert of Europe. The alliance of European monarchies after 1815, designed to prevent or crush any threat to their conservative regimes. Inspired and led by Austrian prince Clemens von Metternich.

constitutional monarchy. A monarchy that is limited in its powers by a written or unwritten constitution, as distinguished from an absolute monarchy.

Council for Mutual Economic Assistance (CMEA or Comecon). An organization created by Moscow in 1949 to coordinate trade and integrate the economies of the Eastern European communist states. Dissolved in 1991.

coup d'état. A violent or illegal seizure of power, effecting a change in government.

Das Kapital. Meaning "capital" (or money), the title of the major work of Karl Marx in which he described his theory of history and the revolutionary overthrow of capitalism. First volume published in 1867.

decolonization. The process by which the colonies of the European empires gained their political independence, occurring mostly in the twentieth century and especially after World War II.

despotism. A form of government led by a tyrant, despot, or absolute ruler.

dialectic. An element of Marxist theory, borrowed and adapted from the philosopher G. W. F. Hegel, that holds that each stage of history both paves the way for the next stage and sows the seeds of its own destruction.

divine right. The doctrine that rulers derive their right to govern from God; claimed by many European monarchs in the seventeenth through nineteenth centuries.

dual monarchy. Created by the *Ausgleich* (compromise) of 1867, a constitutional union of Austria and Hungary under the common crown of the Habsburgs, lasting until 1918.

Eastern Europe. In this text, the term refers to the communist European states outside of the Soviet Union during the Cold War—East Germany, Poland, Czechoslovakia, Hungary, Romania, Bulgaria, Albania, and Yugoslavia—and their postcommunist successor states.

economic determinism. Marx's theory that all aspects of a society (e.g., politics, religion, social structure) are determined by the economic basis of that society.

ECSC. *See* European Coal and Steel Community.

EEC. *See* European Economic Community.

enclosure movement. In British history, the practice of fencing off into private property land formerly considered community property. Reached its peak in the seventeenth century and led to the migration of the poor from the countryside to towns.

Enlightenment. The eighteenth-century philosophy and trend that emphasized reason, individualism, and human rights as opposed to tradition. Found expression in people such as Rousseau, Kant, and Thomas Paine and in the American and French Revolutions.

EU. *See* European Union.

eugenics. The study of methods to improve the human race through control of mating and heredity by society, often by discouraging propagation by those deemed inferior or unfit.

euro. The common currency used by eighteen of the twenty-eight members of the European Union.

European Coal and Steel Community (ECSC). A common market in coal and steel established by France, Germany, Italy, Belgium, Holland, and Luxembourg in 1951; a forerunner of the EEC and the European Union.

European Economic Community (EEC). A successor to the ECSC established in 1957 to establish a complete common market among its member states; a predecessor of the European Union.

European Union (EU). Known as the European Community (EC) until 1994, an intergovernmental organization promoting economic union among its member states, numbering twenty-eight in 2014.

eurozone. An economic and monetary union of the EU member states that have adopted the euro as their common currency.

evolution theory. The theory developed in the nineteenth century by Charles Darwin that animal and plant species developed by gradual, continuous change from earlier forms through a process of natural selection.

fascism. A totalitarian ideology that looks to a strong dictator, reveres the nation or state, and emphasizes order, militarism, and sometimes racism. It was the system developed by Mussolini in Italy in the 1920s but is also a term used to describe other extreme right-wing, nationalist, and authoritarian movements and regimes, like those of Hitler's Germany and Franco's Spain.

feudalism. The social and economic system in medieval Europe (persisting in some places into the nineteenth century), where a vassal (e.g., a serf) held land from a superior (e.g., the lord of the manor) in exchange for allegiance and service.

First World. A term used after World War II to describe the most developed countries in the world, mostly in Western Europe and North

America, as distinguished from the communist Second World and developing Third World countries.

five-year plan. In the Soviet Union, government-controlled economic plans first implemented by Stalin in 1929, with the aim of rapid industrialization.

Fourteen Points. The World War I peace proposal of US president Woodrow Wilson in 1918; included appeals for self-determination of nations and the creation of a League of Nations.

functionalism. The idea that international cooperation and peace can best be achieved through gradual expansion of economic and social cooperation among countries rather than through political venues. A principal idea behind the formation of the Common Market in Europe after World War II.

glasnost. The Russian word for openness or publicity, one of the elements of Gorbachev's reform program in the Soviet Union after 1987, which reduced restrictions on the media.

Great Purge. In the Soviet Union between 1934 and 1938, a repressive wave of terror that Stalin used to eliminate opposition and help establish his own unchallenged leadership.

gross domestic product (GDP). The total value of goods and services produced by a country in a given time period (usually a year). A standard measure of the size of a country's economy.

Helsinki Accords (or Agreements). A diplomatic treaty signed by thirty-five nations in Helsinki, Finland, in 1975, which obliged all signatory states to promote human rights. Became a basis for challenges to restrictions on those rights in the Soviet Union and Eastern Europe.

historical materialism. A part of Marxist theory holding that each stage of the historical development of a society is based on economic factors, particularly the means of production.

Holy Alliance. Formed in 1815 and inspired by Russian tsar Alexander I, an agreement among Russia, Austria, and Prussia to maintain and protect the Christian monarchies of Europe. Most European monarchs adhered to the alliance, which lasted until 1848. *See also* Concert of Europe.

ideology. The system of ideas at the basis of an economic or political theory, for example, communism.

imperialism. The policy of a state to acquire dependent territories or extend a country's influence over other states. European imperialism reached its pinnacle in the mid-nineteenth century.

irredentism. A policy advocating the acquisition of some region included in another country, usually based on ethnicity or historical claims.

isolationism. A policy of the United States up until the early twentieth century to avoid political or military entanglements with the world community, especially Europe. This policy was decisively ended with US involvement in Europe after World War II.

laissez-faire. From the French, meaning "let do," the doctrine that an economy functions best without government interference. In the eighteenth century, Adam Smith developed this principle, a core element of capitalism.

League of Nations. An international organization formed after World War I to promote peaceful settlement of international disputes through collective security; a predecessor to the United Nations.

Leninism. Modifications of Marxist theory by the Russian revolutionary Vladimir Lenin in the early twentieth century, emphasizing the role of the "vanguard of the party" (the Bolsheviks) in stimulating a revolution in Russia, even though it was not yet an advanced capitalist society.

liberalism. A set of ideas in the mid-nineteenth century, promoted especially by the educated middle class, favoring Enlightenment ideas of progress, individual rights, voting rights, and constitutionalism.

mandates system. The arrangement whereby the colonial territories of the defeated states in World War I (e.g., Germany and Turkey) were placed by the League of Nations under the guardianship of Allied nations.

Marshall Plan. A large-scale US aid program to Western Europe from 1947 to 1952 to help rebuild the economies shattered by World War II.

Marxism. The body of economic, political, and social theories developed by Karl Marx and Friedrich Engels in the nineteenth century that included a "scientific" philosophy of history, a critique of capitalism, and a prediction of the revolutionary overthrow of capitalism and its replacement with communism.

mercantilism. An important economic policy in Western Europe from about 1500 until the Industrial Revolution and the advent of *laissez-faire* ideas. Mercantilists held that a nation's wealth and power could best be enhanced by the accumulation of precious metals like silver and gold. Countries that did not have such metals had to rely on government-managed trade to acquire them.

monarchy. A form of government with a monarch (such as a king, queen, or emperor) at its head; characteristic of most European governments before 1789 and of many through the nineteenth century.

nation. A group of people with a common culture, sense of identity, and political aspirations. Usually they have their own state (forming a nation-state), but not always.

nationalism. A political and social philosophy in which the good of the nation is paramount. In the nineteenth century, this was a powerful force in forging nation-states, but it can also be a source of ethnocentrism or militarism, as in Nazi Germany.

national self-determination. The doctrine that postulates the right of a nation to have its own state and to choose its own form of government.

National Socialist German Workers' Party. The Nazi Party of Adolf Hitler.

nation-state. A state (with a government) that is made up largely of one nation.

NATO. *See* North Atlantic Treaty Organization.

natural selection. A key element in Darwin's theory of evolution, which holds that plants or animals within a species with the most useful characteristics would tend to survive and pass on those characteristics to succeeding generations.

Nazi Party. *See* National Socialist German Workers' Party.

nihilist. An adherent of nihilism (from the Latin, meaning "nothing"), a doctrine that rejects all existing moral principles and social, economic, and political institutions. The term was coined by the Russian writer Ivan Turgenev to describe nineteenth-century Russian revolutionaries who called for the destruction of all existing institutions.

Non-Aligned Movement. An organization of countries not formally aligned with or against any major power bloc, formed in 1961 as a reaction against the Cold War, and now including about 120 members.

North Atlantic Treaty Organization (NATO). A regional mutual defense alliance formed by the United States in 1949 to block the threat of Soviet military aggression in Europe. Its membership expanded and its mission changed after the collapse of communism in 1989–91.

old regime. See *ancien régime.*

Ottoman Empire. Formed from the fourteenth to sixteenth centuries by the Ottoman Turks, it reached its height in the sixteenth century and began a slow decline after that, finally collapsing in defeat after World War I. In the nineteenth century, it included Asia Minor and much of the Balkan peninsula of Europe.

Partitions of Poland. In the late eighteenth century, Poland was dismembered and absorbed by its three neighboring empires—Russia, Prussia, and Austria—and disappeared from the map until the country was restored after World War I.

perestroika. The Russian word for economic restructuring, which was the cornerstone of Gorbachev's program of reform in the Soviet Union in the late 1980s.

philosophes. The French word for the French Enlightenment thinkers and social critics of the late eighteenth century.

popular nationalism. Nationalism promoted "from below" by the masses, as opposed to civic nationalism promoted by political leaders.

populists. *Narodniki* in Russian; a nineteenth-century socialist movement of mostly intellectuals, who sought to transform society by basing it on the traditional peasant commune (*mir*).

Prague Spring. The 1968 communist reform movement in Czechoslovakia that tried to create "socialism with a human face" but was crushed by Soviet military intervention in August of that year.

proletariat. The term used in Marxist theory to describe the working class, which would eventually lead a revolution to overthrow the capitalist order.

protectorate. A state that is controlled or protected by another. Britain established protectorates over Egypt and Afghanistan in the 1880s.

Quadruple Alliance. Established in 1815 by Russia, Austria, Britain, and Prussia to preserve the status quo after the defeat of Napoleon, it came to be dominated by the spirit of the Holy Alliance.

quotas. In international trade, a fixed limit on imports of particular products from other countries, a form of protectionism (along with tariffs) that was largely eliminated among member states of the European Union.

Risorgimento. Meaning "resurgence" in Italian, the nineteenth-century nationalist movement for the unification of Italy led by such figures as Mazzini, Cavour, and Garibaldi.

Romanticism. A movement in the arts, especially in the nineteenth century, which favored a return to nature, exaltation of emotion and the senses over the intellect, and a revolt against eighteenth-century rationalism.

Scramble for Africa. The rapid, competitive colonization of Africa by the European powers at the end of the nineteenth century.

Second World. A synonym for the communist states during the Cold War, including especially the Soviet Union and Eastern Europe.

separatism. A form of nationalism in which a national or ethnic group wishes to separate from a larger state or empire to form its own nation-state.

Slav. A member of a group of people in central or eastern Europe speaking Slavonic languages, such as the Russians, Poles, and Serbs.

Slavophiles. A group in nineteenth-century Russia that saw Russia's greatness as springing from traditional institutions like the Orthodox Church or the village commune (*mir*) and therefore opposed the Westernization of Russia.

social contract. An Enlightenment-era philosophy, developed by Locke, Rousseau, and others, that contended that people escape from the state of nature by forming a contract to create a government, which is then responsible for the protection of those people. A core principle of democratic theory.

social Darwinism. The false application of Darwin's theory of biological evolution to the political, social, and economic realms, often used to justify the superior position of dominant countries, groups, or races. Herbert Spencer was the prime exponent of social Darwinism.

socialism. A theory that advocates popular or government ownership or regulation of the economy with the principal aims of providing basic human needs and reducing social and economic inequality.

socialist internationalism. Part of the foreign policy of the Soviet Union that subordinated national interests to international socialist ones; used to justify Soviet intervention in Eastern Europe (i.e., with the Brezhnev Doctrine).

soft power. A concept developed by the political scientist Joseph Nye to describe the ability of a country to do what it wants, and to influence other countries, without using force or coercion, usually arising from the attractiveness of the country's culture, political ideals, and policies.

Solidarity. The Polish social movement and trade union that emerged in 1980 to challenge communist rule, was crushed by martial law in 1981, and reemerged to win national elections in 1989.

Soviet bloc. The alliance of communist states in Eastern Europe during the Cold War dominated by the Soviet Union.

Soviet Union. The shorthand name for the Union of Soviet Socialist Republics (see below).

state. An organized political entity that occupies a definite territory and has a government that possesses sovereignty.

suffrage. The right to vote in political elections.

supranational. Organizations or processes that are "above" the traditional state or transcend it, as with some elements of the European Union.

tariff. In international trade, a form of economic protectionism in which a country attaches taxes to imports, thus reducing their competitive advantage with domestic products; mostly eliminated among the countries of the European Union.

Third Reich. Meaning in German the third realm or empire, the name used by Nazi propagandists to describe Hitler's regime in Germany (1933–45) following the First Reich of the Holy Roman Empire and the Second Reich of the German Empire of 1871.

Third World. A term developed during the Cold War to describe the developing countries of the non-Western world, mostly in Africa, Asia, and Latin America.

totalitarianism. A political system where the state recognizes no limits to its authority and attempts to regulate every aspect of public and private life. The term most frequently refers to the regimes of Joseph Stalin in the Soviet Union, Adolf Hitler in Germany, and Benito Mussolini in Italy.

Triple Alliance. An alliance from the 1880s until World War I between Austria-Hungary, Germany, and Italy (also called the Central Powers). At the beginning of the war, Italy left the alliance and joined the Allies.

Triple Entente. The loose alliance between Britain, France, and Russia from 1907, becoming a formal alliance at the beginning of World War I in 1914 (also called the Allied Powers).

Truman Doctrine. Based on a speech by US president Harry Truman in 1947, a pledge by the United States to support "free people who are resisting attempted subjugation"; the doctrine became a basis for the US policy of the containment of communism.

tsar. The Russian title (from the Latin *Caesar*) for the emperors of Russia (sometimes appears as *czar* or *tzar*).

Union of Soviet Socialist Republics (USSR). The formal name of the Communist Party state formed in Russia in 1922 and lasting until its breakup in 1991. Russia was the largest of the fifteen republics of the union.

USSR. *See* Union of Soviet Socialist Republics.

Velvet Revolution. The peaceful, popular revolution of 1989 in Czechoslovakia that led to the resignation of the communist government and the establishment of a democratic state under the presidency of Václav Havel.

Warsaw Pact. The Warsaw Treaty Organization, the Cold War military alliance of communist states in Eastern Europe, dominated by the Soviet Union; established in 1955 and dissolved in 1991.

Weimar Republic. The democratic government established in Germany after World War I and lasting until Hitler's accession to power in 1933.

Yalta Agreements. The provision concerning the post–World War II order in Europe signed by Roosevelt, Churchill, and Stalin in 1945, in the Soviet resort town of Yalta. Although they called for democratic governments in Eastern Europe, they also affirmed the predominant Soviet influence in the region.

Notes

INTRODUCTION: REVOLUTIONARY EUROPE

1. Norman Davies, *Europe: A History* (New York: Oxford University Press, 1996), 10.

2. Mikhail Gorbachev, *Perestroika: New Thinking for Our Country and the World* (New York: Harper & Row, 1987), 197.

3. This issue was crystalized by the publication in 1983 of an essay by the Czechoslovak writer Milan Kundera titled "The Tragedy of Central Europe." He argued that it was only because the region was "kidnapped, displaced and brainwashed" (by the Soviet Union) after World War II that it was consigned to "East Europe." This essay first appeared in English in *New York Review of Books*, April 26, 1984.

CHAPTER 1: THE OLD REGIME AND THE ENLIGHTENMENT

This chapter is based heavily on Paul R. Hanson's *Revolutionary France* (Acton, MA: Copley, 1996), used by permission of the author.

1. The British constitution, unlike the US Constitution, is an unwritten one consisting of documents (like the Magna Carta), parliamentary acts, legal customs, and tradition.

2. Cited in James Miller, *Rousseau: Dreamer of Democracy* (New Haven, CT: Yale University Press, 1984), 120.

3. From Kant's 1784 essay *What Is Enlightenment?* (available on the Internet).

CHAPTER 2: THE FRENCH REVOLUTION AND NAPOLEON

1. From Robespierre's 1793 speech "On Revolutionary Government."

CHAPTER 3: THE INDUSTRIAL REVOLUTION AND THE BIRTH OF CAPITALISM

1. Great Britain is the largest of the British Isles, and consists of England, Scotland, and Wales, and is itself the largest component of what was then the United Kingdom of Great Britain and Ireland (since 1922, Northern Ireland).

2. R. R. Palmer and Joel Colton, *A History of the Modern World Since 1815*, 7th ed. (New York: McGraw-Hill, 1992), 459.

3. Flora Tristan, *Utopian Feminist: Her Travel Diaries and Personal Crusade*, edited by Doris and Paul Beik (Bloomington: Indiana University Press, 1993), 63.

CHAPTER 4: 1848: THE PEOPLE'S SPRING

1. The Holy Roman Empire was a political body embracing most of central Europe from the tenth century until 1806: it was "Roman" because it claimed succession to imperial Rome and "holy" because it originally claimed authority over Christendom.

2. Cited in Norman Davies, *Europe: A History* (New York: Oxford University Press, 1996), 762.

3. Cited in E. J. Hobsbawm, *The Age of Revolution: 1789–1848* (New York: New American Library, 1962), 362.

CHAPTER 5: MARX, MARXISM, AND SOCIALISM

1. "Marx and Marxism," *The New Encyclopaedia Britannica* (Chicago: Encyclopaedia Britannica, 2002), 534.

2. The dialectic was an idea borrowed and adapted from the eminent German philosopher G. W. F. Hegel.

CHAPTER 6: DARWINISM AND SOCIAL DARWINISM

1. George Bernard Shaw, *Back to Methuselah: A Metabiological Pentateuch* (New York: Brentano's, 1921), lxv.

2. Herbert Spencer, "Poor Laws," in *Social Statics; or, the Conditions Essential to Human Happiness* (New York: Appleton, 1884), 354.

3. Cited in Philip Appleman, ed., *Darwin: A Norton Critical Edition* (New York: Norton, 1970), 497.

4. Heinrich von Treitschke (1834–96), cited in D. R. Oldroyd, *Darwinian Impacts: An Introduction to the Darwinian Revolution* (Atlantic Heights, NJ: Humanities Press, 1980), 217.

5. Adolf Hitler, *Mein Kampf*, vol. 1, chapter 11.

6. Cited in Oldroyd, *Darwinian Impacts*, 218.

7. On the television series *Cosmos: A Spacetime Odyssey: Some of the Things That Molecules Do*, which aired March 16, 2014, on the National Geographic Channel.

8. Cited in Oldroyd, *Darwinian Impacts*, 233.

CHAPTER 7: THE UNIFICATIONS OF ITALY AND GERMANY

1. Cited in Norman Davies, *Europe: A History* (New York: Oxford University Press, 1996), 823.

2. Cited in Davies, *Europe*, 814.

3. Cited in John Merriman, *A History of Modern Europe*, vol. 2 (New York: Norton, 1996), 770.

4. Merriman, *A History of Modern Europe*, 771.

5. Davies, *Europe*, 826.

CHAPTER 8: THE AGE OF IMPERIALISM AND THE SCRAMBLE FOR AFRICA

1. John Merriman, *A History of Modern Europe*, vol. 2 (New York: Norton, 1996), 960.

2. Cited in Merriman, *A History of Modern Europe*, 1000.

3. William Neher, *Nigeria: Change and Tradition in an African State*, 3rd ed. (Acton, MA: Copley, 1999), 27.

4. Neher, *Nigeria*.

5. Stanley had earlier searched for and found the explorer and missionary David Livingstone on the shores of Lake Tanganyika, delivering there the famous salutation, "Dr. Livingstone, I presume?"

CHAPTER 9: WORLD WAR I

1. Cited in Norman Davies, *Europe: A History* (New York: Oxford, 1996), 875.

2. Quoted in John G. Stoessinger, *Why Nations Go to War*, 8th ed. (Boston: Bedford/St. Martin's, 2001), 6.

3. George Frost Kennan, *American Diplomacy, 1900–1950* (Chicago: University of Chicago Press, 1951), 58.

4. Winston S. Churchill, *The World Crisis* (New York: Scribner, 1929), 1–2.

CHAPTER 10: THE RUSSIAN REVOLUTION AND COMMUNISM

1. Paul Valliere, *Change and Tradition in Russian Civilization* (Indianapolis: Butler University, 1995), 111.

2. The Bolshevik seizure of power occurred on October 25 under the old (Julian) calendar and on November 7 under the new (Gregorian) calendar, which the Soviet government adopted in 1918. Thus, the October Revolution was celebrated each year on November 7.

3. Recent research on the *Gulag* suggests that about twenty million people revolved through the labor camps over a quarter of a century. Although some two million died in the camps during World War II, the total number of deaths is not known. Galina M. Ivanova, *Labor Camp Socialism: The Gulag in the Soviet Totalitarian System*, edited by Donald J. Raleigh (Armonk, NY: M. E. Sharpe, 2000).

CHAPTER 11: WORLD WAR II AND THE HOLOCAUST

1. Winston Churchill, *Their Finest Hour* (Boston: Houghton Mifflin, 1949), 25.

CHAPTER 12: EUROPE DIVIDED, THE COLD WAR, AND DECOLONIZATION

The first part of this chapter draws heavily on my book *Revolution in East-Central Europe: The Rise and Fall of Communism and the Cold War* (Boulder, CO: Westview, 1992).

1. The Truman Doctrine speech is reprinted in Gale Stokes, ed., *From Stalinism to Pluralism: A Documentary History of Eastern Europe Since 1945* (New York: Oxford University Press, 1991), 35–37.

2. From the 1953 presidential memoirs interview, at www.trumanlibrary.org.

3. Roosevelt died in April 1945, so it was Harry Truman who presided over the creation of the UN, which must have had special meaning for him. For years, he had carried in his wallet several stanzas of his favorite poem, Tennyson's "Locksley Hall" (see box 3.2), which ended:

> For I dipt into the future,
> Far as human eye could see,
> Saw the Vision of the world,
> and all the wonders that would be . . .
> Till the war-drum
> Throbbed no longer, and
> The battle-flags were furl'd
> In the Parliament of Man,
> The Federation of the World.

CHAPTER 13: 1989: THE COLLAPSE OF
COMMUNISM AND END OF THE COLD WAR

1. The Kremlin is the ancient walled fortress in central Moscow that housed the offices of the Soviet political leadership. Thus, "the Kremlin" became a shorthand description of Soviet leadership in Moscow.

2. Adam Michnik, "Does Socialism Have Any Future in Eastern Europe?" *Studium Papers* 13, no. 4 (October 1989): 184.

3. The absurdities of central planning were sometimes addressed in the Soviet press. Plans calling for the production of chandeliers, for example, specified their weight in terms of kilograms. Smart factory managers thus produced chandeliers made out of lead, making it easier to meet their kilogram quota. No consumers, of course, wanted to buy lead chandeliers, so the products languished in warehouses.

4. *Pravda*, January 28, 1987.

5. Cited in David S. Mason, *Revolution and Transition in East-Central Europe*, 2nd ed. (Boulder, CO: Westview, 1996), 49.

6. Mason, *Revolution and Transition*, 53.

7. Francis Fukuyama, "The End of History," *National Interest* (Summer 1989): 3.

CHAPTER 14: THE EUROPEAN UNION:
EUROPE UNITED AND FREE?

1. In a customs union, a group of countries agrees to eliminate among themselves restrictions to trade (such as quotas or taxes on imports, called tariffs).

2. Cited in Norman Davies, *Europe: A History* (New York: Oxford University Press, 1996), 8.

3. Gabriel Almond, Russell Dalton, and G. Bingham Powell, eds., *European Politics Today*, 2nd ed. (New York: Longman, 2002), 459.

4. All three of these capital cities of the European Community—Strasbourg, Luxembourg, and Brussels—are along the French-German linguistic border, and that area remains, in many respects, the core of the EU.

5. Davies, *Europe*, 1119.

6. Standards of living as measured by per capita gross domestic product (GDP). GDP is the total value of goods and services produced in a country in a year and so is an indication of the size of the economy. This amount, divided by the size of the population, gives a per capita figure that is a rough estimate of income levels, or the standard of living.

7. John McCormick, *The European Superpower* (New York: Palgrave Macmillan, 2007), 89.

8. Richard Bernstein, "Continent Wrings Its Hands over Proclaiming Its Faith," *New York Times*, November 12, 2003.

9. Based on survey data from the European Values Study, reported in Frank Bruni, "Mainline Christianity Withering in Europe," *New York Times*, October 13, 2003, 1, A5.

CONCLUSION: EUROPE IN THE TWENTY-FIRST CENTURY

1. "Putin's Present Fights His Past," *New York Times*, October 9, 2003, A11.

2. David Herszenhorn, "Xenophobic Chill Descends on Moscow," *New York Times*, April 13, 2014.

3. A poll of 7,500 Europeans conducted in October 2003 on behalf of the European Commission, reported in Alan Cowell, "Bush Visit Spurs Protests against U.S. in Europe," *New York Times*, November 16, 2003.

4. A survey of 40,448 respondents in 37 countries conducted by the Pew Research Center between February and May 2017. The researchers found that "in the eyes of most people surveyed around the world, the White House's new occupant is arrogant, intolerant and even dangerous." "U.S. Image Suffers as Publics around World Question Trump's Leadership," http://www.pewglobal.org/2017/06/26/u-s -image-suffers-as-publics-around-world-question-trumps-leadership.

5. Quoted in Melissa Eddy, "In Era of Trump, Germany Seeks a Stronger Role Abroad," *New York Times*, December 6, 2017.

Suggestions for Additional Reading

A short history text such as this one is meant to be supplemented by primary source materials from each era, and perhaps some of the historiography—the differing presentation and interpretation of events by historians. One can find such materials both in documentary sourcebooks and, increasingly, on the Internet.

DOCUMENTS AND PRIMARY SOURCE MATERIALS

An excellent starting point is Fordham University's "Internet Modern History Sourcebook," which is clearly organized by region, country, and era and contains hundreds of links to primary documents (most translated into English) and to other websites with even more documents (https://sourcebooks.fordham.edu/Halsall/mod/modsbook.asp). Another good site, from Brigham Young University, is "EuroDocs: Online Sources for European History" (http://eudocs.lib.byu.edu). The European Union has a helpful website (europa.eu), including some documentary material.

A very useful printed sourcebook, with chapters and organizational structure very similar to this one, is John C. Swanson and Michael S. Melancon, *Modern Europe: Sources and Perspectives from History* (Longman, 2003). A similar book by the same authors, with some overlap with the first one, is *Nineteenth-Century Europe: Sources and Perspectives from History* (Longman, 2007). The twentieth century is covered in Marvin Perry, Matthew Berg, and James Krukones, *Sources of European History: Since 1900* (Wadsworth, 2010). A focus on Eastern Europe is provided by Gale Stokes,

From Stalinism to Pluralism: A Documentary History of Eastern Europe Since 1945 (Oxford, 1996). The Cold War conflict is covered in Edward Judge and John Langdon, eds., *The Cold War through Documents: A Global History* (Rowman & Littlefield, 2017).

BOOKS AND SECONDARY SOURCES

In keeping with the emphasis of this book on short and clear histories, I will focus here on concise treatments for each of the topics addressed in this book, organized by chapter. More comprehensive bibliographies and suggested readings can be found in many of those books. I will also include some fictional works that address important issues or periods discussed in this text.

MODERN EUROPEAN HISTORY—GENERAL

Sometimes the most synthetic coverage of European history can be found in textbooks on world history, and one of the most readable of these is Joel Colton, Lloyd Kramer, and R. R. Palmer, *A History of the Modern World*, 10th ed. (Knopf, 2007), although you should be warned that this is more than twelve hundred pages long! Other versions of this book have a separate, smaller volume covering the period since 1815. The most helpful and entertaining comprehensive history of modern Europe is John Merriman, *A History of Modern Europe, vol. 2: From the French Revolution to the Present* (Norton, 2009). Another good one is Asa Briggs and Patricia Clavin, *Modern Europe, 1789–Present* (Routledge, 2003). Both of these have comprehensive bibliographies organized by topic and era.

CHAPTER 1: THE OLD REGIME AND THE ENLIGHTENMENT

The Old Regime and the French Revolution (Anchor, 1955) is a classic study by eighteenth-century Frenchman Alexis de Tocqueville, who also wrote *Democracy in America*. A more recent and very concise treatment of both France and Europe is William Doyle, *The Ancien Regime* (Palgrave, 2001). Good short overviews of the Enlightenment include Roy Porter, *The Enlightenment* (Palgrave, 2001), and Dorinda Outram et al., *The Enlightenment* (Cambridge, 2013). A book that focuses more on Enlightenment thinkers is Norman Torrey, *Les Philosophes: The Philosophers of the Enlightenment and Modern Democracy* (Perigee, 1980). For a little light entertainment that illustrates some of the manners of the old regime and hints at Enlightenment ideas, you might want to read Pierre-Augustin Caron de Beaumarchais's 1778 comic play *The Marriage of Figaro*, which was the basis of Mozart's opera of the same title.

CHAPTER 2: THE FRENCH REVOLUTION AND NAPOLEON

Short and helpful overviews of the French Revolution include Paul R. Hanson, *Revolutionary France* (Copley, 1999); Jeremy Popkin, *A Short History of the French Revolution* (Prentice-Hall, 2009); and Jack R. Censer and Lynn Hunt, *Liberty, Equality, Fraternity: Exploring the French Revolution* (Penn State University, 2001), which includes many documents and a CD-ROM companion with images, songs, and documents. Napoleon is the subject of a multitude of biographies, most of them thick. A relatively short and nicely illustrated one is David Chanteranne et al., *Napoleon: The Immortal Emperor* (Vendome, 2003).

Many literary masterpieces have been set in the revolutionary or Napoleonic eras, including Charles Dickens's portrayal of a family during the French Revolution in *Tale of Two Cities* (1859); Stendhal's story of a young dreamer fueled by Napoleonic ideas in post-Napoleonic France, *The Red and the Black* (1830); and Leo Tolstoy's epic masterpiece about the Napoleonic wars, *War and Peace* (1869), considered by some to be the greatest novel ever written.

CHAPTER 3: THE INDUSTRIAL REVOLUTION AND THE BIRTH OF CAPITALISM

A classic, short overview of the Industrial Revolution is T. S. Ashton, *The Industrial Revolution, 1760–1830*, first published in 1948 and now available from Oxford University Press (1998). One that focuses on England but includes more discussion of the social and political dimensions is John F. C. Harrison, *The Birth and Growth of Industrial England, 1714–1867* (Harcourt Brace, 1973). Many of Charles Dickens's novels explore the dark side of industrialization, including *Oliver Twist* (1838), *David Copperfield* (1850), and *Hard Times* (1854).

CHAPTER 4: 1848: THE PEOPLE'S SPRING

Good short overviews of the revolutions of 1848 include Georges Duveau, *1848: The Making of a Revolution* (Pantheon, 1967); Jonathan Sperber, *The European Revolutions, 1848–1851* (Cambridge, 2005); and Peter Stearns, *1848: The Revolutionary Tide in Europe* (Norton, 1974).

CHAPTER 5: MARX, MARXISM, AND SOCIALISM

One of the best treatments of Marx's life and thinking is David McLellan, *Karl Marx: A Biography* (Palgrave Macmillan, 2006), although this one does not really fit my criteria of short! A much shorter and more whimsical work is Rius, *Marx for Beginners* (Pantheon, 2003). Many editions of *The Communist Manifesto* include helpful introductions to the work, including the Signet Reprint Edition (1998), with an introduction by the historian Martin Malia. A useful collection of writings by the authors of the *Manifesto* is Robert Tucker, ed., *The Marx-Engels Reader* (Norton, 1978). Elizabeth Gaskell's classic novel *Mary Barton* (1848) is set in the Manchester of Marx and Engels, and epitomizes class conflict.

CHAPTER 6: DARWINISM AND SOCIAL DARWINISM

The text of *Origin of Species* is available in reprinted editions and on the web at http://www.gutenberg.org/ebooks/2009. Steve Jones, *Darwin's Ghost* (Ballantine, 2001), is an update of *Origin of Species*, following the same organization as the original but written in a modern, popular style. Written for his grandchildren when he was sixty-seven years old, *The Autobiography of Charles Darwin*, edited by Nora Barlow (Norton, 1993), describes the years leading up to the publication of his seminal work, the process of discovery, and his changing religious views. A very useful and interesting discussion of the impact of Darwinism and social Darwinism on science, politics, literature, theology, and so forth, is D. R. Oldroyd, *Darwinian Impacts: An Introduction to the Darwinian Revolution* (Open University Press, 1980).

CHAPTER 7: THE UNIFICATIONS OF ITALY AND GERMANY

For a good short overview of Italian unification and the various historical interpretations of that, see Lucy Riall, *The Italian Risorgimento: State, Society and National Unification* (Routledge, 1994). Denis Mack Smith profiles the very interesting personalities involved in Italian unification in *Cavour* (Knopf, 1985), *Mazzini* (Yale, 1994), and *Garibaldi: A Great Life in Brief* (Knopf, 1956). A readable and concise introduction to the German case is D. G. Williamson, *Bismarck and Germany, 1862–1890* (Addison-Wesley, 1998). Giuseppi di Lampedusa's novel *The Leopard* (1958) depicts the political intrigues surrounding Italian unification in the 1860s.

CHAPTER 8: THE AGE OF IMPERIALISM AND THE SCRAMBLE FOR AFRICA

The broadest and most synthetic, reasonably concise coverage is Raymond Betts, *The False Dawn: European Imperialism in the Nineteenth Century* (Oxford, 1975), and carrying the story forward is Woodruff Smith, *European Imperialism in the Nineteenth and Twentieth Centuries* (Wadsworth, 1982). Rudyard Kipling's masterpiece novel *Kim* (1901) is set in colonial India and is played out in the context of the Great Game of imperial competition in South and Central Asia between Russia and Britain.

CHAPTER 9: WORLD WAR I

An excellent short discussion of the causes of World War I and the historiographical debates on the topic is James Joll and Gordon Martel, *The Origins of the First World War* (Routledge, 2006). A long, but thoroughly absorbing, account is Barbara Tuchman's Pulitzer Prize–winning classic *The Guns of August* (Ballantine, 1994). The eminent British military historian Michael Howard covers the war from beginning to end in a concise fashion in *The First World War* (Oxford, 2003). A classic novel on the war, and one of the greatest novels ever written on any war, is Erich Maria Remarque's *All Quiet on the Western Front* (1929).

CHAPTER 10: THE RUSSIAN REVOLUTION AND COMMUNISM

A succinct history and interpretation of the Russian Revolution and the consolidation of the Soviet state under Lenin and Stalin is Sheila Fitzpatrick, *The Russian Revolution* (Oxford, 2017). It is difficult to find a good short history of the Soviet era, but Ronald Hingley, *Russia: A Concise History* (Thames and Hudson, 1991), includes that period in a broader sweep. Robert Massie's long, but fascinating, *Nicholas and Alexandra* (2000) provides a richly detailed account of the last tsar and his family and the last days of the Russian Empire. Boris Pasternak's wonderful novel *Dr. Zhivago* is set in the turbulent years of the Russian Revolution. It was first published in Italy in 1957 and banned for many years in the Soviet Union because of the main character's ambivalent attitude toward the revolution.

CHAPTER 11: WORLD WAR II AND THE HOLOCAUST

The path to World War II is addressed concisely in Joachim Remak, *The Origins of the Second World War* (Prentice-Hall, 1976), and a short overview of the war itself is provided in Gerhard Weinberg, *World War II: A Very Short Introduction* (Oxford, 2014). There are many fine biographies of Hitler and Mussolini; good concise ones include Ian Kershaw, *Hitler* (Longman, 2001), and M. Feldman and Robert Mallett, *Mussolini and the Origins of the Second World War, 1933–1940* (Palgrave, 2003). For an excellent review of the debates surrounding the Holocaust, see Michael Marrus, *The Holocaust in History* (Key Porter Books, 2000). A short, extraordinary, and moving account of the Nazi death camp experience is *Night*, first published in 1958 by Elie Wiesel, who won the Nobel Peace Prize in 1986.

CHAPTER 12: EUROPE DIVIDED, THE COLD WAR, AND DECOLONIZATION

The best and most comprehensive (at 960 pages!) history of Europe since World War II is Tony Judt, *Postwar: A History of Europe Since 1945* (Penguin, 2006), which was a finalist for the Pulitzer Prize. A history of the origins and development of the Cold War conflict between the United States and the Soviet Union, with much attention to Europe, is Walter Lafeber, *America, Russia and the Cold War, 1945–1992* (McGraw-Hill, 1993). A political history of the Eastern European communist states is Joseph Rothschild and Nancy Wingfield, *Return to Diversity: A Political History of East Central Europe Since World War II* (Oxford, 2007), and of Western Europe is Derek Urwin, *A Political History of Western Europe Since 1945* (Longman, 1997). *Decolonization: A Short History* by Jan Jansen and Jurgen Osterhammel (Princeton, 2017) is a clear and concise account. A novel that sheds light on the restrictions and inanities of life under communism is Czech writer Milan Kundera's *The Joke*, first published in 1967. A similar theme is developed in Polish writer Tadeusz Konwicki's novel *A Minor Apocalypse*.

CHAPTER 13: 1989: THE COLLAPSE OF COMMUNISM AND END OF THE COLD WAR

It is the author's prerogative to suggest his own book, covering in brief fashion the establishment and decay of communism, the revolutions of 1989, and the subsequent process of building democracy and markets: David S. Mason, *Revolution and Transition in East-Central Europe*, 2nd ed. (Westview, 1996). The British journalist and historian Timothy Garton

Ash provides first-person accounts of the 1989 events in *The Magic Lantern: The Revolution of '89 Witnessed in Warsaw, Budapest, Berlin and Prague* (Random House, 1990). Padraic Kenney addresses the postcommunist era in *The Burdens of Freedom: Eastern Europe Since 1989* (Zed Books, 2006). The Croatian writer Slavenka Drakulic has written some wonderful essays about life under communism, the civil war in Bosnia, and the joys and difficulties of the transition from communism in *The Balkan Express* (HarperPerennial, 1993), *How We Survived Communism and Even Laughed* (HarperPerennial, 1993), and *Café Europa* (Penguin, 1999).

CHAPTER 14: THE EUROPEAN UNION: EUROPE UNITED AND FREE?

A good short history of the European Union is provided by Mark Gilbert, *European Integration: A Concise History* (Rowman & Littlefield, 2011). The formation of the European Common Market is addressed in Douglas Brinkley and Clifford Hackett, eds., *Jean Monnet and the Path to European Unity* (Palgrave, 1992). A journalist's account of Europe's accomplishments and prospects is T. R. Reid's *The United States of Europe: The New Superpower and the End of American Supremacy* (Penguin, 2004). In *After Europe* (University of Pennsylvania, 2017), Ivan Krastev raises concerns about the future of the European Union in the face of immigration and the spread of right-wing populism. The official European Union website also has much useful information at http://europa.eu.

Index

About the Author

David S. Mason is professor emeritus of political science at Butler University in Indianapolis. He holds a BA in government and Russian from Cornell University, an MA in international relations from the Johns Hopkins School of Advanced International Studies, and a PhD in political science and a certificate in Russian and East European studies from Indiana University. Professor Mason is the author of six books on European politics and history, including *Revolution in East-Central Europe: The Rise and Fall of Communism and the Cold War*. His most recent book is *The End of the American Century*. Besides teaching courses on international, European, and Russian politics, he taught and coordinated Butler's core curriculum global studies course, which included a unit on modern Europe. Professor Mason has received several teaching awards, including Outstanding Teacher in the College of Liberal Arts and Sciences.